NEW AMERICAN PROFILES

NEW AMERICAN PROFILES

LUCETTE ROLLET KENAN

Harcourt Brace Jovanovich, Publishers

Orlando San Diego New York
Toronto London Sydney Tokyo

Copyright © 1986 by Harcourt Brace Jovanovich, Inc.

All rights reserved. No part of this publication may be reproduced or transmitted in any form or by any means, electronic or mechanical, including photocopy, recording, or any information storage and retrieval system, without permission in writing from the publisher.

Requests for permission to make copies of any part of the work should be mailed to: Permissions, Harcourt Brace Jovanovich, Publishers, Orlando, Florida 32887.

ISBN: 0-15-565715-1
Library of Congress Catalog Card Number: 85-81732
Printed in the United States of America

COPYRIGHTS AND ACKNOWLEDGMENTS

For permission to use selections reprinted in this book, the author is grateful to the following copyright holders:

ASSOCIATED PRESS   For excerpts from "Cronkite Truly Ends Era for Many" by Peter J. Boyer. Reprinted by permission of The Associated Press.

DON CONGDON ASSOCIATES, INC.   For *The Fog Horn* by Ray Bradbury. Copyright © 1951, 1979 by Ray Bradbury. Reprinted by permission of Don Congdon Associates, Inc.

JOHN COSTELLO   For "He Changed the World" by John Costello from *The Washingtonian* (December 1983). Reprinted by permission of the author.

HOUGHTON MIFFLIN COMPANY and MARIE RODELL-FRANCES COLLIN LITERARY AGENCY   For excerpts from *The House of Life: Rachel Carson at Work* by Paul Brooks. Copyright © 1972 by Paul Brooks. Reprinted by permission of Houghton Mifflin and Marie Rodell-Frances Collin Literary Agency.

LITTLE, BROWN AND COMPANY   For excerpts from *Imogen Cunningham: A Portrait* by Judy Dater. Copyright © 1979 by Judy Dater. Reprinted by permission of Little, Brown and Company.

HAROLD MATSON COMPANY, INC.   For excerpts from the preface to *The Stories of Ray Bradbury* by Ray Bradbury. Copyright © renewed 1980 by Ray Bradbury. Reprinted by permission of Harold Matson Company, Inc.

NEWSWEEK   For "How the News Media Rate" by The Gallup Organization, Inc., and *Newsweek* from *Newsweek* (May 4, 1981). Reprinted by permission of *Newsweek*.

Continued on page 306.

Preface

New American Profiles is a contemporary reader for high-intermediate and advanced ESL students who have already acquired a working knowledge of English grammar and vocabulary. The purpose of the book is to help those students develop the skills that will allow them to draw maximum benefit from their readings. The book will teach them to approach any material with an alert and critical mind; to make intelligent guesses when confronted with unknown words; to recognize the most important facts provided by the texts; to understand humor, metaphors, and implications; and to follow the logic as well as the chronology of a narrative.

New American Profiles consists of ten chapters, each of which includes an introductory section, a two-part profile of an interesting contemporary personality, and a concluding essay (or other form of reading) related to the field in which the person portrayed has attained fame. Each profile shows the person in the context of his or her environment: Ray Kroc is portrayed with the fast-food business; Rachel Carson with ecology; Ray Bradbury with science fiction writing; Amelia Earhart with aviation and women's search for equality in the working world; Katharine Graham with the role and problems of the press; and Walter Cronkite with televised news. Imogen Cunningham is associated with the art of photography; Jackie Robinson with baseball, sports in general, and racism; Walt Disney with cartoons and amusement parks; and John Mauchly with a survey of computers of the past, present, and future. Nine of the profiles were written expressly for this reader; the last one, John Costello's portrait of John Mauchly, appeared in *The Washingtonian* of December 1984. Other excerpted readings are: *The Fog Horn*, by Ray Bradbury; "There Has Always Been Olympic Mischief," by Erich Segal; and "To Have, To Have Not, or To Have More," by James H. Rosenfield, Senior Executive President of CBS Broadcast Group.

Each chapter begins with preliminary activities designed to familiarize students with the main topic of the chapter and to raise their interest. They are asked to survey the whole chapter to gain a clear understanding of the content of the four sections. They study the special vocabulary and cultural notes and talk about what they already know of the subject of the profile and of his or her field. Each introduction also includes an exercise, based on either a brief essay or a specialized type of information, such as a table, map, or cartoon.

Before reading the profile, the students are expected to skim the text to understand its scope, and to answer specific questions on details of the narrative. The reading is followed by a series of exercises, including:

- comprehension exercises:
    answering factual questions about the story, recognizing key words and main ideas, devising questions, and taking notes

- observation exercises:
    scanning essays, finding implications, recognizing irrelevancies, and understanding figurative speech
- opinion exercises:
    appraising and criticizing the text, giving personal points of view, and discussing the topics provided at the end of each section
- study exercises:
    taking notes, writing summaries and outlines, and scanning and skimming a text for specific information
- vocabulary exercises and the study of prefixes and suffixes
- sequencing
- logical reasoning
    (including cause and effect) and the use of connectors
- understanding tables and graphs
- special projects:
    planning a campus paper, outlining a science fiction story, judging photographs, and so on.

The introductory section of each chapter provides a short, in-context presentation of the vocabulary peculiar to the field covered. Footnotes are also provided to clarify the meaning of foreign terms and idioms that may not be understood from the context and to warn readers about slang words and expressions. But no glosses are otherwise offered, and the students should be encouraged to try to understand new terms through their context before consulting a dictionary. It should be emphasized to the students that, as people do in everyday life, they can perfectly well follow a story, a film, or a conversation even if they are not certain of the precise meaning of every single word. Further encounters with new words (and the book makes full use of the power of repetition) will eventually make clear the meaning of words and expressions that at first seem obscure or vague.

The "Topics for Discussion" at the end of each main section can be used either for general discussion or as a basis for a debate between two groups of students presenting opposite views. They can also be used as written assignments.

The author wishes to express her gratitude to Gwendolyn Z. Verhoff for her review and useful suggestions, and to the experienced people who have helped in the production of *New American Profiles* at the College Department of Harcourt Brace Jovanovich: Albert I. Richards, Mike McKinley, Eleanor R. Garner, Maggie Porter, Merilyn Britt, Kim Turner, and Melanie Rawn.

Lucette Rollet Kenan

To the Instructor: The Distribution of Special Exercises

A number of exercises and activities recur regularly in every chapter. The students are always required to survey the whole chapter to get a clear idea of the material that they are going to study, to skim each text and answer questions before reading, to scan the passages for details, to answer comprehension questions, to study vocabulary and affixes, and to discuss topics suggested at the end of the sections. Other exercises, however, are most appropriate for certain specific readings, and so appear only in certain instances. Table A on the next page shows the distribution of these special exercises.

Activities described in the table as "appraising" cover the study of implications, irrelevancies, literal versus figurative speech, humor, tone, author's attitude, and so on. The section entitled "The Main Idea" is an exercise about the main idea of a paragraph; the section "What Is Important" asks students to decide what is worth remembering from the whole reading.

TABLE A
SPECIAL EXERCISES

	Ray Kroc	Rachel Carson	Ray Bradbury	Amelia Earhart	Katharine Graham
Introduction	Interpreting Figures	Logical Reasoning	Definitions	Summarizing Logical Reasoning	The Main Facts Generalizations
Profile, Part One	Key Words Your Opinion Appraising The Main Idea	Key Words Appraising The Main Idea	Commenting on the Text The Main Idea Generalizations	The Main Idea	Commenting on the Text Project: Starting Newspaper Facts/Inferences/Opinions
Profile, Part Two	Your Opinion The Main Idea Devising Questions	The Main Idea Sequencing	Commenting on the Text Facts/Inferences/Opinions Sequencing	Facts/Inferences/Opinions Taking Notes for a Summary Your Opinion	Key Words The Main Idea Outlining
Reading or Selected Reading	Choosing a Title A Critical Look at the Text Taking Notes for a Summary	Taking Notes for a Summary Appraising Conflicting Opinions	Appraising the Story Project: Devising a SF Story	Finding a Title Outlining Graphs and Tables	Interpreting Public Opinion Polls Writing a Summary

Walter Cronkite	Imogen Cunningham	Jackie Robinson	Walt Disney	John Mauchly
Comparing Two Writings Logical Reasoning	Outlining Logical Reasoning	Your Opinion What Is Important?	Logical Reasoning	Logical Reasoning Commenting on the Text
The Main Idea Sequencing	Appraising Taking Notes for a Summary Facts/Inferences/Opinions	The Main Idea Sequencing	Facts/Inferences/Opinions Sequencing	Appraising What Is Important? Taking Notes for an Outline
Outlining Facts/Inferences/Opinions	Appraising What Is Important?	Facts/Inferences/Opinions Outlining	The Main Idea Generalizations	Your Opinion
Devising Questions Appraising Taking a Survey	Comparing Opinions Project: Judging Photographs		Appraising What Is Important?	Sequencing

Contents

Preface	viii
To the Instructor The Distribution of Special Exercises	ix

Ray Kroc   1

Introduction: Interpreting Figures	2
Profile, Part One	4
Profile, Part Two	12
Reading: McDonald's—How it Works	22

Rachel Carson   29

Introduction: Interpreting a Cartoon	30
Profile, Part One	32
Profile, Part Two	42
Reading: The Publication of *Silent Spring*	50

Ray Bradbury   57

Introduction: Definitions	58
Profile, Part One	60
Profile, Part Two	69
Selected Reading: The Fog Horn, by Ray Bradbury	80

Amelia Earhart   87

Introduction: Amelia's Last Flight	88
Profile, Part One	92
Profile, Part Two	101
Reading: Women in a Man's World	111

Katharine Graham   121

Introduction: The American Press	122
Profile, Part One	126
Profile, Part Two	135
Reading: The Press after Watergate	146

Walter Cronkite   153

Introduction: Two Articles about Walter Cronkite	154
Profile, Part One	157
Profile, Part Two	167
Selected Reading: "To Have, To Have Not, Or To Have More," by James H. Rosenfield	176

Imogen Cunningham   181

Introduction: Photography	182
Profile, Part One	187
Profile, Part Two	195
Selected Readings: About Imogen Cunningham and Ansel Adams	204

Jackie Robinson   209

Introduction: Baseball	210
Profile, Part One	214
Profile, Part Two	224
Selected Reading: "There Has Always Been Olympic Mischief," by Erich Segal	233

Walt Disney 241

Introduction: Animation 242
Profile, Part One 245
Profile, Part Two 254
Reading: Disney Worlds 262

John Mauchly 269

Introduction: "Miracles, Menaces—the 21st Century as Futurists See It," from *U.S. News & World Report* 270
Profile, Part One 276
Profile, Part Two 285
Reading: Computers since ENIAC 294
Word List 301

Ray Kroc

Introduction

The Vocabulary of Business

A small business usually belongs to one person or to several partners who operate it together. The partners can consider their business successful if its gross revenue is large enough to leave a profit (or, a net profit) after all the operating expenses have been paid. Large enterprises gross millions of dollars each year, but of course they net much less.

A large chain of restaurants like McDonald's, which gives its name to thousands of outlets, doesn't own them all. Many are operated by managers who have bought the McDonald's franchise, which entitles them to use the McDonald's name and its methods.

Hamburger restaurants such as McDonald's are often called drive-ins because the customers are either served in their cars or are expected to eat in their cars; the name is often applied now even when the outlet also offers an eating area with tables and chairs. Some banks have drive-up windows where customers can conduct their business without getting out of their cars.

Although he had never studied marketing, Ray Kroc, whose profile you are about to read, was a natural genius in the field; he revolutionized the methods of selling fast foods on a large scale.

He was less successful as a real estate agent in Florida, selling land, houses and buildings at a time when the demand for properties in that state was experiencing a dramatic increase. That land boom, however, didn't last long enough to make Kroc rich.

Looking Ahead

- Leaf through the chapter to get a general idea of its contents:
    Is "business in general" the central topic of the chapter?
    What different sections does the chapter include?
    Who was Ray Kroc?
- Look at the figures in the table on page 3, concerning McDonald's outlets, and try to answer the questions that follow.

Growth of McDonald's

Number of McDonald's Outlets		McDonald's Gross Sales	
1955:	1	1955:	$158,000
1956:	12		
1957:	37		
1958:	80		
1959:	100	1959:	$20 million
1960:	250	1960:	$37 million

Number of McDonald's Outlets		McDonald's Gross Sales	
1964:	657		
1965:	710		
		1966:	$200 million
		1967:	$266 million
1972:	1,500	1972:	$1,300 million (1.3 billion)
1973:	2,200		
1974:	2,700	1974:	$2,000 million (2 billion)
1976:	4,177		
1983:	5,813	1983:	$2,800 million
1984:	6,200	1984:	$6,400 million
1985:	7,778	1985:	$8,600 million

1. Consider the number of outlets opened in the ten years 1955–1964, in the ten years 1965–1974, and in the ten years 1974–1983. Does it seem that McDonald's growth is slowing down, speeding up, or remaining steady?
2. Can you figure the yearly gross revenue per outlet in 1955, 1959, 1974 and 1985 and compare them? Is it growing or diminishing?
3. What do you think of the future of McDonald's?

Cultural Notes for Profile, Part One

Years ago, most drugstores had a counter where soft drinks, ice cream, and perhaps some light food could be purchased. These soda fountains have almost completely disappeared. Some stores and fast-food restaurants had jukeboxes that played a record when a customer dropped a coin in the machine.

Country clubs usually maintain for their members a golf course, a number of tennis courts and swimming pools, and perhaps places to practice other sports. They all have dining rooms and rooms available for social activities. Ray Kroc went to his country club to play bridge. But not all country clubs are equally prestigious—or equally expensive.

Profile
Part One

Born October 5, 1902
Died January, 14, 1984

Skim the text to find out the answers to
the following questions:
- Did Ray Kroc create McDonald's?
- What was remarkable about the first McDonald's outlet?
- Does this part of the profile cover the greater development of McDonald's?

Read the text carefully but without trying
to check every unfamiliar word; try to guess
the meaning from the context.

Thirty years ago, there was in San Bernardino, California, a small hamburger drive-in owned and operated by Maurice and Richard McDonald. Business was good in a conservative sort of way and the brothers, satisfied with their earnings, felt no desire to expand their enterprise.

Someone else did. And today the McDonald's Corporation operates about 8,000 outlets—6,500 in the United States and the rest in Europe, Asia, South America, Africa, and Australia. Its 150,000 employees serve more than three billion hamburgers each year, a quantity of beef that represents the meat of 300,000 head of cattle.[1] The company buys whole crops of Idaho potatoes, is the largest buyer of fish in the country, and has made millionaires of its suppliers of buns, meat, paper goods, and accessories. Its own gross revenue, as we have seen in the preceding table, reached $8.6 billion in 1985, and is still growing. There is nothing small or modest about McDonald's Corporation.

The transformation of the quiet family concern into a fast-food empire was achieved by a man who has become a legend in the marketing industry. His name was Raymond Albert Kroc, and his accomplishment has been put on a par with those of Henry Ford for the automobile and Andrew Carnegie for the steel industry.

When Ray Kroc discovered the McDonalds' small drive-in, he was already fifty-two years old, an apparently unremarkable salesman in bad health. Plagued by diabetes and arthritis, he had lost through surgery his gall bladder and part of his thyroid. Although he was making a fairly good living selling milkshake mixers, the market for this item was declining and a weaker man might have been discouraged. But Ray Kroc could muster more en-

[1] 300,000 head—300,000 animals.

thusiasm and energy in the face of difficulties than most men half his age. It was simply not in his character to despair and give up. Kroc was a dynamic visionary ("I am a dreamer, but a do-er," he would say), and his dreams had always been on a grand scale. Since boyhood he had been determined to become extremely successful—that is, extremely wealthy, for he saw money as the only irrefutable proof of success. At the ripe old age of fifty-two, after several decades of ups and downs and mediocre results for his relentless struggle, he still firmly believed that he would reach his goal sometime, somehow, through hard work and shrewd thinking, and above all through persistence.

Persistence had been Kroc's key word throughout his life. In his twenties he was struck by a declaration of President Calvin Coolidge about this humble virtue—so much so that for sixty years he kept the words reverently framed on the walls of his homes, his offices, and all the kitchens of his hamburger empire.

> "Nothing in this world [Coolidge had said] can take the place of persistence. Talent will not: nothing is more common than unsuccessful men with talent. Genius will not: unrewarded genius is almost a proverb.
> Education alone will not: the world is full of educated derelicts.
> Persistence and determination alone are omnipotent."

Coolidge's observation may have been particularly comforting to young Ray because he had no reason to think of himself as gifted or fortunate in any way. Except for a certain musical ability, there was nothing in his background that might ease his steps on the road to riches. He could not expect much assistance from his parents, low-middle class people of German descent, who lived and struggled in a modest suburb of Chicago. The Krocs were poor. Ray's father died in debt, "having worried himself to death," according to his now famous son. Nor could young Kroc boast of a good education. Always bored with studies, he had left school at fifteen to enlist as an ambulance driver at the end of World War I. To please his father, he did make a half-hearted attempt to finish his schooling after the war; but he soon dropped out again, announcing that algebra had not improved in his absence. Kroc never developed any respect for formal education, and never missed an opportunity to make disparaging remarks about "college boys" or "guys[2] from Harvard."

Besides the taste for hard work that he inherited from his parents, Kroc's only assets were his personal qualities—his courage, his optimism, his determination, and his absolute faith in the American Dream, that old belief that unlimited possibilities are open to the enterprising and the persevering. After a few odd jobs that couldn't lead anywhere, Kroc decided to try

---

[2]guys—slang for *men*.

his luck as a professional pianist. Perhaps he felt that this was his destiny: when Kroc was four years old, a phrenologist, after studying the shape of the boy's skull, had predicted that he would someday make a fortune either in food or in music. Music seemed the most promising of the two, and for a number of years it seemed that Ray had made the right choice. He played popular tunes in cafes, theaters, and dance halls; and he apparently made a name for himself, for he became musical director of a radio station, keeping at the same time his very full schedule of engagements. But after he was married and the father of a girl, Kroc began to look around for a second career that might be more respectable; he didn't think that the late hours, the surroundings, and the associations of a musician added up to a proper kind of life. For a short time he tried selling real estate in Florida, only to end up broke[3] when the Florida land boom collapsed. He had better luck selling paper cups for the Lily-Tulip Company. Paper cups were a new item then, not very well received because they were considered unhealthy. The public's reluctance gave Kroc a chance to prove his mettle. A superb salesman, pleasant, shrewd, untiring, and resourceful, he managed to find steady customers who appreciated his product—pushcart vendors selling refreshments in the streets of Chicago, small businesses, then soda fountains. By 1929 he was selling five million cups a year to two large drugstore chains. In 1937 he became sales manager of the Lily-Tulip Company for all the Midwestern states.

It was not a bad living. But Kroc had never envisioned remaining an ordinary salesman, nor living forever in a merely "nice" house in a merely "nice" neighborhood, and playing bridge in an ordinary country club. These were not the spectacular results that he had dreamed of, and he knew that he could do better. In this frame of mind, he began to build great hopes on a newly invented appliance, an electric mixer that could prepare five drinks at a time. There seemed to be a chance there. Kroc was ready to take risks ("I wanted adventure!" he admitted later). Although the move was forcing him to borrow heavily, he bought the exclusive rights to the Multimixer and paid $85,000 to Lily-Tulip to terminate their contract. Then, hopeful and excited in spite of his debt, he proceeded to find a market for his gadget.

The mixers sold very well for a while to bars and small eating places. In the process of demonstrating his wares, Kroc learned a good deal about the fast-food business. Most of the establishments he visited shocked him, however, because he judged them to be inefficient and generally dirty. If Kroc loved efficiency, about cleanliness he was truly fanatic; no eating place, in his view, deserved to flourish if it didn't have spic and span[4] kitchens, gleaming floors, and sparkling rest rooms.

[3] broke—slang for *out of money*.
[4] spic and span—perfectly clean.

When soda fountains began to go out of fashion in the early fifties, Kroc became concerned about his narrowing market, and once again he looked around for new products to champion. In 1954, while he was pondering the possibilities, he noticed that someone named McDonald, in Southern California, had bought eight of his mixers. The discovery puzzled him: what kind of place could possibly need to mix 40 drinks simultaneously? Never one to leave a question unanswered or a stone unturned, Ray Kroc flew to California to investigate the matter. What he found was the McDonald's drive-in, a small white cube decorated with two golden arches, with a steady line of customers.

After observing the scene for a while from across the street, Kroc took his place in the line to sample the fare. What he saw filled him with admiration. The store was spotless, the prices low, the food fresh and good, the menu as simple as the decor. Nothing was sold but hamburgers (15 cents), cheeseburgers (19 cents), french fries (10 cents), coffee (5 cents) and milkshakes (20 cents). There was no place to sit, no telephone or jukebox, nothing that could slow or complicate the service, and encourage loafers to hang around.[5] No waitresses to attract young men in an undesirable way. Nothing to break or steal. "It was the most amazing merchandising operation I had ever seen," said Kroc, years later.

This time, he knew that he had stumbled onto something remarkable, and he made up his mind at once that he would—somehow—become part of this affair. Why, if the owners of the place could be persuaded to open a hundred such drive-ins, he, Kroc, would be able to sell them 800 mixers! His fortune was made! Unfortunately, the McDonald brothers refused to consider ten more outlets, let alone a hundred; it would entail, they said, too much extra work and too much traveling. As for granting franchises, that notion didn't appeal to them either. They already had granted a few, and were not at all pleased with the way these places, which bore their name, were being run. Moreover, unlike Kroc, they were satisfied with their life as it was and didn't wish for anything more.

Kroc was not about to take no for an answer. After a few days of discussions with the brothers and their lawyer, he finally extracted from them the permission to sell McDonald's franchises, on the condition that he would do all the work: he would find locations, recruit and train managers, collect the money, and make sure that the new McDonald's adhered rigidly to the high standards of the original one. Victorious and happy, Kroc flew back to Illinois with the contract in his pocket, having learned—he thought—all there was to learn about drive-in floor plans and the fine art of frying potatoes.

---

[5] to hang around—an informal expression.

Understanding the Text

1. Many other men have built large corporations. Why then is Ray Kroc's career remarkable?
2. What did President Coolidge say, basically?
3. Why does the author say that Ray Kroc didn't have anything that might help him on the way to riches?
4. Did Ray Kroc do well in his jobs?
5. What proof do we have that he was an outstanding salesman?
6. Why was he so impressed by the brothers' establishment?
7. Was he qualified to judge a fast-food restaurant?
8. What rights did his contract with the McDonalds give him, exactly?

Key Words and Implications

Recognizing key words (i.e., the most significant words) and implications (i.e., facts that are not directly expressed but merely suggested) are two important ways of getting the full meaning of a story.

The key words of the first paragraph, which describes the first McDonald's outlet, are "good" and "conservative" (or "in a conservative way"). For the second paragraph, describing what has happened to the McDonald's business, the key words would be "a corporation," "8,000 outlets," "billions," "largest buyer," and "millionaires."

It is implied in the text, for example, that young Ray didn't like algebra and was probably no good at it. When Ray Kroc is quoted as saying: "I am a dreamer *but* a do-er," we can infer (i.e., reach the understanding) that usually dreamers are not doers. In this case the word "but" was a clue.

1. Read the last paragraph of the profile again. Do you feel that Kroc had learned "all there was to know about drive-in floor plans and the fine art of frying potatoes"? Explain your answer.
2. Does anything in the profile make you think that Ray Kroc had strict moral principles?
3. Scan the text to make a list of (a) the key words, and (b) the implications that give a clear idea of Ray Kroc's personality. Suppose you were asked to describe the 40-year-old Kroc to a person inquiring about his character, what could you say (or write) briefly but accurately? What inferences could you make?

Scanning for Details

1. Who told Ray's father that the boy would make a fortune in food or music?
2. What did Calvin Coolidge say, exactly, about genius?

3. Can you figure approximately when Calvin Coolidge was president of the United States?
4. How does the author define "the American Dream"?
5. How old was Ray Kroc when he became sales manager of the Lily-Tulip Company?
6. How much did Kroc pay to terminate his contract with Lily-Tulip?
7. Did the author say that Kroc considered money the only *irreducible* proof of success?
8. What proof, or proofs, can you find in the text that Kroc was a courageous optimist?
9. What proof do you find that he was a very ambitious man?
10. Did Kroc show before leaving Lily-Tulip that he had the spirit of adventure?

Your Opinion

1. In the early thirties, many people thought that paper cups were unhealthy, mainly because a number of children had been sick after drinking from the same dirty cup. Do you agree that paper cups are unhealthy and anti-hygienic?
2. The author states that Kroc had a certain (which implies a limited) musical ability. Does the text support that statement?
3. Do you think that Kroc's failure in Florida shows that he was not a good property salesman?
4. Do you agree that waitresses in restaurants "attract young men in an undesirable way"?
5. The text implies that fast-food restaurant owners have to be prepared for theft and damage to their equipment. Do you think that this is true, false, exaggerated?

Does It Mean What It Says?

Words and sometimes whole sentences may be used in a way that is not meant to be taken literally. The words may be used as metaphors (images) to make the story more colorful. In other cases, they are used "tongue-in-cheek," that is, jokingly.

1. Can you find a metaphor in the paragraph beginning with line 109?
2. What tongue-in-cheek expression can you find in the last paragraph?

Vocabulary

A. *Choose in the list the word or expression that would best replace the underlined word of each statement. When called on by the teacher, read the whole statement with the substitute word.*

10 RAY KROC

> reluctance
> to put on a par with
> to decline
> very wrong
> comforting
> fanatically
>
> spotless
> relentless
> a loafer
> let alone
> inherited
>
> mettle
> disparaging
> visionary
> a do-er
> irrefutable

1. A stern man, Calvin Coolidge first showed his strength of character as Governor of Massachusetts when he broke a strike of the Boston Police.
2. He declared that "there is no right to strike against the public safety." The Americans, obviously finding the argument impossible to disprove, elected him President in 1923.
3. Coolidge was almost excessively devoted to big business.
4. Besides his contemptuous remarks about talent and education, he is remembered for saying "The business of America is Business."
5. Many people would not agree that perseverance should be considered equal to talent, much less genius.
6. Coolidge was a shrewd and practical man of rather short views, not a dreamer of great dreams.
7. Coolidge, who spent his own money with great unwillingness, was an untiring opponent of government spending.

B. *You may check the text before answering the following questions.*

line 22–23   Kroc had reasons to complain about his diabetes, his arthritis, his thyroid, and his gall bladder. Do you have the impression that all four belong to the same category of things? Decide whether each is:
a) a disease
b) a financial problem
c) an organ of the body
d) a member of his family

line 32   If you were asked to describe the ups and downs of your life, would you describe your travels?

line 57   To please his father, young Kroc made a halfhearted attempt to complete his education. Was he trying
a) very hard, or
b) with limited enthusiasm?

line 126   In the first McDonald's there was no place for young people to hang around. How could you say in your own words: "Joe and his friends always hang around at the corner of Vine Street and 10th"?

line 140   Kroc was not the kind of man who takes no for an answer. This means:
a) he insisted that people say "No, Sir"

b) he was not discouraged by a "no"
c) he didn't understand "no" because he was of German origin

Prefixes

omni

1. Coolidge said that "persistence and determination alone are *omnipotent.*" Some people would say: "Money is *omnipotent.*" What does the word mean? What does omni seem to mean?
2. According to most religions, only God is *omniscient* and *omnipotent.* How else can you express the same idea?
3. What meaning does omni have in the following sentence?
   In the United States, Coca-Cola, hamburger places and pizza parlors are *omnipresent.*
4. While some animals are called carnivorous because they eat only meat, and others are called herbivorous because they eat only grass, man is described as *omnivorous.* Why?

The Main Idea

Check the statement in each group that best expresses the essential meaning of each paragraph, rather than supporting facts or nonessential details.

Par. 1–2 together:
a) In 1983 the McDonald's Corporation was selling 3 billion hamburgers per year.
b) In 30 years, someone turned McDonald's, once a small, family business, into a giant, worldwide corporation.
c) The first McDonald's was located in San Bernardino, California.

Par. 4
a) Ray Kroc was 52 when he saw his first McDonald's.
b) Ray Kroc at one time sold milkshake mixers.
c) The man who built up the giant McDonald's corporation was an old man in bad health.

Par. 5
a) Calvin Coolidge said that nothing is more common than unsuccessful men of talent.
b) Persistence remained Ray Kroc's key word all his life.
c) Kroc so admired Coolidge's words that he had them framed.

Par. 6
a) Kroc started with no money and little education.
b) Kroc enlisted in the Ambulance Corps to get out of school.
c) Kroc's father wanted him to complete his education.

12 RAY KROC

Par. 7
    a) Kroc was a pretty good piano player.
    b) After trying several professions, Kroc found success as a salesman.
    c) Someone had predicted that Kroc would make a fortune in food or music.

Par. 8
    What is the main idea of this paragraph?

Topics for Discussion

1. Kroc thought that a musician's life was neither good nor respectable enough for a family man. Do you agree with him?
2. President Calvin Coolidge seemed to think that persistence was much more important than education and even intelligence. What do you think of this idea? If you had a choice, would you rather be intelligent, persistent, or educated (assuming that you can have only one of the three qualities)?
3. Kroc tried several lines of work—first as a musician, then as a real estate agent, then as a salesman, and finally as organizer of a chain of eating establishments. Do you think that this is the best way to find success, or would it be surer to get training in one type of work and concentrate one's efforts on that one profession?
4. "I wanted adventure!" said Kroc, speaking of the way he felt when he was around forty, and leaving the Lily-Tulip Company. He probably felt the same way at fifty-two, when he embarked on another career. What do you think about his attitude—is a spirit of adventure likely to help a man get ahead, or to wreck him? Was Kroc foolish to start a new career at fifty-two? Would you have done it?

Profile
Part Two

What was Ray Kroc doing when we left him at the end of Part One?

Had he already understood how the McDonald's idea would make his fortune?

Skim the text to find the answers to the following questions:

- Is Ray Kroc still the head of the McDonald's Corporation?
- Are the McDonald brothers still part of McDonald's?
- Did Ray Kroc have any interests or hobbies besides his business?

Now that he had found his lifework, Ray Kroc threw into the task all his formidable energy and dedication. To begin with, he built himself a McDonald's in Des Plaines, near his home, in order to learn the hamburger business "from the inside." This undertaking immediately revealed a major flaw in the terms of his agreement with the McDonalds. The contract stipulated that all new outlets should be identical in every detail to the San Bernardino drive-in. In his eagerness to reach an accord, Kroc had not given a thought to the diversity of American climates. In the dry heat of Southern California there was no need for a furnace; and since the stock of potatoes could safely be stored on the roof, there had been no reason to provide the building with a storage basement. Not so in Illinois. Although Kroc did obtain by telephone the authorization to make the necessary adjustments in cold states, the McDonalds never confirmed the permission in writing, and Kroc had to live for years in fear of a lawsuit from the wily brothers.

This first cloud in his sky didn't prevent Kroc from pursuing his mission with zeal. On the road all day long with his mixers, he would come back to Des Plaines to cook, clean, and serve at his drive-in until closing time. He worked twelve to eighteen hours a day, carried the bags of potatoes, sliced the fries if need be, and applied his meticulous attention to every detail of the operation, including the appearance of the restrooms. Nothing was too small for an all-out effort. The french fries, for example, gave him much trouble, and the way he handled the problem is so typical of Kroc's tenacity that it can serve as an illustration.

Kroc was not satisfied with his french fries. No matter how hard he tried to find the right way to prepare and cook them (and he tried many), they never came out as crisp and delicious as those he had enjoyed on that fateful day in San Bernardino. After uncounted experiments and worried consultations by phone with the McDonalds, Kroc took his problem to the Potato and Onion Association, which had no answer to offer. The undaunted Kroc then insisted on taking his potatoes to the Association's laboratory. The scientists, finding no other explanation, suggested that perhaps the sun and hot breezes of Southern California had a drying and curing effect on the potatoes kept outdoors. This turned out to be the right idea. Kroc found a way to cure his potatoes in their basement through the use of large electric fans, and the french fries have been the pride of McDonald's ever since. They remained Kroc's favorite item on the menu.

The Des Plaines outlet opened in the spring of 1955. Shortly thereafter, Kroc, who throughout his career displayed a superior flair for choosing associates and subordinates, took on a partner—Harry Sonneborn, a former vice-president of Tasty-Freeze.[1] Sonneborn lacked Kroc's fanatic drive, aggressiveness, and passion for detail. But though he was never the force that moved the enterprise, he was its financial genius.

Sonneborn suggested to Kroc that instead of selling franchises, he should buy the lots, build the outlets, and rent them to his franchisees; he would thus make money both ways—on the franchise and on the rents. It was

---

[1] Tasty-Freeze—a fast-food chain serving soft ice cream.

Sonneborn also who arranged to borrow the $1.5 million needed to acquire the first lots and to erect the first outlets. (The idea worked splendidly: to this day McDonald's Corporation draws more profit from its real estate holdings than from its franchises.)

By the end of 1956, Kroc had managed to establish eleven additional drive-ins in California. In 1957, fifteen more were operating in various states. Kroc was prospecting furiously for new locations while still selling his Multimixers. But despite his backbreaking work load, he was not accumulating much money. For all his shrewdness, he had made a miscalculation at the time of his contract with the McDonald brothers: still thinking in terms of mixers, and counting on the sales of his gadget to make his fortune, he had agreed to keep only 1.4 percent of the gross revenue from the McDonald's outlets. Since Kroc was putting practically all of his share back into the business to offset his expenses, he had no choice but to support himself and his family with the proceeds from the mixer sales. As time went by, he became increasingly irritated with the McDonalds, who were doing absolutely nothing to deserve the money that they were receiving from him. It was high time, he thought, to get rid of these inactive partners.

In 1960, Sonneborn negotiated a loan that enabled Kroc to free himself from his contract. The McDonalds were demanding $2.5 million to relinquish their interest in the chain and to let Kroc use their golden arches and their name (which certainly sounded better than "Kroc's"). With the interest on the loan, Kroc ended up paying $14 million—still a bargain, he declared in the 1970s, since by that time he would have been giving the brothers $30 million per year.

1960 was a turning point in Ray Kroc's life. He was now entirely committed to his McDonald's chain; there was no reason to waste more time on the Multimixers. Kroc sold his rights to the mixer for $100,000, a sum that came just in time to pay for his divorce. As always, he was short of cash. He was also deep in debt at an age—fifty-eight—when it might have been wiser to use some caution. But Kroc was unafraid. "I was going for broke,"[2] he said to a journalist after his retirement years later. "Don't get me wrong, I am not a gambler. But when I like something, I go all the way." In 1963, Kroc decided to put the McDonald's stock on the market at $22 a share. At the end of the day, it was selling briskly at $30 a share, and before the end of the month at $50. The move, besides creating the McDonald's Corporation, made Kroc a multimillionaire overnight, with more than 50 percent of the stock.

Finding himself with a fortune at last didn't incline Kroc to take life easy. Far from it. From then on he applied himself to the task of enlarging the network of hamburger stands across the country, and at the same time of

---

[2] to go for broke—to risk everything.

perfecting and polishing what came to be known as "The System"—the combination of rules and methods and sentimental ties that still govern (it is claimed) the giant corporation, and that bind its employees, from executives to kitchen help, into a tight family. Kroc loved to boast that he didn't have to give contracts to his people. "There is an esprit de corps[3] at McDonald's that is a religion," he would say proudly. He took great pains to establish that family feeling throughout the company by encouraging a friendly informality at all levels, by keeping all members informed of what was going on in the McDonald's community, by giving praises and bonuses for a job well done, and by trying to keep the employees proud of "belonging."

During those busy years, Kroc meticulously worked out every step of the preparation and service of the food in the outlets: the equipment of the kitchens, the timing of the operations, the training of the workers, the length of their hair, nails and moustaches, the size and weight of the ingredients—everything was determined carefully. All the while, Kroc was crisscrossing the country to find interesting locations and to observe the eating habits of the population. Soon he began to work out the details of establishing McDonald's abroad; the first foreign outlets opened in 1972, marking a new phase in the history of the corporation.

While Kroc travelled, Sonneborn was left "home" to take care of the administrative side of the business and of the financial situation, all of which he had always done brilliantly. But now that, like Kroc, he had become very wealthy, Sonneborn was losing his eagerness to exert himself. After 1965 he began to disappear for a week or two at a time in Alabama, where he had built a house. Kroc couldn't understand Sonneborn's attitude, and he resented it as much as he had resented the McDonalds' inactive status in the late fifties. Out of patience with his partner in 1966, he pushed him out of the association with a pension of $100,000 a year to supplement his comfortable cushion of McDonald's stock. Kroc himself was beginning to think of stepping down, although he had no intention of neglecting the company as Sonneborn had done. He was grooming his favorite aide, Fred Turner, to take his place at the head of the corporation. Turner was named President of McDonald's Corporation in December 1973. Kroc remained Chairman of the Board. He never completely ceased injecting his dynamism and his ideas into the operation. His fortune when he retired was estimated at about $500 million. Ray Kroc had finally fulfilled the dream of his youth.

Until he died in January 1984 from a heart attack, Kroc enjoyed the life of the super-rich in the company of his third wife, a former professional organist, and of her daughter (his own daughter Marilyn had died of dia-

---

[3] esprit de corps—a French expression describing a strong feeling of solidarity and loyalty to a team, family, or group.

betes in 1973). He divided his time between a luxurious apartment in Chicago, a 210-acre ranch in Southern California, and a mansion in Florida—complete with yacht, pools, butler, and a front-door bell that chimed "You Deserve a Break Today . . ."[4] whenever a visitor rang.

The ranch still serves as headquarters for the Kroc Foundation, an organization dedicated to research on diabetes, arthritis, and multiple sclerosis (the disease of Ray's sister), under the direction of Dr. Robert L. Kroc, Ray's brother. Mrs. Kroc is in charge of a $1 million "alcoholic education" program, financed also by the foundation. A very generous man, the Hamburger King gave massively to charities—mostly hospitals, zoos, and scientific establishments. But he always refused to contribute to higher education. Whenever a college or university approached him for help, he answered that he would consider their request if they added a trade school to their campus. In 1972 he celebrated his seventieth birthday by giving $7.5 million to charity and $9 million in stock to the McDonald's employees. He also presented the corporation with a jet plane, and a fleet of especially equipped busses for the use and pleasure of his employees.

In 1974, Kroc startled the sports community by buying for $12 million ("Just for the fun of it!") what was then an extremely unsuccessful baseball team, the San Diego Padres. The Padres had distinguished themselves by losing 500 games in five years. "It's the losing-est[5] team in a major league!" laughed Kroc. But he was not always in a laughing mood when he watched his boys play, and the Padres soon learned that their new boss had a hot temper and a direct approach. At the end of a particularly bad game, Kroc roared in the public address system: "We are putting on a lousy show for you. I apologize for it. I am disgusted with it. This is the most stupid baseball playing I have ever seen!"[6]

Although he never intended to run the team himself, Kroc had great fun planning all sorts of changes and events for his Padres: "Children's Days" at the stadium, with free hamburgers and Cokes for each youngster; beautification of the ballpark and of the surrounding areas, which of course weren't clean enough; pleasure cruises on his yacht for the players who did well and their families. To the end he was bubbling with new ideas and projects. In a long interview for *Baseball* magazine in 1974, he explained the reasons for his purchase and, incidentally, his attitude toward wealth: "I just wanted a hobby. It's an extravagant hobby, for sure. I could make more money out of one hamburger stand than I can on baseball. But I love baseball and I have no interest in money. Never in my life have I sought money, and yet I have never been poor. . . . The only enjoyment I get out of making money is from the knowledge that people always say: 'If

---

[4]"You Deserve A Break Today . . . At McDonald's!" is the theme song of McDonald's.
[5]losing-est—a superlative made up by Kroc.
[6]The Padres went on to win the National League championship in 1984.

you are so smart, why aren't you rich?" Well, I am rich, so I guess you
could say I am smart. I am in baseball so I can have fun. Money has nothing to do with it. . . . All money represents for me is pride of achievement."

Understanding the Text

True or False? If the statement is partly true only, explain why.

1. Kroc must have wished that he had given more thought to the terms of his contract with the McDonalds.
2. Kroc should have stopped selling Multimixers as soon as he came back to Illinois.
3. Kroc was irritated with the McDonalds and he was afraid of them.
4. Kroc always regretted the high price he had to pay to get rid of the McDonalds.
5. Kroc was a good boss who cared about the feelings of his employees.
6. Sonneborn was the financial genius and the driving force of the partnership.
7. The idea of building and renting the outlets to the franchisees was a disaster for McDonald's.
8. Kroc never stopped being involved in the running of his company, even after his retirement.
9. Kroc didn't mind spending money for good causes, but he never spent money to please himself.
10. Kroc always refused to contribute to colleges and universities.

Scanning Exercises

A. *Scan the profile section you have just read, for the following details:*

1. What was the name of Ray Kroc's brother?
2. When did Kroc open his first outlet?
3. How does the author define the "System"?
4. Why did Kroc call his San Diego Padres "the losing-est" team in a major league?
5. When was the McDonald's stock put on the market?
6. What metaphor can you find in the text?

B. *This exercise requires scanning both parts of the profile.*

Sum up in the brief list below the progress of McDonald's since the opening of the first outlet by the McDonald brothers. The dates of the turning points are indicated as guides. It is not necessary to write complete sentences.

1. _____ Ray Kroc discovers the McDonald brothers' restaurant in San Bernardino _____ (before 1954)

18 RAY KROC

2. _____ (1955)
   _____ other significant
   _____ facts, same year
3. _____ (1960)
4. *issue of stock MCD $22% → 80% - Kroc Martin Allen → 50%* (1963)
5. *First MCD outlet* (1972)
6. *December became retainer person with $500* (1973)
7. *January he died from heart attack* (1984)

Go back to the list of figures provided at the beginning of the chapter. What do those figures show after 1972? What is the explanation, or at least one of the explanations?

Your Opinion

1. What do you think of Kroc's statement: "I am not a gambler"? Do you agree with him? How do you justify your answer?
2. Do you think that Kroc was telling the truth when he said: "Never in my life have I sought money"?
3. How do you see Ray Kroc? Do you feel that he was: intelligent, refined, calm, sentimental, a realist in business, stupid, hot tempered, cold, formal, informal, generous, proud, modest, ambitious, or . . . ?

Vocabulary

For each of the following, find the meaning of the underlined word.

line 6	Kroc's contract with the McDonald brothers <u>stipulated</u> that all new outlets should conform to the original one. What word could you use instead of *stipulated*?
line 14	The author states that Kroc lived in fear of the <u>wily</u> brothers. Is this likely to be a compliment? From the context, *wily* is likely to refer to the brothers' a) kindness b) honesty c) judgment
line 32, 34	The California sun <u>cured</u> the potatoes. This means: a) the sun improved the health of the potatoes b) the sun had a good effect on the potatoes c) the sun destroyed the potatoes
line 40	Sonneborn never had Kroc's fanatic <u>drive</u>. In this context, *drive* refers to Kroc's a) energy b) driving skill c) belief
line 48	McDonald's <u>holdings</u> must refer to

PROFILE 19

	a) its property
	b) its agents
	c) its sales
line 59	Kroc used his revenue to <u>offset</u> his expenses.
	a) hide *make up for*
	b) expand
	c) balance
line 66	For $2.5 million the McDonald brothers <u>relinquished</u> their interest.
	a) renewed
	b) gave up
	c) expanded
line 79	"<u>Don't get me wrong</u>, I am not a gambler," said Kroc.
	a) Don't misunderstand me
	b) Don't hurt me
	c) Don't think badly of me
line 97	When Kroc is pleased with an employee, he gives the person a <u>bonus</u>, which is likely to be
	a) extra work
	b) good words
	c) extra payment
line 99	Kroc worked out every step of the preparation of food <u>meticulously</u>.
	a) partially
	b) reluctantly
	c) in great detail
line 103	Kroc <u>crisscrossed</u> the country to find new locations. How would you express the same idea in your own words?
line 152	If you want a person to know what you think, you can take the <u>direct</u> or the <u>indirect approach</u>. What is the difference?
line 153	Kroc apologized for the <u>lousy</u> performance of his team. Lousy (a slang word) obviously means:
	a) very bad
	b) very good
	c) interesting

Prefixes

<u>mis</u> and <u>mal</u>

Mis and mal indicate that something is either wrong or bad. When Ray Kroc agreed to receive only 1.4 percent of the revenue from the franchises, for example, he made a *miscalculation*—a bad calculation. He certainly realized later that he had made a *mistake*.

1. If someone says: "I was misinformed" what does it mean?
2. Doctors and lawyers are sometimes sued for *malpractice*. What might this refer to? *malpractical*

3. Do you ever *misspell* or *mispronounce* words?
4. Do you think that television ads sometimes *misrepresent* products?
5. What can be done to help people fight *malnutrition*? Is malnutrition always a matter of money?
6. A felony is a serious crime, which can be punished by long prison terms or even death. A *misdemeanor* is a minor crime, usually punished by a fine or a short jail term. What, in your opinion, should be considered a misdemeanor?
7. Is *mistreating* a child a felony or a misdemeanor? Is mistreating an animal a felony or a misdemeanor?

The Main Idea

Check the statement in each group that best expresses the essential meaning of the paragraph.

Par. 1
   a) Kroc found out that the climate of Illinois is different from the climate of California.
   b) In cold states it was impossible to adhere to the clauses of the contract.
   c) Kroc couldn't get a written authorization from the McDonalds.

Par. 2
   a) Kroc worked hard, doing anything that needed to be done.
   b) Kroc paid attention to the appearance of the restrooms.
   c) Kroc had much trouble with the french fries.

Par. 3
   a) Kroc couldn't make good french fries.
   b) The french fries were Kroc's favorite item on the menu.
   c) Kroc took great pains with every detail of his business.

Par. 4
   a) The number of outlets grew rapidly.
   b) Kroc, who was making little money, became irritated with the McDonalds.
   c) Kroc was keeping only 1.4 percent of the gross revenues of the outlets.

Par. 5
   a) Kroc found a partner who could help in financial matters.
   b) Sonneborn was a former vice-president of Tasty Freeze.
   c) It cost Kroc $14 million to terminate the contract with the McDonalds.

Par. 6   What is the main idea of the paragraph?

Devising Questions

After reading the passage below, prepare a few questions for the class to answer. These should be:

   a) questions about the main facts or the meaning of the story, such as the questions usually found in "Understanding The Text"; or
   b) questions of opinions ("Do you think that . . ." etc.)

The purpose of this exercise is to separate the main facts or ideas of a story from the less significant details. It would hardly be worthwhile, for instance, to ask whether June Martino had $70 or $72 million when she retired.

JUNE MARTINO

When Ray Kroc was still selling Multimixers, a woman named June Martino approached him for a job. A good judge of people, Kroc was impressed by the woman, who seemed eager and very bright; and even though she admitted that she didn't know anything about bookkeeping, he hired her as a bookkeeper. He had a feeling that she would be a fast learner, and once again his instinct proved right. June, who at that time desperately needed to earn a salary, was happy to get any kind of job. Kroc couldn't pay her much, as he explained regretfully, but he promised to give her a raise as soon as he could.

Kroc was delighted with his new bookkeeper, for she was not only as intelligent as he had surmised, but extremely hardworking. He was not quite as pleased, however, with his secretary, whom he eventually fired. By then, Kroc had begun to work full-time on the McDonald's franchise, and since he was away much of the time, he needed a dedicated and reliable secretary who would be a real assistant to him. The best solution, he decided, was to give the position to June Martino. June's situation had changed since she had come to work for Kroc; her husband was making a good living and as a consequence she didn't really need her salary. She therefore suggested to Kroc that he pay her in McDonald's stock instead of cash, an idea that her boss found excellent.

Later on, June Martino persuaded her husband to give up his own electronics business in order to organize a special workshop where he would invent and build the many gadgets that Kroc wanted for improving his kitchens. Mr. Martino did well over the years, but his wife did even better. When she decided to retire, she had accumulated about $70 million worth of McDonald's shares. Kroc, who was usually displeased when an old and trusted member of his staff left the corporation, didn't show any ill humor toward June Martino. She was a nice lady who had earned her wealth, he said, and who had a right to enjoy it. Besides, he added, "I like to make people happy."

Topics for Discussion

1. Over the recent past, the fast-food industry (hamburgers, hot dogs, fried chicken, pizzas) has been increasingly popular throughout the world. In your opinion, what accounts for that popularity? Do you think that the trend will continue? What improvements would you suggest to McDonald's and other such places?
2. How healthy do you think it is to eat regularly in fast-food outlets?

3. The original McDonald's had a very simple menu, and today's menu at the chain is still limited. Other fast-food outlets offer many choices. Which do you prefer? What are the advantages and disadvantages for the customer?
4. What do you think of the saying quoted by Kroc: "If you are so smart, why aren't you rich?" Is there a connection between smartness and financial success?
5. Kroc said once: "It takes a particular kind of mind to find beauty in a hamburger bun." What do you think he meant? Do you agree with him?
6. Kroc demanded that universities start a trade school if they wanted to benefit from his generosity. Was this unreasonable? Should colleges and universities teach trades, or should they remain places of academic learning, leaving separate establishments to take care of other types of training?

Reading

The piece that you are about to read has been left intentionally without a title. Skim it rapidly to find out what it is about.

The heart of the McDonald's empire, known as Hamburger Central, is an ultra-modern, eight-story building in Oak Ridge, near Chicago. As chairman of the board, Ray Kroc kept an office there, but since 1974 the corporation has been run by his most devoted disciple, Fred Turner, who started his career as cook in Kroc's Des Plaines drive-in. Turner so impressed his demanding boss with his dedication to the pursuit of the perfect hamburger that Kroc kept promoting him regularly and eventually put him in charge of his beloved corporation. Through every step of his ascension, Turner proved himself worthy of Kroc's trust. "Fred didn't go to college," Kroc commented once. "But he has what we need: spirit and grit and dedication and integrity. Forget the brains. Fred is a multimillionaire, but it hasn't slowed him down!"

The basic principles governing the McDonald's operation have remained unchanged since Kroc adopted the motto "Q.S.C.V." for Quality, Service, Cleanliness, and Value. The aim is still to serve good food at reasonable prices and to offer pleasant and efficient service in spotless surroundings. Since the responsibility for maintaining the high standards established by the Founding Father rests on the managers of the outlets (now called "restaurants" by the corporation), it is essential to prepare them for their task. Therefore, after paying $20,000 for the franchise (1983 figure), the would-be manager is required to undergo a period of training at Hamburger University, which is located in Hamburger Central. There, before receiving his degree, he studies the 385-page Operations Manual, the company's bible, and takes courses in subjects such as marketing, operations, building maintenance, competition and cash control—not to mention cooking techniques. Since most of the McDonald's employees under the managers are teenagers or students in their early twenties, the future operators are also instructed in the best ways to communicate with the young generation. When the candidate has completed his academic training and received his degree (either as Bachelor or Master of Hamburgology), he still has to spend about 500 working hours in a McDonald's.

There is a purpose to this careful preparation that goes beyond the practical knowledge required to run a fast-food outlet worthy of its golden arches. The managers must be able to inspire in their subordinates that love and respect for the company, that esprit de corps so dear to Ray Kroc which, in his mind, was the strength and the distinction of his corporation.

Once they have gone through the different phases of their training, the managers can be relied upon to insure the perfect uniformity imposed by Kroc. It is their business to guarantee that you will eat the same Big Mac in Buffalo as in New Orleans or San Diego, and hopefully as in Paris or Tokyo. All the kitchens are uniformly equipped with stainless steel counters and stove (for easy cleaning) and with all the computerized gadgets that can improve the efficiency of the work—such as the electric light that warns the cook that the meat patties must be turned ("never flipped!" said Kroc). The cooking area, like the restrooms and the parking lot, must be kept immaculate at all times. The windows are washed inside and outside every morning. And woe to the cook caught with a spot on his clothes! The measurements and weights of all ingredients have been determined by Kroc once and for all, after much experimenting: the size of the buns (3½ inch) and their content in sugar (higher than in commercial buns to produce the right degree of crispness); the size and weight of the patties (1.6 ounces), the precise amount of onion (1/4 ounce) and of the pre-packaged mustard and ketchup. We know with what devotion Kroc studied the frying of the potatoes; but he also had a special scoop devised to serve exactly the same number of fries in each bag—not one more or less. The help are allowed fifty seconds to serve a hamburger with fries and a milkshake.

To make sure that the food is always as good and fresh as advertised, the only grade of beef used is "prime" and all "old" food is promptly thrown away. Unsold hamburgers are disposed of after ten minutes, fries after seven minutes, coffee after thirty minutes. Any bun slightly dented by the fingers of a worker has to be discarded too. Each outlet is told how much food it is expected to discard per day.

Just in case an unworthy operator should be tempted to forget the rules, a small army of inspectors is constantly on the road, checking each McDonald's about twice a month. It is not unusual for a top executive of the corporation to show up at one of the stores, and the Founding Father himself used to do the same, becoming furious if he spotted cigarette butts on the parking lot. Such inspections are very important for the managers, who can receive a bonus for good performance, but can lose their franchise if they are repeatedly found below standard.

Some changes have occurred over the years, some of them at the instigation of Kroc himself, and surely all of them approved by him, for he would not have been too shy to express his displeasure otherwise. The stores are now larger, while the gaudy arches have been reduced to a more discreet and elegant size. McDonald's seems indeed to be aiming at elegance. Some stores are decorated with murals to fit the location—palm trees in Hawaii or fishnets near the seashore. Tables and chairs and sometimes even china were introduced as early as 1968. In Los Angeles and Maryland, some managers have tried candlelight on the tables and hostesses in long gowns, and an outlet in Atlanta once served its Coca-Cola in crystal glasses.

The menu itself has been expanded, although the new items had to be kept simple in order not to interfere with the efficiency of the service. First to appear was the Big Mac—two patties sandwiched between three half-buns; then came the Egg McMuffin (an egg on a bun) and a successful fish sandwich called Filet o' Fish; and finally Chicken McNuggets, introduced in 1983, which made McDonald's the nation's second-largest chicken retailer after Kentucky Fried Chicken. The Quarter Pounder, advertised as offering 4 ounces of beef to hungry customers, got McDonald's into trouble. Competitors were prompt to point out that the Quarter Pounder patty weighed no more than 2 $4/7$ ounces. A very popular television ad (for Wendy's) showed three old ladies trying to find the meat on an enormous bun—one of them inquiring "Where's the beef?" over and over again. McDonald's Corporation angrily countered that the patty of the Quarter Pounder indeed weighed 4 ounces—*before cooking!* The battle is not over.

The most important change in Hamburger Central's policies may be the one affecting the location of the stores. Like its main rivals (Wendy's, Jack-in-the-Box, Burger King, and Kentucky Fried Chicken), Kroc had first built his outlets along well-travelled routes or in the outskirts of towns, where middle-class families with children could be expected to patronize often the fast-food drive-ins. Kroc, through a specially conducted survey, had found out that in such families it is usually the children who choose the eating places. After 1958, Kroc began to open stores in the heart of big cities, where none of his competitors would venture. The results were remarkable—those outlets grossed twice as much as a typical suburban site. On the other hand, the new locations brought all sorts of new problems: higher fixed costs, difficulty in finding good help, theft, vandalism, racial tensions, and sometimes the hostility of the neighborhood.

McDonald's had to fight other difficulties due to its employment policies. Since the very beginning, the chain had relied almost exclusively on the work of teenagers, college students, and unemployed women, all eager to find part-time jobs. Such employees fit perfectly McDonald's needs, because the manager can schedule a larger staff at rush hours, and a small one in between. There is a further advantage: the part-time, unskilled workers are paid the absolute minimum wage and aren't entitled to fringe benefits such as medical insurance, social security payments, retirement, or vacations. The seventies saw several fierce anti-McDonald's campaigns, which Kroc fought furiously. He did his best to oppose in Washington any attempt to raise the legal minimum wages, won most of the battles, lost a few. But he must have been saddened to find his youthful employees so lacking in "esprit de corps." He was unhappy and irritated also when his competitors and even some scientists expressed doubts about the nutritional value of the McDonald's meal, and when his rivals started making fun of the fixed McDonald's menu and tried to beat it with "individually prepared" hamburgers and a choice of seasonings. The worst blow was to have the McDonald's famous cleanliness put in question when an outlet was closed for a while by a health inspector.

Is the Ideal fading in an overextended empire? Not much, surely, for the inspections remain severe in the franchised outlets and in the large proportion of outlets belonging directly to the corporation. In the foreign McDonald's, spread over 31 countries, allowances have to be made for the customs and tastes of the public, and control is more difficult. But Kroc, and Turner after him, have always maintained that the standards would never be allowed to decline.

Will McDonald's keep expanding? One might think that the ever-growing competition, the public's interest in gourmet or health food, and perhaps a certain boredom with the McDonald's menu, will eventually stop the multiplication of golden arches. But the corporation is putting up a good fight, by massive advertising (McDonald's is the second largest advertiser on television) and simply by keeping its fanatical attention to details and its willingness to try new approaches when the old ones fail. Kroc laughed at the predictions that the corporation might slow down in the future—he predicted 12,000 stores, worldwide.

Choosing a Title

Which of the following titles would be best for the text that you have just read?

> The Employment Policies of McDonald's
> McDonald's—The Future
> The McDonald's Empire
> The Training of McDonald's Managers
> Hamburger University
> McDonald's, Inc.—How It Works
> The New Face of McDonald's

Understanding the Text

What have you learned about:

1. the McDonald's motto:
   a) what qualities does it claim?
   b) is it still unchanged?
   c) has it been challenged?
2. the changes that have occurred:
   a) in the stores?
   b) in the menu?
   c) in the locations?
3. the kind of problems that McDonald's has faced?

A Critical Look at the Text

lines 24–29   Were Kroc's remarks about Fred Turner meant to be complimentary, or to be patronizing (i.e., meant to make Turner feel inferior)? Do you agree that brains are less important than spirit, courage, dedication, and integrity?

line 29   Could that last sentence refer to someone that Kroc had in mind?

line 34   The Founding Fathers of the United States were the men who wrote the Declaration of Independence and the Constitution. Who is the "Founding Father" here? Is the author serious, respectful, or lighthearted?

line 51   Is it necessary to learn to communicate with teenagers? How?

lines 92–99   What do you think of the "old food" policy?

Taking Notes for a Summary

Skimming through the text, note down what a person who wishes to manage a McDonald's outlet must do before being accepted as manager, and what his/her responsibilities will be then.

Write a brief summary based on your notes:

1. A man who wants to operate a McDonald's outlet must first _____

2. When he (she) is in charge of the outlet, the manager is expected __

Vocabulary

Complete the following sentences, from memory if you can, or after consulting the list provided below, which includes more words than necessary.

Ray Kroc didn't build his first drive-in in Chicago, but in a small community on the _____ of the big city. It was a small and simple building: two enormous, bright and _____ yellow arches attracted the attention of motorists. There was no decor inside, no _____ painted on the walls. Fred Turner and Kroc himself spent a great deal of time sweeping, washing, and scrubbing to keep the place _____. The extra workers hired to help during the _____ hours were expected to do the same. Those who did their best found a _____ of a few dollars in their pay at the end of the week. But _____ to the employees who failed to check the restrooms or who showed up for work with dirty hair.

disciple	gaudy	grit
fringe benefits	outskirts	motto
woe	rush	immaculate
bonus	manual	mural

Topics for Discussion

1. Have these texts about Ray Kroc and McDonald's changed your opinion of McDonald's? In what way?
2. Kroc opened McDonald's outlets in the hearts of big cities, which are often the sections of town inhabited by the poorest part of the population. Are you surprised that these outlets grossed more than the typical suburban places? Why would fast-food chains hesitate to open stores in the hearts of towns?
3. What do you know about health foods, and what do you think of them?
4. What do you think of McDonald's as an employer (based on the second part of the profile and on the preceding text)? Would you like to work for McDonald's?
5. If you have seen McDonald's outlets in countries other than the United States, how do they compare with those in the United States? Are they different? Do you think that they'll succeed there?

Rachel Carson

Woman environmentalist
(Cared about nature, animal)

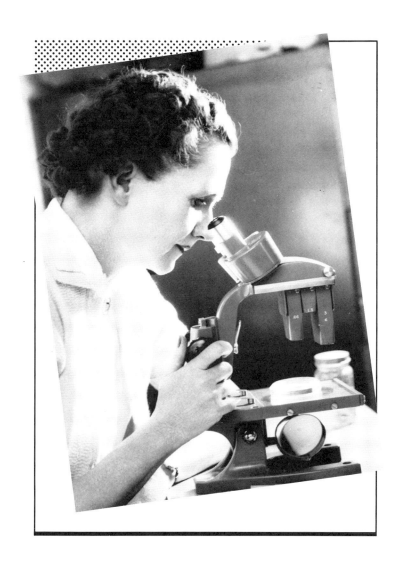

Introduction

The Vocabulary of Ecology

The last two sections of this chapter touch on the question of <u>ecology</u>, i.e., the relationship of all living things with each other and with their <u>environment</u>. Until *Silent Spring* appeared on the market, few people had been clearly aware that man was endangering the <u>ecological</u> balance, and indirectly his own survival, by his careless use of <u>toxic</u> substances—particularly by his use of the poisons known in laboratories as chlorinated hydrocarbons, the most famous of which is DDT.

Toxic wastes poured into the rivers by factories <u>pollute</u> the water and kill the fish. Other <u>chemicals</u> sprayed over fields and orchards are meant to <u>exterminate</u> <u>insects</u>, <u>rodents</u> (rats and field mice in particular) and other creatures that we call <u>pests</u> because they are a nuisance or an annoyance to us. Unfortunately the chemicals kill indiscriminately all animals living in the sprayed area, either directly or because the animals eat plants or other animals <u>contaminated</u> by the <u>pesticides</u>.

Some species of insects, we know, have already developed a natural resistance, an <u>immunity</u> to the chemicals used repeatedly against them. Other animals are not so fortunate; some species of birds, for example, face <u>extinction</u> because of the large number of adults destroyed, and also because the surviving birds, after eating toxic substances, produce eggs that are either sterile or too fragile to be hatched.

A great effort has been made to limit the use of harmful chemicals. In certain countries the use of DDT has been <u>banned</u> entirely.

A number of areas have been set aside as <u>sanctuaries</u> for birds and other endangered creatures; in such places, people are forbidden to hunt or fish, to interfere with the lives of the creatures living there, or to tamper in any way with their <u>habitat</u>. One such sanctuary, located in Maine, bears the name of Rachel Carson.

Looking Ahead

- Survey the chapter: what different sections does it include?
- Are you familiar with the problems concerning the protection of the environment? Which, in your opinion, are the most pressing?
- Can individuals or small groups of people do much to protect the environment? Suppose that this class decides to do something, what could it do?
- Does the name *Rachel Carson* mean anything to you? If it does, explain the meaning of the cartoon on the opposite page.

If you do not know about Rachel Carson, what can you guess from her photograph and from your survey of the chapter? Describe the cartoon

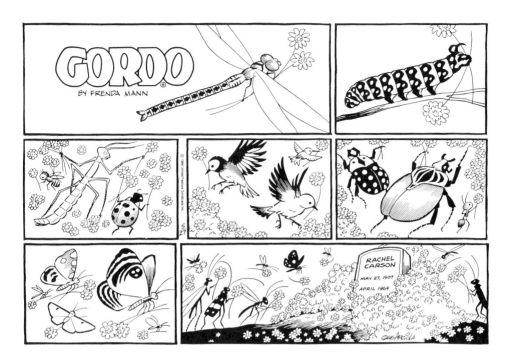

and give a possible interpretation of the action—what are the birds and insects doing? What reasons could they possibly have to act in such a fashion?

Cultural Notes for Profile, Part One

Greek Letter Societies: Three different kinds of American organizations bear names that consist of one or several Greek letters. Some are honorary associations, designed to further the social and intellectual interests of their members; such is the case of the Omega Club, a literary society to which Rachel Carson belonged. Another kind of Greek letter association gathers college and university students who want to live in the same house; these organizations are known as "fraternities" for men and "sororities" for women. Their purpose is purely social. Finally there are professional associations such as the Phi Delta Phi association for lawyers. We will encounter several of these Greek letter societies in later chapters.

Being accepted (or elected) as a member of an honorary or professional society is usually a sign of distinction in a particular field.

Logical Reasoning

The logical relationships between clauses (such as relationships of cause, purpose, consequence, contrast, condition or time sequence) is often marked by the use of a *connector*—which can be an adverb such as however, therefore or moreover, or a conjunction such as because, although, unless or until.

For the sentences of the following passage, choose from the list the connector that is most likely to make the story coherent. In some cases, any one of several connectors indicating the same relationship would do equally well.

Cause	Consequence	Contrast/Restriction
for, as	therefore	but
since	as a consequence	however
because	consequently	although
		even though

1. Gus Arriola drew the cartoon strip about the death of Rachel Carson. He signed the cartoon with the name Frenda Mann ("friend of man") _____ he wanted to suggest that the woman who tried to save insects and other small creatures from widespread poisoning was also a friend of mankind.
2. Arriola often draws animals in his cartoons; he is better known, _____, for the character called "Gordo."
3. Gordo, the hero of the strips, is a happy bachelor, a Mexican tourist guide who drives an old bus called "La Cometa Halley"—probably, _____ Gordo drives it at astronomical speed.
4. He has never had an accident, _____.
5. _____ he is fat, balding, and middle-aged, Gordo sees himself as a lady-killer.*
6. _____ poor Gordo is far from attractive, he doesn't have much success with the girls.
7. As a cartoon character, _____, Gordo is thoroughly lovable. The public likes him and _____ the strip has been published in a large number of newspapers.
8. You won't be able to find it now, _____, _____ Gus Arriola has retired, and no longer draws the strip.

*Lady-killer—a man who attracts women.

Profile
Part One

Born May 27, 1907
Died April 14, 1964

When Rachel Carson published *Silent Spring,* her critics accused her of being ignorant, inaccurate and unscientific.

Skim the text to find out if the charges
are likely to be true.

What was Rachel Carson's great interest during
the part of her life covered by this first
half of her profile?

Rachel Carson was born in Pennsylvania on a 65-acre farm belonging to her father, Robert Waldo Carson. Although close to the town of Springdale, the property was in a beautifully rural part of the state, still untouched, with trees, wildflowers, and animal life in all its variety. There Rachel Louise spent an uneventful and free childhood, close to nature. Mrs. Carson, a former teacher who was fond of books, music, and wild things, was anxious to impart her tastes to her daughter and to share her pleasures with her. She began to read to Rachel when the child was barely two years old. She took her for walks in the countryside and encouraged her to roam by herself. Rachel Louise hardly needed to be prompted: "I can remember no time when I was not interested in the out-of-doors and the whole world of nature," she later wrote to a friend. "Those interests, I know, I inherited from my mother and have always shared with her. I was rather a solitary child and spent a great deal of time in woods and beside streams, learning the birds and the insects and flowers."[1]

Solitary perhaps—but Rachel Carson never gave any indication that she had been lonely or unhappy. True, she didn't have many opportunities to make friends of her own age, other than her brother and her two sisters. Her mother, concerned over the child's delicate health, kept her out of school much of the time. Even so, Rachel kept up with the rest of the class without difficulty, thanks to her mother's tutoring and to the friendly interest of her teachers, who were attracted by her quick mind and her gentle personality. All the way through school and college, Rachel was to find devoted friends among her professors. But she doesn't seem to have achieved the same closeness with her classmates, to whom she appeared aloof and perhaps too serious. The students who prepared the high school yearbook printed under her photograph:

> Rachel's like the mid-day sun,
> Always very bright.
> Never stops her studying
> 'Til she gets it right.

Little Rachel loved books. What's more, she had made up her mind at an early age that she would some day write a few of her own. Her first attempts in the practice of her chosen craft were nothing short of spectacular. At the age of ten she won a Silver Badge for a story that she had sent to the *Saint Nicholas Magazine* for children, and the following year the

---

[1] This and other quotes of Rachel Carson in this profile are from Paul Brooks, *The House of Life* (Boston: Houghton Mifflin, 1972).

same magazine published another of her essays about Saint Nick. For this literary masterpiece she received three dollars and a few cents, at the magnificent rate of a penny a word. "I doubt," she said years later to a group of women journalists," that any royalty check in recent years has given me as great a joy as the notice of that award. Perhaps the early experience of seeing my work in print played its part in fostering my childhood dream of becoming a writer."

All through high school and during her first year at the Pennsylvania College for Women, Rachel Louise clung to her literary dream and concentrated on studying English, composition, and all the courses best suited to enrich and perfect her natural talent. She belonged to the literary Omega Club and contributed to the college paper. Her professors were unanimous in encouraging her to remain on that course. As for Rachel herself, although she was still uncertain of what form her inspirations would take, there was no question in her mind about the kind of career that lay in her future.

Rachel's plans took an abrupt turn in the course of her second year in college, when she enrolled in a required course in biology. It was her first taste of science. The course immediately appealed to her; so did the discipline and the precision of scientific work, the painstaking search for accuracy "til you get it right." She became so engrossed in the natural sciences that the following year she switched her major from English to marine zoology. The decision, coming so late in her studies, forced her to spend her remaining time in college in the laboratory, observing and probing organisms with the passionate concentration of the born scientist. But she was happy. Literature seemed almost forgotten then, although she did find time, occasionally, to write some poetry.

After graduating *summa cum laude*[2], Rachel Carson went on to Johns Hopkins University, where she took more scientific courses, including genetics, and received her master's degree in zoology in 1932. Since 1930 she had been teaching at the Johns Hopkins summer school. She also taught for five years as part-time instructor in the Zoology Department of the University of Maryland. But her happiest summer weeks were the ones she spent doing research at the Marine Biological Laboratory at Woods Hole, Massachusetts. There she could immerse herself completely in the kind of work she loved and in the captivating and awesome world of the ocean. Until then she had only known the sea through novels and poetry; and yet she had always felt strongly attracted to it. Her biographer, Paul Brooks, quotes her as saying:

> Years ago on a night when rain and wind beat against the window of my college dormitory room, a line from *Locksley Hall* burned itself in my mind:

---

[2] A degree is granted *summa cum laude* ("with high praise," in Latin) when the student has achieved a particularly high academic standard.

"For the mighty wind arises, roaring seaward, and I go. . . ."
I can still remember my intense emotional response as that line spoke to something within me, seeming to tell me that my own destiny was somehow linked with the sea. And so . . . it has been when I finally became its biographer, the sea has brought me recognition and what the world calls success.

The laboratory, where she was "almost literally surrounded by the ocean"—the beaches and their tiny inhabitants, the tide pools and rocks alive with small creatures laboring to feed and protect themselves—that was her blessed universe. There she never felt discomfort, fatigue, or cold. Toward the end of her career, when she was in her fifties and preparing *The Edge of the Sea,* she took her illustrator, Bob Hines, with her to the rocky shore where she was searching for the minuscule objects of her study among the seaweeds. For hours Hines watched her as she worked in the icy water, until finally she was so stiff with cold that she had to be carried home.

Much as Rachel Carson would have liked to remain at Woods Hole, other obligations were soon to require her presence at home. The death of her father forced her to take steps to support herself and her mother. She had to seek a job that would provide more income and security than her part-time teaching in summer schools. She did find a position—albeit a temporary one—in the Department of Fisheries in Washington, D.C. The work seemed to have been invented to make use of her abilities as a scientist and as a writer; it consisted in making up scripts for a series of broadcasts officially entitled "Romance under the Waters" but known in the Department as "The Seven Minute Fish Tales." Whether she realized it or not, Rachel Carson had stumbled onto something much more important, in the long run, than her modest salary: the subject matter of the books that were to make her famous, and to turn into knowledgeable sea-lovers her thousands of fascinated readers.

The Fish Tales series was nearing its end, in 1936, when Rachel's married sister died, leaving in the care of Rachel and her mother her two grammar-school daughters. The extra burden made it imperative for Rachel Carson to find a permanent position. As it turned out, there was an opening for a Junior Aquatic Biologist at the Department of Fisheries. Rachel Carson took the civil service examination that was required to qualify, and won with the highest score of all the candidates. Her first assignment was, again, to write scripts for more broadcasts, a task that she found most congenial.

In those years Rachel Carson was a gentle, frail-looking woman with an attractive, serious face and a great deal of quiet dignity. She was reserved with strangers and never had much small talk—probably a result of her shyness. With friends and family she was warm and gay, with a fine sense of humor that was particularly appreciated around her office. As a young woman, and even in middle age, she was by no means an austere and compulsive worker. She loved to go to parties and to entertain, and for a woman so shy and so private she collected a remarkable number of loyal and distinguished friends. All her life she remained close to her mother, who shared her interests and kept house for her, as Rachel hated to cook and never had much time for domestic chores anyway. She cared deeply for her relatives and was always ready to listen and to assist when needed. Her niece Virginia, who spent years with Rachel Carson, considered her more like an elder sister than an aunt, and remembered with pleasure the time that she had spent in Rachel's house. Virginia married, but Rachel Carson never did ("never had time," she claimed). Because of her career, of her single status and of her apparent self-sufficiency, it seemed that she might be a confirmed feminist, and a journalist once asked her if this was the case. "Oh no," she said. "I am not interested in things done by women or by men, but in things done by people."

For about a year Rachel Carson kept working on her broadcasts. When the series was completed, she was asked to prepare a different kind of script—something "about the sea in general". Many years later she was to describe the ensuing set of events: "I set to work, but somehow the material rather took charge of the situation and turned into something that was, perhaps, unusual as a broadcast for the Commissioner of Fisheries. My chief read it and handed it back with a twinkle in his eye. "I don't think it will do," he said. "Better try again. But send this to the *Atlantic*." Eventually I did and the *Atlantic* accepted it. Since then I have told my chief of those days that he was really my first literary agent."

Actually, the *Atlantic* piece was not her first article in print. For almost five years she had been supplementing her income by contributing articles to the *Baltimore Sun,* always about fisheries and sea creatures. She had also tried repeatedly to get some of her poems published; but her efforts in that direction had only brought her a rich collection of rejection slips.

The piece published by the *Atlantic* under the title "Undersea" is a marvelously clear and evocative introduction to the ocean, its changing moods, its mysterious depths and its beaches—all in the flowing and lyrical style that marked all her writings, scientific or not. She managed to convey to her readers some of her understanding and love of the sea, with all the accuracy and care of the biologist, but without pedantry or specialized jargon. She denied that there was such a thing as "scientific writing"—only writing, and science did not have to exclude beauty. "If there is poetry in my books about the sea, it is not because I deliberately put it there, but because no one could write truthfully about the sea and leave out the poetry."

Undersea was her first bright step into the career that she had contemplated years ago when she was sending stories to a children's magazine. It brought her much more than a momentary pride of authorship. Shortly after the publication of the article, Rachel Carson received a letter from Quincy Howe, who was then an editor with the Simon and Schuster publishing company. Howe wanted to know if she had ever considered writing a book in the vein of *Undersea,* in which case Simon and Schuster would be interested in hearing about it. The meeting with Quincy Howe resulted in Rachel Carson's first "sea book," *Under the Sea Wind.* It took her three years to write it for, busy as she was at the Fisheries, she could only work in the evening, alone with two of her staunchest supporters: "In those concluding months of work on the book, I often wrote late at night in a large bedroom that occupied the entire second floor of our house on Flower Avenue. My constant companions during these otherwise solitary sessions were two precious Persian cats, Buzzie and Kito. Buzzie in particular used to sleep on my writing table, on the litter of notes and manuscript sheets. . . ."

Cats held a special place in Rachel Carson's heart. She wrote once about what she considered their special qualities in a letter to the Cat Welfare Association: "I have always found that a cat has a truly great capacity for friendship. He asks only that we respect his personal rights and his individuality; in return he gives his devotion, understanding and companionship. Cats are extremely sensitive to the joys and sorrows of their human friends; they share their interests."

Understanding the Text

Is it true?

1. Almost from birth, Rachel Carson was likely to turn into an ecologist.
2. A required college course changed the direction of her life forever.
3. But she always loved literature much more than science.
4. Rachel chose marine biology because she had always enjoyed her trips to the sea shore.
5. Her family responsibilities forced her to find increasingly better sources of income.
6. If you had been introduced to Rachel Carson, it would have been easy to have a lively conversation with her.
7. She was not to particularly interested in feminism.
8. Her job at the Department of Fisheries was a lucky step for her and for the rest of her career.
9. When her boss refused *Undersea,* Rachel Carson sent the article to Simon and Schuster.

Appraising the Text

1. Did you find any "tongue-in-cheek" word or expression in the text?
2. One sometimes finds in a story some sentences or a whole paragraph that seem *irrelevant* to the main line of the tale. Is there anything in this first part of the profile that doesn't seem essential to the knowledge of Rachel Carson's career?

38 RACHEL CARSON

3. Can you infer from the text
    a) whether or not Rachel Carson's family was wealthy?
    b) whether or not she had a pleasant relationship with her chief?
    c) whether or not her poetry was better than her prose?
4. Does it seem to you that the tone of the profile is: serious, ironic, friendly, antagonistic, neutral?

Scanning for Details

1. What degree did Rachel Carson receive in 1932, a Ph.D. in zoology or a Ph.D. in biology?
2. Who was Rachel Carson's illustrator?
3. Complete the line from *Locksley Hall*:
   "For the _____ and I go."
4. What are the titles of the two books by Rachel Carson mentioned in the text?
5. What newspaper published Rachel Carson's articles?
6. What did she answer when she was asked if she was a confirmed feminist?
7. What were the names of her cats?

Vocabulary

A. *Complete each sentence with the most appropriate word from the list below, which includes more words than necessary. Be sure to make all needed adjustments in articles, verbs and nouns.*

to probe	to convey	to impart
pedantry	engrossed	congenial
twinkle	compulsive	imperative
spectacular	evocative	rejection

1. Rachel Carson wrote four books, three of them about the sea. In these three she tried to _____ to her readers some of her knowledge of the subject, and to _____ the awe and wonder that the ocean inspired in her.
2. One of the reasons for the success of the books is the _____ _____ power of Rachel Carson's style, which makes the illustrations almost unnecessary.
3. Although she was not a cold person, she was ill at ease with people who didn't share her interests or tastes. In more _____ company, however, she was gay and witty.
4. As a young girl, Rachel had been too _____ in her studies to take part in the sports and games of her classmates.
5. She was serious and hardworking; but she never showed any signs of intellectual arrogance or _____.
6. Ray Kroc was a _____ worker, but Carson didn't really

PROFILE 39

have the same obsession; she only worked hard because she had to.

B. 1. When Rachel Carson met people for the first time, she couldn't find anything to say to them. She admitted that she was not good at small talk. What could she have talked about that would qualify as small talk?
2. Rachel Carson looked in tide pools for crabs and other small creatures. What is the expression *tide pool* likely to describe?
3. She said that her Silver Badge pleased her more than any royalty check that she received later as an author. What are *royalties* likely to be in such a context?

Prefixes and Suffixes

A. A chapter about scientists and universities usually includes many words ending in graphy and logy.

Graphy refers to something that has to do with writing. *Epigraphy* is the study of old inscriptions on monuments. *Stenography* is a sort of rapid writing using symbols. Logy indicates a science or a study. *Geology* is the science (or study) of the Earth history, and *speleology* is the study of natural caves, for example. In the chapter about Ray Kroc, we found a *phrenologist*. What did *phrenology* seem to be? What would you expect *graphology* to be?

B. Bio, at the beginning of a word, indicates that the word has to do with life or with living organisms of some kind: animals, plants, germs, etc.

1. What is the difference between *biology* and *biography*?
2. Medical students have to take *biochemistry* courses. What do you think they might study there?
3. Humanity is accumulating an enormous amount of trash: household refuse, papers, empty bottles and containers, broken objects, etc. People are concerned about the large number of bags and containers made of plastic, because such things, not being *biodegradable* like paper or wood, will last forever. What happens to biodegradable materials like wood and paper, or kitchen refuse?
4. Can you imagine what *biological* warfare would be?

C. The meaning of auto is comparable to the meaning of *self*. An *automatic* washing machine does the washing (almost) by itself.

1. In the same vein, what definition could you give for *automobile*?
2. What is the difference between a *biography* and an *autobiography*?
3. In the 1950s, many colonies won their *autonomy* from the great colonial powers. What does that mean?

4. Collectors pay a high price for *autographed* letters from famous people. Why are those letters particularly interesting, even if their content is not? When Rachel Carson was asked for her *autograph*, what did she have to do?

Key Words (Taking Notes)

Consider the first six paragraphs of Rachel Carson's profile. In each paragraph, select two words or groups of words that in your opinion are important in revealing Rachel Carson's personality or explaining her career. It would be correct, for example, to note down for paragraph 5 (lines 55–56): *science appealed to her* and *accuracy* (although you can make a different choice).

(*Instructor's Note:* One student can write on the blackboard the key words chosen for each paragraph. The class can then discuss which are the best choices.)

The Main Idea

Check the statement in each group that best expresses the essential meaning of the paragraph, rather than supporting facts or examples.

Par. 1
a) From an early age, Rachel Carson learned to enjoy nature and solitude.
b) Rachel's mother was an educated woman and a good mother.
c) Rachel Carson was the daughter of a Pennsylvania farmer.

Par. 2
a) She was not very healthy as a child.
b) To her classmates she looked like a perfectionist.
c) She was a serious student, closer to adults than to other children.

Par. 3
a) Even as a child, Rachel was a gifted writer.
b) She had two articles published in a magazine for children.
c) *Saint Nicholas Magazine* didn't pay much.

Par. 4
a) Rachel Carson went to a college for women in Pennsylvania.
b) All her friends and Rachel herself thought that she would be a writer.
c) Rachel Carson didn't know what to write about.

Par. 5
a) Biology was Rachel's first scientific source.
b) She still wrote poetry in college.
c) In college she discovered that she was even more interested in science than in literature.

Topics for Discussion

1. Rachel Carson attended a college for women. What do you think of such colleges:
   a) What are the advantages and disadvantages?
   b) Would you prefer to attend a school or college for members of your sex only?
2. Most colleges and universities have newspapers that are prepared and published by the students. The paper covers campus events, reviews plays and concerts performed at the college, gives practical information, and occasionally interviews important people who have come to the college or to the town.
   a) What is the value of such papers?
   b) Can such papers create problems?
   c) Suppose you were on the staff of your school paper. What topics would you suggest for the next issue?
3. Is the sea an important part of the Earth? In what way? Is the sea particularly important in the life of the country where you live or have lived? Can you think of countries for which the sea has been particularly important?

Cultural Notes for Profile, Part Two

Book clubs and book guilds offer to the public books of interest that have been recently published. Because of the large volume of sales, the books are offered at a reduced price. One of the best known such organizations, the Book-of-the-Month Club, was started in 1927. The club doesn't publish books, but chooses every month a number of works that its selection committee judges to be particularly good, and offers them to its subscribers across the nation. A book selected by the club is therefore assured of a large printing.

There are a number of specialized book clubs, such as the Scientific Book Club and the History Book Club.

The National Audubon Society is named for John James Audubon, a naturalist and artist born at the end of the eighteenth century, who devoted himself to the study of nature and especially to making drawings of American birds.

The National Audubon Society was founded in 1886 "to promote the conservation of wildlife and the natural environment, and to educate man regarding his relationship with, and his place within the natural environment and ecological system."

The society has established many sanctuaries and provides an educational program that includes publications and workshops for adults and children. It also sponsors a field research program.

Idioms

You will find in the text a few expressions that are used in informal speech:

To be at sea: to be confused, to be lost
To be out of one's depth: to be involved in something too deep, too complicated for one's abilities.
To make one's point: to explain one's ideas or argument clearly.

Profile
Part Two

Skim the text to find out the answers to the following questions:

- Did Rachel Carson keep her job at the Fish and Wildlife Services after the publication of her first book?
- What other books did she write?
- Did Rachel Carson ever have anything to do with television?

Under the Sea Wind came out in November 1941, one month before the attack on Pearl Harbor. It is difficult to understand now how this enchanting and engrossing book, so full of the romance and drama of life among sea-birds and ocean dwellers, could have passed unnoticed. But unnoticed it went, at least as far as the general public was concerned, in that first year of the American involvement in World War II. In scientific circles, however, the book did receive much attention and warm praise. It was chosen as the 1941 selection for the Scientific Book Club.

This limited but significant success, and the letters from scientists who had been impressed by her work, encouraged Rachel Carson to launch bravely into a second volume. She knew that the task would be even harder than the preparation of the *Sea Wind*. Her responsibilities at the Department (soon to become the Fish and Wildlife Services, under the Department of the Interior) were growing steadily. Between 1941 and 1952 she was promoted from Assistant Aquatic Biologist to Aquatic Biologist, then to Information Specialist and finally to Chief Editor. She described her job as "the work of a small publishing house": planning the publications of the Department's information program, overseeing the work of the writers, editing, illustrating, etc. It was a high-pressure position, involving long hours and take-home work. With each promotion Rachel Carson's burden increased, and when the time came to do the actual writing of her second book, the task seemed overwhelming.

Still, her main difficulty continued to be of a financial nature. With four persons to support on a salary that was never lavish, she had to keep writing articles for newspapers and magazines. She attempted several times to free herself by securing a well-paid job, first as editor of the *Readers' Digest,* then—when that attempt failed—with the New York Zoological Society and with the National Audubon Society. Nothing came of that either, and she had no choice but to struggle as best she could through the preparation of her book.

    Since *Under the Sea Wind* had been primarily devoted to the life of the shore and surface dwellers of the ocean, Rachel Carson was now planning to depict life in the deeper layers of the sea, all the way to the lightless, hardly explored ocean floor. She began to research her material, carefully and thoroughly as always, calling upon other scientists' expertise to supplement her own considerable knowledge. One of the experts that she consulted was William Beebe, the deep-sea explorer who, in the 1930s, had made a descent of 3,028 feet in his special diving-chamber, the bathysphere. Beebe was most willing to contribute his share of information, but he remarked, tongue-in-cheek, that Carson couldn't write about the abyss without having some first-hand knowledge of those mysterious regions. He would be delighted, he said, to take her deep-sea diving off the Bermudas. Rachel, amused, wrote to a friend that Beebe was making all advance preparations to insure that she meet "all the proper sharks, octopuses, and other members of the local fauna." The project seemed a bit ambitious for a woman who was not even good at swimming, let along diving. At the end, they reached a compromise, and Rachel Carson went down fifteen feet, off the coast of Florida, with a diving helmet and lead weights attached to her feet. It was well worth the effort and the risk. A delighted Carson reported the joy that she had felt at the sight of the "exquisitely delicate and varied colors displayed by the reef creatures, and of the misty green depths of a strange, nonhuman world."

    She worked slowly, steadily, on her book. Her first draft, written in longhand, was edited over and over again until the sound of the phrases, which she read aloud to herself, satisfied her critical ear. Through 1949 and 1950 she labored—doing her job at the office during the day, and writing late into the night. And the book slowly took shape. The title itself was giving Rachel a lot of trouble. At first she had thought of *Mother Sea,* but as time went on, and she despaired of ever finishing her task, she dubbed the book "Sea Without End". Her friends cheerfully suggested "Out of My Depth" or "Carson at Sea"—which didn't help. Eventually, Rachel Carson hit upon what looks in retrospect like the obvious and perfect title: *The Sea Around Us.*

    The Sea came out in July 1951. It was eagerly awaited by the public, who had already been able to read a few chapters in the *Yale Review* and the *New Yorker*. The sensation created by these excerpts, and then by the book, was far beyond anything that author and publisher had been prepared for. The book went immediately to the bestseller list, where it remained for 86 consecutive weeks—39 in the first place. The only problem for the publisher was to keep the book in stock. By December it was selling at the rate of 4,000 copies a day. Already selected by the Book-of-the-Month Club, *The Sea Around Us* received the National Book Award, the most coveted in the publishing trade. Medals and honorary doctorates followed, and also, unfortunately, a flood of requests for public appearances that threw the shy author into a panic. She did manage to give talks and lectures, but she never become too enthusiastic about it.

The Sea Around Us has been translated into thirty-two languages. While the book's triumph was heartening, it was also making life difficult for Rachel Carson. All of a sudden she was a public figure, and she didn't find the honor enjoyable. The curiosity of her fans, and their often rude intrusion into her private life, were distasteful to her. She wrote to a friend about an incident that happened in a beauty shop where she was having her hair done during a trip. As she was sitting under the dryer, the operator turned the machine off, explaining that someone wanted to talk to Miss Carson. "I admit," wrote the disgruntled author, "I felt hardly at my best, with a towel around my neck and my hair in pin curls." Another time, someone knocked at the door of the motel room where Rachel and her mother were staying. When Mrs. Carson opened the door, a woman pushed her aside and presented two books for autographing to the author, who was still in bed and "very much annoyed."

Happily there were compensations. For the first time in many years, Rachel Carson's financial problems were eased, at least (she thought) for a while. In fact, her royalties remained such that she allowed herself a luxury—the purchase of a good binocular microscope. Then, as *The Sea Around Us* continued to run from edition to edition, she realized that she could now reasonably expect to live off her pen. In June 1952 she retired from the Fish and Wildlife Services. Already she was at work on a sequel to her two sea books, while trying to keep abreast of the mountains of mail that came to her every week.

The new volume, planned as a "Guide to the Seashore Life on the Atlantic Coast," is now known as *The Edge of the Sea*. The research for that book took Rachel Carson up and down the coast from Maine to Florida. But she had her own place there where she could spend time thinking and enjoying the proximity of the ocean. In 1953 she had built a small cottage on the coast of Maine as a summer residence, but her stays became longer and longer, starting early in spring and lingering into the fall. She worked in the cottage and entertained many of the friends who came to share her retreat. Her widowed niece Marjie spent some time there with her little boy Roger. When Marjie died in 1957, Rachel Carson kept Roger with her, and eventually adopted him.

Amidst all of Carson's activities, the *Edge of the Sea* got written and came out in 1955, bringing more acclaim and more awards. Now that she was established as a best-selling author, Rachel Carson could afford to choose among the many projects suggested to her. She agreed to write a television program about clouds, because the subject fascinated her; she had at one time considered writing a book about "The Air Around Us." The script of the television show flowed as easily as any of her other works:

> Hidden in the beauty of the moving clouds is a story that is as old as the earth itself. The clouds are the writing of the wind on the sky. They carry the signature of masses of air drifting across sea and land.
> They are the aviator's promise of good flying weather, or an omen of furious turbulence hidden within their calm exterior. But most of all they are cosmic symbols, representing an age-old process that is linked with life itself. Our world has two oceans—one ocean of water and an ocean of air. In the sea the greatest depths lie about seven miles down. Life exists everywhere. Corals, sponges, waving sea-whips inhabit the bottom. We, too, live on the floor of an ocean. . . .

She also wrote, with deep feelings, an article entitled *Help Your Child to Wonder*, which was later published in book form, handsomely illustrated with photographs taken around Rachel Carson's Maine cottage. Many of the pictures included young Roger, whom she had introduced to the beauty of the natural world since he was a very small visitor.

Perhaps she had other projects in mind. But they were not to be realized, because of a disturbing letter that she received in January 1958 from Olga Owens Huckins, one of her regular correspondents in Connecticut. Mrs. Huckins and her husband were concerned by the damage done in a bird sanctuary near Cape Cod by the spraying of pesticides; it had occurred to them that perhaps Rachel Carson could help save the birds and other creatures indiscriminately killed in the name of protecting nature from "pests."

Rachel Carson was indeed very interested. Her friends' appeal had not come as a complete surprise to her, for she had long been aware of the danger of sprays and particularly of DDT. As early as 1945 she had offered an article on the subject to the *Readers' Digest*, which turned it down. To Rachel Carson, nature and all the living things in it were sacred, and the thought of man's tampering with it disturbed her profoundly. A member of the Audubon Society, she loved birds; but her compassion for living creatures embraced all of them, no matter how tiny or apparently insignificant—a spider residing in the pile of wood behind her house was a neighbor to her, that deserved to enjoy its web without human interference. During her research on shore animals, she always put back gently among the rocks the crabs or other creatures that she had picked up for observation. That love of all wildlife had made her unsympathetic to the hunters and fishermen with whom she had to deal at the Fish and Wildlife Services. "We cannot have peace," she said once, "among men whose heart finds delight in killing any living creature. By every act that glorifies or even tolerates such moronic delight in killing, we set back the progress of humanity."

After receiving the Huckinses' letter, Rachel Carson began to investigate the matter of pesticides, and became increasingly distressed as she discovered the extent of the ravages done to the natural environment by the massive use of chemicals. It took her four years to complete her documentation and to write the book that she called *Silent Spring*. She was in pain during much of that time with arthritis and various ailments that made it difficult for her to walk. Her mother, who was also in poor health, died during that period. Then Rachel Carson learned that she had cancer. She died on April 14, 1964. But she had made her point: *Silent Spring* had come out in September of 1962, awaking the world to the fact that it was in the process of poisoning itself, and turning—as we shall see—the gentle scholar into a very controversial figure.

Understanding the Text

1. Was Rachel Carson known as an ecologist during most of her life?
2. Can it be said that her first book was disappointing and at the same time encouraging to the author?
3. How did Rachel Carson "prepare" for a book like *The Sea Around Us*?
4. Do we know why Rachel Carson's writing *sounds* so beautiful?
5. What sort of impact did the success of *The Sea Around Us* have upon the life of the author—good or bad?
6. How did Rachel Carson happen to have a son when she died?
7. What prompted the writing of *Silent Spring*?
8. Was concern for *land* environment and *land* creatures new to Rachel Carson?

Scanning for Details

True or false?

1. William Beebe became famous in the 1930s when he went down 3,208 feet in his bathysphere.
2. Rachel Carson retired from the Fish and Wildlife Services in 1952.
3. *The Sea Around Us* remained number one on the bestsellers list for 86 weeks.
4. Before writing about the deep sea, Rachel Carson did go down 30 feet off the coast of Florida.
5. The person who wrote to Rachel Carson about the damages caused by pesticides was Olga W. Huckins.
6. Roger was the son of Rachel Carson's niece.

7. Rachel Carson wrote: "The clouds are the writing of the wind on the sky."
8. According to Rachel Carson the deep sea off Florida is dusty green.

Vocabulary

A. *line 2*   Since Rachel Carson's first book is praised as "enchanting and engrossing," engrossing must mean something like:
    a) too heavy
    b) interesting
    c) boring

line 21   Since she found it difficult to live on her salary, which was not lavish, the salary must have been:
    a) very generous
    b) small
    c) sufficient

line 35   Rachel Carson had to go deep-sea diving to have some knowledge of the abyss of the ocean. In an ocean, the *abyss* must be:
    a) the deep region
    b) the coastal region
    c) the surface

line 39   ". . . sharks, octopuses and other members of the local fauna." *Fauna* obviously refers to:
    a) animals
    b) rocks
    c) plants

line 59   The book remained at the top of the list for eighty-six consecutive weeks:
    a) a total of eighty-six weeks
    b) eighty-six weeks in succession

line 89   Rachel Carson built a house where she could enjoy the proximity of the ocean:
    a) the smell of the ocean
    b) the rage of the ocean
    c) the nearness of the ocean
  How would you compare the meaning of proximity and approximately ("The distance from the house to the beach was approximately two hundred feet")?

line 105   The clouds are a promise of good weather and an omen of furious weather.
    a) a sign
    b) an effect
    c) a request
  What is the apparent implication, good or bad?

48 RACHEL CARSON

B. Rachel Carson wrote all her drafts in <u>longhand</u>; if she had dictated the drafts to a secretary, the secretary would have taken the dictation in <u>shorthand</u>. What is the difference?

It is difficult to <u>stay abreast</u> of a friend who walks very fast. For Rachel Carson the great problem was to <u>keep abreast</u> of her fan mail. What does this mean? <u>Abreast</u> is related to <u>breast</u>—how would you explain the relationship?

Suffix

<u>cide</u>

1. What do *insecticides* and *pesticides* do to insects and pests?
2. If you found a product called *herbicide* on a shelf, would you be tempted to drink it? Where would you use it and to what purpose?
3. The police department has a *homicide* section. What does that section deal with?
4. There are many articles in newspapers nowadays about the *suicide* of teen-agers. What are they about?
5. Rachel Carson said that chemicals used indiscriminately are not just pesticides, but *biocides*. What did she man?
6. Civil wars are described as *fratricidal*. Why?
7. Why was the mass killing of Jews and Gypsies by the Nazis called *genocide*?

The Main Idea

Check the statement in each group that best expresses the main idea of each paragraph.

Par. 1
a) *Under the Sea Wind* came out in November 1941.
b) *Under the Sea Wind* was selected in 1941 by the Scientific Books Club.
c) *Under the Sea Wind* didn't have much success among the general public, but it made an impression in scientific circles.

Par. 2
a) Rachel Carson was so encouraged by the response of scientists to her first book that she decided to write a second one.
b) In spite of the demands of her government job, Rachel Carson began to work on a second book.
c) Rachel Carson did so well at the Fish and Wildlife Services that she was promoted several times between 1941 and 1952.

Par. 3   a) She tried several times, unsuccessfully, to get a well-paid job.
           b) Since she didn't make enough money at the Department, Rachel Carson had to write magazine articles.
           c) Neither the *Readers' Digest* nor the Audubon Society agreed to give her a position.

Par. 4   a) Rachel Carson didn't swim well and had never tried to dive.
           b) She went down to see what the ocean was like under the surface, and was delighted by what she saw.
           c) Her main adviser was the famous William Beebe, who thought that she should go deep-sea diving with him.

Par. 5   a) She wrote the first draft in longhand and read it to herself until she was pleased with the sound of the sentences.
           b) She wrote slowly and had much trouble finding the best title.
           c) She had so much trouble finding a title that her friends made fun of it.

Par. 6   What is the main idea of the paragraph?

The Right Order

Put the following sentences in the proper chronological order to make a coherent story.

__1__ The Fish and Wildlife Service had a boat, the *Albatross*, that was used to study the fish population, the currents, and the water temperature of certain areas.

____ The Department refused to give her the authorization on the grounds that no one from the office had gone on such an expedition before.

____ Rachel Carson persuaded her literary agent, Mary Rodell, to go with her.

____ Because of her work, Rachel Carson was interested in the operations of the boat.

____ Miss Rodell said later that she too was going to write a book, entitled: "*I was a chaperone* on a fishing boat.*"

____ Besides, some of her superiors didn't like the idea of sending a woman alone to sea for ten days with a bunch of fishermen.

---

*A chaperone is usually an older woman who accompanies young girls and watches over them at social occasions.

50   RACHEL CARSON

___ Carson protested that it was her duty to go and that, furthermore, she was old enough to take care of herself.

___ They said finally that she could go if another person was going with her.

___ And so she asked for permission to go on the next long fishing trip of the *Albatross*.

Topics for Discussion

1. Does it seem to you that Rachel Carson's life was a happy one?
2. During most of her adult life, Rachel Carson took care of relatives—mother, nieces, grand-nephew—toward whom she felt that she had an obligation. In the same circumstances, would you do the same? What other alternatives exist? What is the best alternative?
3. Rachel Carson called hunting ("delight in killing") *moronic*—which means extremely stupid. Do you agree with her? Do you think that hunting and fishing serve a good purpose? Should they be forbidden? Would it work?
4. Several groups and organizations are concerned about the pollution of the sea. What have you heard about this? Do you think that it is a dangerous problem?

Reading
The Publication of Silent Spring

Survey this section of the chapter: What does it include?
Would you say that the first text is

- an attack on the book?
- a defense of the book?
- a description of the book?
- an opinion on the book?

The publication of *Silent Spring* produced a kind of shock wave totally different from the sensation created by Rachel Carson's previous books. While the sea volumes had brought her universal love and admiration, *Silent Spring* was, as soon as it came out, a controversial success and the object of hot dispute. The public had been alerted to the substance of the book by the publication of several chapters in the *New Yorker*; and so had the great chemical companies, who felt threatened, and who were ready to fight back and, if possible, to discredit the book and its author. One of the companies actually tried to prevent the publication by threatening Carson's publishers with a lawsuit if *Silent Spring* came out.

Silent Spring is an exposition of the harm done to nature—and indirectly to man—by the widespread and uncontrolled use of toxic chemicals, and of dangers of such use for the future of the planet. The book opens with a striking chapter, entitled "A Fable For To-morrow," which describes a town "somewhere in the heart of America," where birds have disappeared from the trees and fish from the brooks; where mysterious diseases kill cattle, sheep, and barnyard fowl; where doctors are puzzled by unknown sicknesses affecting farmers and townspeople; where children die suddenly. Everywhere patches of white powder can be seen on roofs, on lawns, on the banks of the streams.

Having shocked her readers with this desolate scene, Rachel Carson explains that it is fictitious: to her knowledge, no town has been affected by the *totality* of the ills described; but those ills are real and are playing havoc throughout the country. Birds have indeed disappeared for miles around orchards sprayed with DDT; fish have been seen floating by the thousands down rivers polluted by plants manufacturing toxic chemicals. The death of horses has been reported, and even the deaths of people who had inhaled the substances meant to protect them from bothersome insects and rodents. The rest of the book is a detailed, precise study of the numerous harmful pesticides used for spraying.

Until *Silent Spring* sounded the alarm, chemicals had been used enthusiastically by farmers and ranchers to protect their crops and trees, by developers of new residential buildings anxious to get rid of mosquitoes and other undesirable creatures, and by communities eager to attract tourists. The spraying, usually done by airplanes, was hailed as the best thing that had ever happened to farming and to the well-being of humanity. It was well known that the pesticides (and in particular DDT) were not only allowing larger and better harvests, but that they were also a great help in controlling such diseases as malaria and typhus by eliminating the creatures likely to spread these epidemics. Few people, if any, had given a thought to the fact that a spray that kills mosquitoes and assorted bugs will surely kill other species—such as the birds dwelling in the trees and feeding on contaminated insects—and that such a spray could hardly be healthy for larger animals (including man) who breathe the polluted air and eat poisoned flesh. Neither did the public at large know that DDT persists indefinitely in the soil and the water, and that it spreads uncontrollably around the world. DDT has been detected in the fatty tissue of Eskimos living in areas that have never been sprayed with chemicals. Few people outside the scientific world had understood clearly that all the elements of nature—water, plants, animal life—are bound together and that what affects one directly or indirectly affects the others. With *Silent Spring*, Rachel Carson had introduced her readers to the concept of ecology—the solidarity of all living things.

At the end of the book, after twenty chapters full of detailed data, facts, figures, and grim stories, Rachel Carson had provided fifty pages of documentation and sources. The book ended on an appeal for serious study of the effects of chemicals on the environment and for a search for alternatives to the present disastrous policy.

The public was understandably shaken. Carson's book, written in her graceful style in spite of the dreariness of the subject matter, became an immediate bestseller throughout the world—it was to be translated in 32 languages. As Rachel Carson had expected, *Silent Spring* was attacked by the manufacturers of chemicals, and also by scientists who didn't share her beliefs. She was ridiculed, accused of ignorance and fanaticism. The book's critics, ignoring the measured conclusions that she had drawn, asserted that without pesticides it would be impossible to keep the production of food at the needed level, and that famine would ensue. Rachel Carson repeated patiently the point that she had tried to make clear in the final chapter of *Silent Spring*—that she was not opposed to the use of pesticides. "We must have insect control," she would say over and over again, "I do not favor turning nature over to insects. I favor the sparing, selective and intelligent use of chemicals. It is indiscriminate blanket spraying that I oppose."

The very bitterness of the controversy that surrounded her book helped it make the impact that Rachel Carson had hoped for. President John F. Kennedy formed a special committee of scientists to look into the effects of chemical spraying. In 1963 the committee reported its findings and warned against the indiscriminate use of pesticides. The uncontrolled use of toxic substances, said the committee's chairman, Dr. Jerome B. Wiesner, was potentially a much greater danger than radioactive fallout.

Existing legislation on the use of pesticides was tightened, and limits were put on the amount of DDT allowable in food products such as flour or cereals. Sweden was the first country to ban altogether the use of DDT and related compounds. In the U.S. and many other nations research got under way to find nontoxic exterminating substances.

Even though chemicals are still used to control pests, all nations are now aware of their ill effects and of their danger to the balance of nature. Governments and farmers alike have been alerted, citizens groups have been formed, and greater caution is used. Carson herself had said that she didn't believe that one book could bring much improvement, but *Silent Spring* certainly started the ball rolling.

Understanding the Text

1. What was the purpose of *Silent Spring*?
2. What ill effects of pesticides did Rachel Carson describe in her fictional town?
3. Who disagreed with Rachel Carson?

4. What good effects of chemicals could the critics of *Silent Spring* point out?
5. Was Rachel Carson opposed to the use of chemicals?
6. Did *Silent Spring* achieve some result?

Taking Notes

Skim the text on *Silent Spring,* and the *Vocabulary of Ecology* provided at the beginning of the chapter, and note down, without details (a) the reasons why chemical pesticides are dangerous to all living creatures, and (b) the beneficial aspects of the use of such products.

Write a brief summary, based on your notes, to include:

1. an introductory sentence about the main idea of the summary.
2. one or two short paragraphs presenting both sides of the matter.
3. a one-sentence conclusion about what should be done in the future.

Reading Opinions

You will find below six samples* of the kind of comments that were written after the publication of Silent Spring. *As you read them, do not stop at unfamiliar words. Try to understand the general meaning of each excerpt, its tone, and the attitude of the author.*

Miss Carson's book adds no new factual material not already known to such serious scientists as those concerned with these developments; nor does it include information essential for the reader to interpret the knowledge. It does confuse the information and so mix it with her opinions that the uninitiated reader is unable to sort fact from fancy. In view of the mature, responsible attention which this whole subject receives from able, qualified scientific groups (whom Miss Carson chooses to ignore); in view of her scientific qualifications in contrast to those of our distinguished scientific leaders and statesmen, this book should be ignored. . . . The responsible scientist should read this book to understand the ignorance of those writing on the subject, and the educational task which lies ahead."

W. J. Darby, M.D.
Chemical and Engineering News
October 1, 1962

It is a devastating, heavily documented, relentless attack upon human carelessness, greed and irresponsibility—an irresponsibility that has let

*All from *Book Review Digest* (H. W. Wilson Company, 1962). Reprinted by permission.

loose upon man and the countryside a flood of dangerous chemicals in a situation which, as Miss Carson states, is without parallel in medical history. . . . In case after case Miss Carson succeeds in documenting her thesis with complete adequacy. . . . If her present book does not possess the beauty of *The Sea Around Us*, it is because she has courageously chosen, at the height of her powers, to educate us upon a sad, an unpleasant, an unbeautiful topic and one of our own making. *Silent Spring* should be read by every American who doesn't want it to be the epitaph of a world not very far beyond us in time.

Loren Eiseley
(famous anthropologist and author)

The major claims of Miss Rachel Carson's book, *Silent Spring*, are gross distortions of the actual facts, completely unsupported by scientific, experimental evidence, and general practical experience in the field. Her suggestion that insecticides are in fact biocides destroying all life is obviously absurd in the light of the fact that without selective biologicals these compounds would be completely useless. The real threat then to the survival of man is not chemical but biological, in the shape of hordes of insects that can denude our forests, sweep over our crop lands, ravage our food supply and leave in their wake a train of destitution and hunger, conveying to an undernourished population the major diseases, scourges of mankind.

Dr. Robert White-Stevens
(a spokesman for the chemical industry)

Miss Carson is a scientist and is not given to tossing serious charges around carelessly. When she warns us, as she does, with such a profound sense of urgency, we ought to take heed. *Silent Spring* may well be one of the great and towering books of our time. This book is MUST reading for every responsible citizen.

Chicago Daily News

Miss Carson's scientific credentials are impeccable . . . she documents her statements; she cites the tragic facts of the disappearance of birds and wildflowers; she quotes chapter and verse* on stream and open-water pollution. . . . This is a shocking and frightening book. It ought to be placed on the required reading list of every community leader, every

---

*To quote chapter and verse: to give exact and precise references.

lover of nature and every citizen who cherishes the great natural resources of our nation.

Christian Century

Many scientists sympathize with Miss Carson's love of wildlife and even with her mystical attachment to the balance of nature. But they fear that her emotional and inaccurate outburst in *Silent Spring* may do harm by alarming the nontechnical public, while doing no good for the things that she loves.

TIME Magazine

Appraising the Comments

1. Do all the authors agree on the value of *Silent Spring*?
2. Which of these excerpts are against the book? Compare their tone: are they all alike?
3. Make a list of the criticisms and attacks directed at Rachel Carson, and a list of the praises coming from her supporters. With what you know of Rachel Carson, which accusations seem unfair, or absurd, and which ones might be true to some degree?
4. What kind of people attack Rachel Carson? Do you understand their reasons for feeling the way they do?
5. Read carefully W. J. Darby's text. What does the writer *imply* about Rachel Carson's character and knowledge in the sentence: "In view of the mature, responsible attention which this whole subject receives from able, qualified scientific groups (whom Miss Carson chooses to ignore), in view of her scientific qualifications in contrast to those of our distinguished scientific leaders and statesmen, this book should be ignored. . . . The responsible scientist should read this book to understand the ignorance of those writing on the subject."

Topics for Discussion

1. Do you think that too much importance is given to environmental problems in general, or to any environmental problem in particular?
2. Have you ever been involved in the struggle against any environmental problem—such as air or water pollution or any other?
3. What do you think of organizations that try to stop the killing of whales and seals?
4. Do you think that people become overly alarmed after reading a book like *Silent Spring*?
5. Do you think that large companies and industries are apt to do things

that are harmful to the public or to nature? Do they have good reasons to be cautious?
6. If you are familiar with a country other than the United States, compare the ecological problems faced in each country.

Ray Bradbury

Science fiction (writer)

Introduction

The Vocabulary of Fantasy and Fun

Once in a while, a carnival comes into town with its shows, its exotic or trained animals, its games of chance, its candy vendors, its freaks (a bearded lady perhaps, or a three-headed camel), and its magicians ready to perform miracles, making watches disappear or pulling rabbits out of an empty hat. A monster can be defined as something abnormal, whether real or imaginary. But we also use the term monstrous to describe the size of things that are merely unusually large.

Traveling carnivals may bring merry-go-rounds and other rides of reasonable size for children. But they can't bring a roller coaster, which needs enormous structures to provide the steep dips and curves on which carriages will speed. Roller-coasters are found in permanent amusement parks.

Magicians perform tricks that they have carefully practiced. But a fey person performs some kinds of tricks without having learned them. He or she may be able to foretell future events, or to see and hear things that other people do not perceive. People consider them weird, and they certainly seem to have strange powers.

Although it is often based on serious scientific discoveries, science fiction belongs to the world of fantasy. It is a form of escapism in the sense that it takes its readers away from their own problems into a fantasy land. Readers who are antagonistic to science fiction (known as SF by serious fans) say that it is superficial, stupid and worthless. And of course those who are addicted to science fiction resent such derogatory remarks.

Looking Ahead

- Leaf through the chapter: what form of reading do you find in section three?
- Are you familiar with science fiction stories or science fiction movies? For example?
- In what way does a science fiction story differ from an ordinary story:
    in time?
    in location?
    in its type of characters?
    in any other way?

A Few Definitions and Opinions

Read the following definitions and remarks, and take note of the mood in which each statement has been made: serious, amused, flippant (not at all serious), favorable, derogatory?

Which are acceptable definitions, stating clearly and precisely what science fiction and technology are or deal with?

1. Science fiction is fiction dealing with recent or imaginary discoveries and technological advances.
2. Science fiction is that branch of literature that dares look into the future of mankind.
3. Science fiction is whatever science fiction editors buy.
4. Science fiction is a branch of literature that deals with human responses to change in the level of science and technology.
5. Science fiction is a type of semi-literature in which the main characters communicate in brief technical sentences, display no fear and very few feelings that can be recognized as human.
6. Science fiction is escapism.
7. Science fiction describes travels through time and space.
8. Science fiction deals with probable, possible, and impossible scientific discoveries and inventions.
9. What I like most about science fiction is that all the experiments work.
10. Technology is the science of industry and mechanical or practical arts.
11. Technology is what everybody does with what a few people know.
12. Technology is the application of scientific and industrial skills to practical uses.

- Did you find serious definitions in the list?
- Did you find derogatory definitions?
- Which of the statements are not definitions at all?
- Who, in your opinion, may have given definition number 3? (You will find the answer later in this chapter.)
- Who may have made remark number 9? (The answer is provided later.)
- Which are the best definitions?
- Is definition number 11 different from definition number 12?
- Which are your favorite statements? Why?
- How can you modify statements 7, 8 and 9 to make them into the more usual form of definition: "Science Fiction is . . ."?
- Define, in your own words:
   Science fiction
   Escapism
   Semi-literature

Cultural Notes for Profile, Part One

Ray Bradbury grew up during the Great Depression, a period extending roughly from 1929 to the late 1930s, during which the American economy went into a severe decline and many businesses failed. During that time, a large number of people were unemployed, due to the collapse of plants and businesses. Those who couldn't support themselves received some welfare assistance from the government.

"Prince Valiant" and "Buck Rogers" were two very popular comic strips. The first one presented the adventures and exploits of a prince in an ill-defined period several centuries ago. It can still be found on the comic pages of newspapers. The second strip was a futuristic science-fiction cartoon.

Profile
Part One

Born August 22, 1920

What kind of person do you expect a science fiction writer to be? Skim the text to find the answers to the following questions:

- What does Bradbury read?
- Does he become rich and famous in this section of the profile?
- There is a fairly long quote from an interview of Bradbury for *Writer's Digest*. What is it about?

While you read, take notes of words and expressions that are not meant literally.

Waukegan, Illinois, where Ray Bradbury first opened his eyes on the world, was a typical, small Midwestern town, quiet and conventional, with tree-lined streets, neatly painted houses, and the normal quota of people, lawns, cats, children, and steepled churches. Bradbury's readers are well acquainted with Waukegan; they often find it in his books, either renamed Green Town and sitting right where it belongs—on Earth—or surprisingly relocated on the planet Mars. In either case, queer events are apt to happen in the town in spite of the apparent normalcy of the place. The real Waukegan of the 1920s and 1930s was of course neither strange nor alarming; nothing out of the ordinary happened there that might frighten a small boy growing up with his elder brother, surrounded by loving parents and assorted relatives who all lived within walking distance of the house. With such a warm start in life, it is small wonder that Ray Bradbury grew into a man who favors small towns and who cares for families, whether on Earth, on Mars, or anywhere else in the universe.

During the grim years of the Depression, Ray's father was not concerned with life on alien planets; he had enough problems with his own life in Illinois. A power* lineman by trade, he had lost his job like many other Americans at that time, and found it nearly impossible to make enough

---
*electric power

money to support his family. He worked as a milkman when he could, accepted welfare for a while, and even tried to find employment in Tucson, Arizona—his former home town. In 1934, Leonard Bradbury took his wife and children to Southern California, which was then regarded as the golden land of opportunity. His dreams of prosperity were never completely satisfied, and life remained hard for the Bradburys throughout Ray's adolescence.

Ray Bradbury is now a tall and powerful man. Journalists who interview him like to compare him to a teddy bear or a koala. He must have been a sturdy boy in his early teens but, perhaps because of his near-sightedness, he was not good at sports. To make matters worse, he didn't like to fight—a fact that caused him to be poorly regarded by the boys in his neighborhood. For his part, he didn't much admire their amusements or their character. To this day he professes to dislike what he calls "the male animal," and particularly the young members of the species.

> We are not a very nice sex. Men and boys are real destroyers. . . . Being a boy from, say, the age of eleven to fifteen is really horrifying. I would not go there for anything. . . . Boys are dreadful. They are absolute totalitarians. . . . If you diversify in any direction, or if you let them see that you have an I.Q.[1]—if you dare let anyone know that you are brighter than they are, if you are dumb enough to let your brightness out, they KILL you! They slaughter you! They pull your skin off! . . . So I went off and hid and became a writer. Now you have asked about my environment; that's it. My environment, what affected me as a writer, was the lousy world of the twelve-year-old boys who wanted me to conform. This hasn't anything to do with the great wide world out there. It has to do with the male animal, the machismo[2] or whatever you want to call it. If you don't join the gang, if you don't play baseball or football, if you don't run fast enough, if you think too much, you are in big trouble. So I pulled away and formed my own world. [Bradbury's interview with Robert Jacobs, in *Writer's Digest*, February 1976.]

Ray's own world was the world of imagination, peopled with the characters he liked best: monsters and ghosts. He loved mysteries, prodigies, carnival freaks, dinosaurs, "things in jars," and dark corners. At night he entertained himself with fearful stories, which he wrote in the attic while the rest of the family was asleep. He had a wonderful time. In fact—and despite the neighborhood bullies—Bradbury remembers his childhood as "very happy."

---

[1] I.Q. (Intelligence Quotient) is a controversial measure of intelligence. The average I.Q., 100, is the I.Q. of persons whose mental age corresponds exactly to their actual age. Bradbury means: "If you have a high IQ, if you are more intelligent. . . ."
[2] *Machismo* describes the quality of men who exaggerate their manliness, and make a point of acting "rough."

Ray Bradbury says that from the age of three, when he saw his first motion picture, *The Phantom Of the Opera,* he was addicted to the movies, with a preference for horror films and fantasies. *King Kong* and Disney's *Fantasia* have remained two of his favorites. He collected comic strips, which he clipped out of the newspapers, and he stills cherishes the stacks of *Prince Valiant* and *Buck Rogers* that he keeps, neatly filed, in the basement of his home.

He was—and still is—a voracious reader. "There has never been a day since I was ten," he says, "that I haven't been in a library or a bookstore!" At first he preferred the works of Jules Verne (*From the Earth to the Moon, 20,000 Leagues Under the Sea,* etc.) of H. G. Wells (*The Time Machine, The Invisible Man, The War of the Worlds*) as well as Edgar Rice Burrough's adventure Stories of Mars and *Tarzan of the Apes.* Later he became interested in all kinds of authors, including historian Arnold Toynbee. Today he agrees with Toynbee's theory that man's greatest achievements have been accomplished as a response to great challenges, or in an effort to overcome man's frailty. And what greater and more inspiring challenge could there be than the conquest of space? Bradbury believes that men will not only colonize Mars but also that, in the process of overcoming the hardships of their mission, they will attain a higher level of intelligence and morality. At least he hopes so; some of his *Martian Chronicles* seem to indicate that a certain amount of doubt remains in his mind.

Young Bradbury completed his education without difficulty and graduated from his Los Angeles high school in 1938. He was still inventing fanciful tales—an unending stream of tales—which he loved to try on anyone kind enough to lend him an ear. Science writer Henry Kuttner, an early friend, finally put an end to the flood. "Ray," he said. "Stop running around bothering people with your grand ideas. Go home, get your typewriter and WRITE! You can't SAY you want to be a writer, you have to WRITE to be a writer!" Properly impressed by the wisdom of this advice, Bradbury set to work in earnest. Soon he began to offer his production to the kind of magazines (called "pulp magazine" because they were printed on cheap paper) that might be interested. He was 20 when a story of his was accepted for the first time by a magazine specializing in weird tales. Gradually more were published. Since they never paid much, and since even a dedicated author has to eat more or less regularly, Bradbury supported himself by selling newspapers in downtown Los Angeles.

When he was not pounding away on his typewriter or selling his papers, Bradbury was visiting the city's bookstores. One day he noticed among the stacks of new books an attractive young woman whose name—he made it his business to find out—was Marguerite. She accepted his offer of a date— then more dates. While their friendship was thriving, Bradbury was delighted to learn that "Maggie" was, like him, fond of literature, and that she didn't consider wealth an essential element for a happy marriage. As a consequence they were married about a year later, and established themselves in a less-than-luxurious apartment in Venice (a suburb of Los Angeles). Forty-odd[3] years later they are still happily married and have raised four daughters, one of whom is a struggling author. No sons; Bradbury must have been relieved to be spared the handling of a young male animal.

All through the forties and early fifties, Bradbury kept writing the stories that popped effortlessly into his mind. It went very smoothly; he would start a tale on Monday, drafting it in three or four hours. Tuesday, Wednesday, and Thursday would be spent polishing it with the help of Maggie's comments. The piece was mailed on Friday and on Saturday Bradbury would start contemplating the next one. With luck, he could make $50 a week, enough to keep his family fed and sheltered, if not rolling in luxury. Inspiration was no problem, for anything, *anything*—a street scene, a remark from Maggie, the front page news, or last night's dreams—could be the seed of a fantastic tale. In the preface of his latest anthology, *The Stories of Ray Bradbury* (Alfred A. Knopf, 1981), Bradbury relates how one of his best loved stories, *The Fog Horn*, came about:

> One night when my wife and I were walking along the beach in Venice, California, where we lived in a thirty-dollar-a-month newlywed apartment, we came upon the bones of the Venice pier, and the struts, tracks and ties of the ancient roller-coaster collapsed on the sand and being eaten by the sea. "What is that dinosaur doing there on the beach?" I said. My wife, very wisely, had no answer. The answer came the next night when summoned from sleep by a voice calling, I rose up, listened, and heard the lonely voice of the Santa Monica fog horn blowing over and over again. "Of course!" I thought, "the dinosaur heard that lighthouse fog horn blowing, thought it was another dinosaur arisen from the deep past, came swimming in for a loving confrontation, discovered it was only a fog horn, and died of a broken heart there on the shore!

This is the way you come up with a good story—if you are Ray Bradbury.

Until 1949, science fiction was not published in books—only in magazines, and the most highly regarded of these publications was *Astounding Science Fiction*, edited since 1937 by an enthusiastic young man named John Wood Campbell, Jr.[4] Campbell is now revered as the guiding light of early science fiction. His standards were high; he only published the very best "hard" science fiction stories, featuring the exploits of engineers, inventors, and scientists, and preferably written by people who were fully qualified to talk about scientific matters, present or future. The authors he chose then are now considered to be the great names of science fiction—

---

[3] forty-odd—between forty and fifty years later.
[4] Campbell is the man who defined science fiction as "whatever science fiction editors buy."
"What I like most about science fiction is that all the experiments work!" was said by a physicist.

such as Arthur C. Clarke *(2001, A Space Odyssey)*, Robert Heinlein, and Isaac Asimov. Asimov, who has a Ph.D. in biochemistry, has written many scientific books, in addition to his science fiction novels. Another well-known author, scholar L. Sprague de Camp, specializes in archaeology.

For Campbell, Bradbury's tales were not specific enough, not "hard" enough; sometimes they were not even science fiction. Says Asimov:

> Among the stars of the 1940s Ray Bradbury was the only one who was not a Campbell author. He had not gone to college; he knew no science and was, indeed, antagonistic to science; he had an odd and choppy style; his characters tended to be fey, his mood nostalgic, his plots veering toward the weird and the fantastic. Campbell could make nothing of him and, with one or two very minor exceptions, he didn't buy anything from him. Bradbury's first published story appeared in *Super Science Stories* in 1941, and thereafter he published in other minor science fiction magazines. To publish in the "minors" was the kiss of death as far as serious SF fans were concerned. [Isaac Asimov, *Asimov on Science Fiction* (New York: Doubleday, 1981.)]

Surprisingly enough it was not at all the kiss of death for Ray Bradbury, who continued to write and to flourish, gathering a widening circle of readers, many of whom would have refused indignantly to be classified among SF fans. Little by little Bradbury's stories began to appear in prestige magazines such as the *New Yorker*. One of his non-science fiction tales, *The Big Black and White Game*, was included in *The Best Stories of 1946;* another one, *The Homecoming*, was published in another anthology, *The O. Henry Prize Stories of 1947*. When a great publishing house decided to launch the first hardcover science fiction collection in 1949, Ray Bradbury was one of the three authors chosen. The Bradbury book, a group of short stories about the colonization of Mars entitled *The Martian Chronicles*, is still one of his best-selling works. It won an award in 1949 from the National Institute of Arts and Letters.

Even if his financial situation remained rather modest, Ray Bradbury in the early 1950s had every reason to feel that he had achieved a certain amount of success. What's more, he was enjoying himself.

Understanding the Text

1. What kind of background has produced this particular science-fiction writer?
2. What kind of handicaps did Ray Bradbury have as a teenager?
3. Why does he dislike boys so much?
4. Can it be said that young Bradbury was unconventional, or at least "different" in many ways?
5. From what you have read about Rachel Carson and Ray Bradbury, did they have the same approach to writing?
6. How is Ray Bradbury regarded by other science fiction writers?

7. Why were his stories not published in book form before 1949?
8. Was Bradbury rich and famous when we left him at the end of the first part of his profile?

Commenting on the Text

1. What is the tone of the profile: formal, informal, serious, lighthearted, ironic, antagonistic, sympathetic, critical, or? How does the tone of this piece compare with the tone of the passage on *Silent Spring*? Why the difference?
2. Did you notice anything in the text that should not be taken literally?
3. What do you think of the way Ray Bradbury expresses himself (lines 30–40)?
4. What do you think of Bradbury's brand of imagination and of his tastes in films and books, which have not changed visibly to this day?
5. What kind of scenes does the text suggest to you about Ray Bradbury at school or among the neighborhood boys?
6. What is "hard" science fiction?

Scanning for Details

1. Who wrote *The Time Machine*?
2. Even if you don't know what the words mean, what elements of a roller-coaster can you name?
3. Write down the titles of all the Bradbury stories mentioned in the text.
4. Who invented Tarzan? What was the title of the original book?
5. In what science was Asimov trained?
6. Was Bradbury's father a native of Waukegan?
7. Who is Sprague de Camp?
8. Bradbury said: "If you are dumb enough _____ your skin off!"

Vocabulary

For each of the following, find the meaning of the underlined words.

    line 3   The normal quota of people, cats and trees must refer to
                  a) quality
                  b) number
                  c) location
    line 12   Young Ray was surrounded by assorted relatives.
                  a) loving
                  b) in large number
                  c) of various kinds
    line 17   Ray's father was a power lineman. Since "power" here is electric power, what was Mr. Bradbury's job likely to be?
    line 45   The boys wanted Ray to conform. From the context it seems that they wanted him:

a) to obey them
b) to fight with them
c) to be like them

line 37 Boys are <u>totalitarians</u>, according to Ray Bradbury. Germany under Hitler was a <u>totalitarian</u> nation. What does that mean?

line 57 Ray thought that the other boys who wanted to force him to conform were <u>bullies</u>. He found them:
a) brutal
b) ignorant
c) friendly

line 60 He was <u>addicted</u> to movies as other people are addicted to drugs.
a) he couldn't do without them
b) he was forced to go to the movies
c) he didn't like them

line 154 Campbell <u>could make nothing</u> of Bradbury.
a) could not make money publishing him
b) didn't like him at all
c) could not understand his work

Generalizations

A generalization is a statement about a whole group of people ("Teenagers love rock music") or possibly a statement including "never" or "always," as in, "He never returns telephone calls" or "I always walk on the right side of the street." Generalizations are often based on a small number of facts that do not quite justify them.

In the following paragraphs, find the statements that express a generalization rather than a particular fact (a supporting fact or an example, for instance).

Small Midwestern towns are very nice places to live in. Waukegan in the 1940s was friendly and quiet; it had lovely green lawns and well-tended gardens, and it didn't matter if one forgot to lock the front door at night. It was not very sophisticated, but the college's plays were well attended; for *Private Lives,* all three performances were sold out.

Young Ray was not well liked by his neighbors because he was too different from them. They didn't understand that his nearsightedness was making it difficult for him to take part in many games. Boys of that age don't think of such things. Besides, they are cruel. Ray's schoolmates laughed at him, often tried to hurt him, and once they stole and broke his glasses.

Life was hard for Americans during the Great Depression. Bradbury's father could not find any work. Most of his neighbors were in the same situation. The federal government did try to give some assistance, but wel-

PROFILE 67

fare was not as well organized as it is now and a lot of people went hungry and lost their homes.

"Bookstores are the most wonderful places in the world" says Ray Bradbury. The bookstore where he met Maggie was a large one, with hundreds of books on the shelves. Although he could not buy many new books, Bradbury liked to browse among the latest publications on the big counters. However, he always managed to have enough money to take Maggie out for dinner or for a movie. A year and a half after their first meeting, Bradbury and Maggie were married. They first rented a small apartment in a cheap section of Venice, California. Newlyweds can't afford expensive houses.

The Main Idea

Check the statement in each group that best expresses the most essential idea in each paragraph.

Par. 1
a) Ray Bradbury likes families because he has good memories of his own family.
b) Although he writes about weird people and places, Ray Bradbury grew up in a normal family and a normal town.
c) Ray Bradbury has often used his small hometown as a model for the towns in his stories.

Par. 2
a) Bradbury grew up in a poor family.
b) Ray Bradbury's father was a power lineman from Tucson.
c) Even in California, Ray Bradbury's father never became rich.

Par. 3
a) Ray Bradbury thinks that boys are mean and totalitarian.
b) Ray Bradbury escaped into the world of imagination because he didn't fit in with the boys of his age.
c) Ray Bradbury was not liked by the other boys because he was different.

Par. 4
a) Ray Bradbury had a very happy childhood.
b) Ray Bradbury used to stay up at night to write stories.
c) Ray Bradbury was always attracted by things weird and frightening.

Par. 5
a) Although he loves horror films, comic strips and adventure books, Bradbury is interested in deeper subjects.
b) Ray Bradbury believes that man will improve when he colonizes Mars.
c) Ray Bradbury agrees with Arnold Toynbee that man's greatest achievements come as responses to great challenges.

Par. 6   What is the main idea of this paragraph?

Topics for Discussion

Most of the topics below could be used for a debate between two groups of students holding opposite views on the subjects.

1. Do you agree with Ray Bradbury's opinion of teenage boys? Does a boy have to "conform" to be accepted and befriended? Is it the same for teenage girls?
2. Is it the same in countries other than the United States?
3. Do you agree that "men are not a very nice sex"? Are women better?
4. Do you think that men will colonize Mars and live there in large numbers?
5. Do you think that men will become better, intellectually and morally, while colonizing other planets?
6. Does science fiction appeal to you? Why?
7. What do you think of horror movies?
8. Can science fiction be called "literature"?

Cultural Notes for Profile, Part Two

Talking in one of his stories about the wife of a pioneer who settled on Mars ahead of his family, Bradbury compares her to the wives of the Vikings and to the wife of Ulysses in Homer's *Iliad*. The Vikings, great seamen who ventured far to plunder rich lands and to explore unknown territories (8th to 10th centuries A.D.), were away from their homes for long periods. Ulysses was gone from his home for twenty years—ten years besieging Troy and ten years after the fall of Troy trying to go back to the island where his loyal wife Penelope was waiting for him.

Vocabulary: More Definitions

Aesthetics	is the philosophy of beauty in art and literature.
Ethics	is the part of philosophy dealing with moral conduct.
Logic	is the science of reasoning.
Gravity	is the force that attracts objects toward the center of the Earth.
Telepathy	is communication of thoughts from mind to mind, sometimes over great distances.
Parody	is a humorous imitation of a person, or of a literary or musical work.

Profile
Part Two

Skim the text to find the answers to the following questions:
- Is Bradbury still writing science-fiction stories?
- What has he done besides writing?
- One of the paragraphs is a summary of one of Bradbury's stories. Which paragraph, and which story?

John Campbell was right in deciding that *Astounding Science Fiction* was not the place for Ray Bradbury's work; Bradbury is an oddity among science fiction writers. He doesn't conform, he doesn't fit into their ranks any better than he fitted among the neighborhood boys when he was twelve years old. As a matter of fact, does he write science fiction at all? In the first place, he is not limited to one genre: he has produced a considerable number of straight stories, parodies, films and television scripts, and he has written about 35 plays, many of which have been performed in New York or Los Angeles. As for the rest of his stories, described as science fiction for lack of a better term, they are seldom the kind of tale in which Asimov, Heinlein, Clarke, or their successors excel. True SF authors take great care to be accurate and up to date in their technology and to follow with proper respect the laws of science and logic. Bradbury doesn't. His planet Mars would make a ten-year-old laugh. It has a breathable atmosphere and an earth-like gravity; it has plenty of water in canals and lakes; it has trees, flowers, and grass. And it was inhabited once by people who lived in human-like families and who left magnificent traces of their civilization—cities of marble, crystal and precious metals, libraries, monuments, and reflecting pools. Earthlings don't need special equipment to picnic on Bradbury's Mars.

Bradbury knows, of course, that his planet is pure fantasy. He has read the astronomers' recent findings about the solar system; he has visited the Manned Spacecraft Center in Houston and talked with the scientists and technicians there. He is well informed. But accuracy is irrelevant in Bradbury's universe because the real Mars has little to do with the meaning of the stories he wants to tell. Bradbury doesn't write about space, rockets, and astronauts. He writes about people—ordinary people faced with new situations and dangers; about their feelings, their mistakes and their courage, about their inner life. He thinks: "What would it be like to be an average woman on the night before she goes off to Mars to join her husband? That has nothing to do at all with science fiction in the usual sense. You don't confront the planets, you don't confront a machine, you confront an ancient concept: the wife of the Viking, the wife of Ulysses. . . ."

It has been said that Bradbury sees space as the new frontier to be conquered, just as the old ones—first the ocean and then the North American continent—were conquered in the past by families of pioneers. His Martians play the part of the American Indians of old. One of his *Martian Chronicles* is actually based on a tale that Bradbury remembered about a sixteenth-century American Indian who, one day, felt a sudden pang of fear, a premonition of disaster. Without knowing exactly why, he walked and walked for days until he reached the shore of the ocean. There on the beach were a few bearded men wearing metal hats; their skin was white. Three fat ships were bobbing on the sea. The Indian ran back home with a heavy heart. In the story entitled *Ylla*, Bradbury's main character is a Martian woman who "feels" the approach of the first spaceship from Earth just as the Indian had sensed the landing of the Spaniards on the Atlantic shore of their continent. This first invasion of Mars fails, however, when Ylla's husband shoots the astronauts.

The Martian Chronicles describe four landings and the progressive settlement of Mars. Although most of the stories are thoughtful and often sad, a few belong to the domain of black comedy.[1] In *The Earth Men*, the astronauts of the second landing, bursting with pride of their exploit, try in vain to impress the Martians of the town near which they have landed. Any reaction—admiration, surprise, fear, even anger and hostility—would be more acceptable than the profound indifference of the natives, who seem too busy with their own affairs to pay attention to the strange invaders. The only Martian who eventually shows interest in the Earth men is a psychologist who judges them insane, and who congratulates the rocket's captain for being a "psychotic genius." He thinks that the captain, by some telepathic power, makes him and the other Martians see an imaginary spaceship full of nonexistent instruments. In his opinion, the captain has succeeded, by the sheer power of his mind, in creating an illusion.

While as a novelist he often sympathizes with the invaded Martians, Bradbury is not opposed to the real colonization of Mars. In fact he maintains that man's future lies in space, since mankind can't possibly survive on Earth, now that their blue planet is polluted, overpopulated, and threatened with nuclear extinction. The only thing to do is to move out, and to do so without a backward look. Despite his affection for small towns and their old-fashioned ways, Bradbury is persuaded that men would spoil their chances of success if they clung to their old habits and their homeland. Those of his characters who indulge in nostalgia are always doomed; the victors are those who looked ahead.

The Martian Chronicles established Bradbury as an author; they also brought him some unexpected admirers. One of them, the British essayist Aldous Huxley, told Bradbury that he was a poet. As Bradbury looked un-

---

[1] black comedy is a kind of comedy that, although amusing, has sad or tragic overtones.

convinced, Huxley proceeded to read aloud passages from the *Chronicles* to prove his point. After this demonstration, Bradbury felt obliged to write at least one poem every day. Rather hesitant at first, he gained enough confidence by and by to present his work to his publisher, who accepted it. Eight volumes of Bradbury's poetry have been published to date.

In 1953 a letter addressed to Ray Bradbury arrived from Italy; it was signed Bernard Berenson. The eighty-year-old art historian, an expert on Italian Renaissance painters, had been intrigued, he said, by an article in which Bradbury talked about his work. "It's the first time," wrote Berenson, "that I have encountered the statement by an artist in any field, that to work creatively you must enjoy it as a fascinating adventure." The letter ended with an invitation to come to Florence. Given the Bradburys' financial status at the time, the idea of going to Italy was preposterous. At least it seemed to be until another admirer, film director John Huston, appeared with a timely offer. Having read *The Fog Horn,* Huston wanted Bradbury to adapt Herman Melville's classic, *Moby Dick,* for the screen. Since Huston's home was in Ireland, Ray and Maggie joined him there and Bradbury spent three happy months writing the script and collecting Irish anecdotes to be used in later stories. Apparently he also found the time to indulge in some mild mischief, for he was once arrested by the Irish police, who charged him officially with "being drunk and in charge of a bicycle."

As soon as the script was completed, the Bradburys flew to Florence, carrying as a small present for their host Bradbury's most recent work, the just published *Farhenheit 451*.[2] Friendship blossomed immediately between the elderly art expert and the maverick science fiction writer. Bradbury now refers to Berenson as his "second father," no mean compliment from a man who deeply loved the first one. Not only did Berenson read *Fahrenheit 451* attentively, but he came up with some good suggestions for other stories. Meanwhile, Bradbury and his wife visited the treasures of Italian art in the museums of Florence, and reported to their host in the evening about their discoveries of the day.

All through the 1950s Ray Bradbury kept writing his tales of terror, hope, satire, and tenderness. His inexhaustible imagination, his ability to create moods and suspense, attracted a host of readers. By 1960 he had become enough of a celebrity to be interviewed by Oriana Fallaci, an Italian journalist who doesn't waste her time on second-rate figures. In 1966 the film based on *Fahrenheit 451* brought Bradbury to the attention of a segment of the public who had never heard of his books before. He liked the film, but was less pleased a few years later with the adaptation of his *Illustrated Man.*

Bradbury says that his professional life has run like a snowball—each project, each success leading to another project and another success. The

---

[2]451 degrees Fahrenheit is the temperature at which paper burns.

adaptation of *Moby Dick,* for example, inspired him to write about Melville's and Jules Verne's heroes in his introduction to a new edition of *20,000 Leagues Under the Sea.* This introduction in turn caught the eye of one of the directors of the New York World's Fair of 1964–65, who asked Bradbury to be designer-consultant for the U.S. Pavilion. Bradbury, who loves designing and planning, accepted with enthusiasm. The problem he had to solve was to move large crowds of visitors through 400 years of American history, a task that he accomplished deftly with moving platforms, cinema screens of various shapes and sizes, a narrator and a symphony orchestra for background music. The results obviously impressed the Disney Corporation representatives who had been involved with the Fair, for designer Bradbury was hired as a consultant for the futuristic section of the planned Disney World in Florida, Spaceship Earth.

Nowadays Bradbury lives in one of the best sections of Los Angeles and keeps an office in Beverly Hills where he can work uninterrupted. He relaxes occasionally in Palm Springs, mainly by swimming. But he admits that he would find it difficult to live without writing at least four hours a day, and apparently the flow of inspiration has not diminished at all with the years. He gets up every morning brimming over with ideas, he said in an interview for the *Wall Street Journal* in 1985, sits at his typewriter, "and the words come tumbling down." Turning to a new genre, he published in 1985 his first detective novel, *Death Is a Lonely Business* (A. Knopf) and was so happy with it that he proceeded without a pause to work on another one. Now recognized as a master of fiction, he is sought after by publishers, interviewers, and television and film directors; he is also in great demand as a lecturer at colleges and universities. He claims, however, that despite all the fame, his greatest personal satisfaction comes from the fact that he is at last writing what he considers excellent poetry.

In response to those who criticize his work and his attitude toward science fiction, Bradbury protests strongly that he is not antagonistic to technology. But he doesn't show much liking for machines in his everyday life. He hates television, and doesn't find a kind word to say about the telephone, "a barracuda that doesn't leave you any time of your own!" He doesn't drive and refuses to fly. "It's just fear," he says. "I like planes and I like the idea of flying; I just don't want to do it." His attitude toward automobiles is understandable; when he was a child in Waukegan, he was deeply affected by the sight of a car that crashed into a telephone pole in front of him, killing its four passengers. Bradbury's horror of cars, stemming from this accident, was reinforced when he and his parents passed wreck after wreck on their way from Illinois to California. Yet he doesn't object to being driven around, either by his wife or by taxi drivers. In fact he claims that he does his best thinking when he is in motion. The one mode of transportation that he truly favors is trains, because trains, unlike airplanes, allow their passengers to see the world and their fellow humans. "We fly high, see nothing, and yet wonder at our alienation. Give me the train, then, so I can see and know and truly feel and be stirred by the history of our people . . . Then, in a wild impulse, get off the train to admire strangeness and welcome surprise."

Machines are fine, in Bradbury's opinion, and even automobiles, which he once described as "the worst invention in the history of mankind," are not really bad in themselves. Machines are not evil—man is, man who is "capable of misusing anything," and who uses machines to kill, maim and destroy. Worse still, man ends up believing that machines can take care of anything, replace anything—even love. In his usual symbolic vein, Bradbury has given a dramatic illustration of this idea in one of the tales of *The Illustrated Man*, entitled *The Veldt*. The story centers around a family of the future—father, mother, and two children. The parents, having no desire to spend their time caring for their offspring, have bought for them a splendid electronic nursery, a room whose walls and ceiling serve as one large television screen. Whatever the children wish to see, the nursery senses it through some mysterious and refined telepathic device, and the desired scene appears, realistically, on the walls and ceiling, producing a complete environment. The scene can be repeated as often as wanted. After a few years of being ignored by their parents, the children have given up leaving the nursery, the cocoon in which they find the only warmth they have ever known. Eventually the father becomes irritated by the children's refusal to come out of their room; he is also worried by the fact that the nursery seems to provide the same "scene" most of the time, an African plain (a veldt) complete with lions. Recently the lions have been roaring a lot, and objects belonging to the parents have been found in the room, covered with blood. Father unplugs the nursery like a vulgar television set, announcing that he will dispose of it the next day. The children plead for one more day in the nursery, and when their wish is reluctantly granted and the room again in operation, they entice their parents to come in with them. The veldt is on, as usual, and so are the lions, looking very real. Unnoticed, the children tiptoe out of the room, locking Father and Mother inside with the hungry cats; both of them, as it happens, are wearing the items that had been found previously inside the room.

The author of this grim tale is a benign father, a good-natured giant who describes himself as an optimist. He may be right; who but a determined optimist would say that the hydrogen bomb is a great invention because it will make humanity behave? Bradbury is indeed interested in the happiness of humanity and he does take a hand, once in a while, in some community project that might help. In the 1960s he organized a citizens' group, whose purpose was to create a decent rapid-transit system to compete with (and perhaps eliminate) the automobile in Los Angeles.

Improving the quality of life is Bradbury's great concern. The quality of life, he thinks, can be preserved best in small towns such as Waukegan.

The way he sees it, these small towns must be rebuilt or restored, each with its own public malls, universities, radio and television stations, and their own entertainment centers, including ballet and theater companies. Big cities like New York, Chicago, and Los Angeles are obsolete and doomed to fall apart under their own weight like so many dinosaurs.

Bradbury says that he owes the diversity of his interests to the fact that he was immersed in science fiction at an early age. "As a result of reading science fiction when I was eight, I grew up with an interest in music, architecture, city planning, transportation, politics, ethics, aesthetics on any level, art . . . It's just *total*. It is complete commitment to the whole human race on all the Earth." Yet Bradbury is not certain that he is truly a science fiction writer. He accepts the label, for convenience's sake, but he rather sees himself as a fantasist, a moralist and a visionary. "What I do is sometimes called magic realism. I am a poetic maker of metaphor and a trapper of ideas." He doesn't take himself seriously—in fact he deplores serious people, "the long-faced, the self-destroyers!" At ease with his present fame, he considers himself fortunate to have become a celebrity rather late in life. "I have been lucky. We hanker after instant fame, but that's wrong. If fame comes too quickly, it spoils us. For me recognition came just at the right pace."

Understanding the Text

1. Why doesn't Bradbury write a "proper" science fiction story that takes into account the realities of space?
2. Is Bradbury antagonistic to science and technology, as Asimov claims?
3. What is Bradbury's attitude toward the Martians?
4. Is he opposed to man's colonization of Mars? Why?
5. What other creative work has he done besides writing?
6. Does Bradbury have a very good opinion of humans?
7. What kind of cities does he consider best suited to provide a happy life?
8. What portrait of Bradbury emerges from this profile—how would you describe him?

Commenting on the Text

1. What does Bradbury's remark about the telephone suggest about his own life?
2. Bradbury has mentioned the automobile wreck at Waukegan as the reason for his refusal to drive a car. Does the text offer other possible reasons?
3. What do his remarks about trains suggest about Bradbury's personality and about his life?
4. Do you feel that the author likes or dislikes Bradbury or is neutral about him?
5. Would you like to read *The Veldt*? Why?

Facts, Inferences, and Opinions

The following passage offers a combination of facts, inferences and opinions. Inferences are conclusions that the reader derives from the text, but which are not expressly stated. Opinions are sometimes easy to recognize, particularly when they include judgmental words. "This is stupid!" clearly expresses an opinion; so does "This should not be allowed!" It often happens, however, that the difference between fact, opinion, and inference is difficult to detect. "Bradbury is an intelligent man," could be a statement of fact, the speaker's opinion, or a truth implied by Bradbury's actions or by a story written about him. Such ambiguity ("uncertain meaning") occurs constantly in written or spoken statements. The reader should accept this and say: "This could be either fact or opinion; I think it is an opinion, because. . . ."

Read the passage below carefully, trying to recognize facts, inferences and opinions.

1. Apparently Bradbury is a man with multiple talents.
2. He can write stories, parodies, plays, poems, and movie scenarios; he authored many scripts for the Alfred Hitchcock Presents series on television; he is involved in community projects and dabbles in urbanism.
3. Bradbury's plays must not be all equally good.
4. Only some of them have been performed and even those were performed in small theaters.
5. This is not surprising.
6. Bradbury's weird taste cannot appeal to large crowds of theatergoers.
7. Over the last 40 years, at the rate of one per week, Bradbury has written an enormous number of short stories.
8. Some are very funny.
9. *Tyrannosaurus Rex* is an amusing satire of Hollywood's movie producers.
10. Many other stories are too grim to be recommended as middle-of-the-night reading for anyone who is alone and impressionable.
11. Many Bradbury stories deal with death or with evil supernatural happenings.
12. But they obviously appeal to a large public.
13. And however morbid* it may sound, *The Veldt* is an excellent, suspenseful tale.
14. Bradbury is a gentle giant with a sense of humor, a good family man, and a kind father.
15. His opinion of boys doesn't seem to have changed; but he has come to enjoy certain sports.
16. As a concerned citizen he is eager to make life more pleasant for his fellow Los Angelenos by banishing automobiles from their city.

*morbid—sick, unhealthy.

17. Evidently he doesn't have a very high opinion of the present public-transportation system.
18. Some of his ideas on the towns of the future are queer and impractical.
19. Bradbury doesn't drive and travels only moderately.
20. He probably went to Italy by boat.

Based on the preceding passage and on the profile of Ray Bradbury that you have just read:

Which statements are clearly
    a) inferences?
    b) opinions?
Which statements seem debatable?
Does the author seem to know Bradbury's plays?
Do you feel that the author likes Bradbury as a person? Do you think that she likes his ideas and his stories?

Scanning for Details

1. Who wrote *Moby Dick*?
2. What exactly, in Bradbury's article, caused Bernard Berenson's interest in a man so different from himself?
3. Who interviewed Bradbury in 1960?
4. What was the charge against Bradbury when he was arrested by the Irish police?
5. When was *Fahrenheit 451* filmed?
6. What is the title of the *Martian Chronicle* that describes the second landing on Mars?
7. How does he describe himself: "I am a . . . . ideas."?
8. When did Berenson write to Bradbury?

Vocabulary

Complete each of the following sentences with the most appropriate word from the list below, which includes more words than necessary. Be sure to make all needed adjustments in articles, verbs, and nouns.

1. It is not unusual for a science fiction writer to show _____ landing on Mars; they arrive in spaceships, ready to _____ the hostile natives—if there are any.
2. But the idea of men walking around on Mars or Venus without special clothing and helmets is _____.
3. John Campbell considered Bradbury an oddity, a _____ among serious science fiction writers.

4. He tried to _____ Bradbury to change his way of writing by promising to publish any *real* science fiction story that he could produce.
5. Obviously Campbell had no _____ of Bradbury's future appeal to the public; otherwise he would have been proud to add him to his "stable" of authors.
6. Many of Bradbury's characters are _____, like Ylla, who feels that people from another planet are on their way to invade her world, and who knows that they'll destroy it.
7. Bradbury's most dangerous characters often have a nice, mild, _____ appearance.
8. To the reader of the *Martian Chronicles,* it is obvious that scientific accuracy is _____ to Bradbury's style of science fiction.
9. The most tragic element in *The Veldt* is the lack of understanding and communication between parents and children, the total _____ that exists between them.
10. Some of Bradbury's characters cannot adjust to living on Mars; they feel a strong _____ for their former life on Earth and for their familiar surroundings.

maverick	barracuda	alienation
a snowball	to confront	to alienate
nostalgia	preposterous	fey
to misuse	to entice	earthling
psychotic	enticement	offspring
irrelevant	confrontation	premonition
nostalgic	benign	

Prefixes

<u>Tele</u> at the beginning of a word implies the idea of *distance*. The *telephone* is a device that carries the voice of the speaker over great distances.

1. How do you explain the words *"television"* and *"telegraph"*?
2. What is the difference between a *telescope* and a *microscope*—and who uses them?
3. What is *telepathy*? Do you believe in telepathy?
4. How would you define *telephotography*?

<u>Pre</u> means *before*. A *prefix* is a group of letters added at the beginning of a word.
   It comes before the original word—it *precedes* it.

1. How could you express: "The old Indian had a *premonition* of disaster"?
2. Since history is the knowledge of past events through written records and inscriptions, what period of time does *prehistory* cover?

3. What is likely to bring a heavier sentence, a *premeditated* crime or an *unpremeditated* crime? Why?
4. When Rachel Carson asked for the authorization to go on a fishing expedition on a Fish and Wildlife Service boat, her superiors objected that there was no *precedent* for such an action. What did they mean?
5. When does a speaker make his *preliminary remarks*?
6. When a person applies for a job, the employer usually asks the applicant about his or her *previous* experience. What does the employer want to know?
7. Clothes sometimes bear a label indicating that they have been *pre-shrunk*? Is this good? Why?
8. What is the purpose of *preventive* medicine?
9. What makes a person look *prematurely* old?

The Right Order

The following story is a brief summary of *Fahrenheit 451*. Put the sentences in the right chronological order to make the story coherent.

  1 The action takes place in a totalitarian country where it is forbidden to own or read books.

____ Montag runs away, hiding from the police helicopters searching for him.

____ One day, Montag opens a book of poetry that he is supposed to burn.

____ They hope to be able to pass on their knowledge to humanity when it becomes possible to do so.

____ The Captain tells Montag that he has been denounced by his wife.

____ When a person is suspected of having books, the firemen are sent to burn the books, and often the house.

____ Those people are intellectuals who have memorized a book, or part of a book.

____ Montag revolts and kills the Captain.

____ He runs out of town into a forest where he is welcomed by a group of men and women.

____ Montag takes the book home and reads some poems to his wife, who is horrified.

____ Montag is ordered by his Captain to go with the other firemen to burn a house, and discovers that the house is his own.

____ One of the firemen is a young man named Montag.

Topics for Discussion

1. Is it important for a science fiction story to be scientifically accurate? Would you lose interest in a story that wasn't?
2. Do you agree with Bradbury that the automobile is the worst invention of mankind? Would we be happier without it? In your opinion, what is the worst invention of mankind? What is the best one?
3. Do you agree with Bradbury that science fiction gives people an interest in music, architecture, city planning, transportation, politics, ethics, and art?
4. What do you think of his plans for small towns? What would be the advantage of such a plan? From a financial point of view, would the plan be feasible? What would be the quality of small towns' ballet and theater productions? What about television and radio?
5. Are people who take themselves too seriously "self-destroyers"?
6. What do you think of *The Veldt*? Does it justify any of Bradbury's descriptions of himself as an optimist, a moralist, a maker of metaphor, a visionary? Is the story "morbid"?
7. Among the stories summarized in this chapter, do you find any that show Bradbury as
   a) a moralist
   b) a humorist
   c) a compassionate man

Preliminary Notes for Selected Reading: *The Fog Horn*

One of the characters in *The Fog Horn* mentions that the monster rising from the depth of the sea had to depressurize itself gradually before it could swim near the surface. Deep-sea divers, as well as the creatures of the ocean's abyss living under high pressure of water, must go to the upper layers, where the pressure is lower, in careful stages. If they come up too fast, fish die and men are apt to get "the bends," a painful affliction caused by the liberation of air bubbles in the blood stream, which can maim or even kill them.

Colloquialisms

The conversation between the two characters of *The Fog Horn* is very informal, and at times ungrammatical; you will notice, for example, that one of the men uses the adjective "slow" where he should have used the adverb "slowly." The effect, however, is to give the narration more strength and evocative power.

The two men also use colloquialisms:

"I sort of think that's true"	*I tend to think that it's true*
"Is all"	*That's all*

| "He thought it over from every which way" | *He examined it from all points of view; he re-examined every detail of what had happened.* |

Selected Reading

The Fog Horn
by Ray Bradbury

While reading The Fog Horn, *try to catch the mood of the narration, and to see how Bradbury tells us what attracted their strange visitor.*

[The action of *The Fog Horn* takes place in a lighthouse, somewhere on a rocky island off the coast of an unnamed country, in our time.

The lighthouse and its fog horn are manned by Mr. McDunn, who has worked there for a number of years, and his assistant Johnny, a younger man, who is the narrator of the story. Johnny is due to go to the mainland the next day for a brief period of rest. It's November, the night is dark, the sea is dark, and the fog is getting thicker, as it usually does at the time of year. McDunn, who seems worried, has just warned his companion that perhaps they should prepare themselves for some strange happening. The preceding year, at about this time and in the same kind of weather, McDunn had seen something in the ocean, something that circled the lighthouse as if looking at it. McDunn feels that the "something" might come again soon. The two men climb all the way to the top of the lighthouse, where the light and the horn are located. After a while, McDunn suddenly points outside: "something" is indeed swimming in the sea.

And here is the rest of the story as Bradbury tells it.]

It was a cold night, as I have said; the high tower was cold, the light coming and going, and the Fog Horn calling and calling through the raveling mist. You couldn't see far and you couldn't see plain, but there was the deep sea moving on its way about the night earth, flat and quiet, the colour of grey mud, and here were the two of us alone in the high tower, and there, far out at first, was a ripple, followed by a wave, a rising, a bubble, a bit of froth. And then, from the surface of the cold sea came a head, a large head, dark-colored, with immense eyes, and then a neck. And then— not a body—but more neck and more! The head rose a full forty feet above the water on a slender and beautiful dark neck. Only then did the body, like a little island of black coral and shells and crayfish, drip up from the subterranean. There was a flicker of tail. In all, from head to tip of tail, I estimated the monster at ninety or a hundred feet.

I don't know what I said. I said something.

"Steady, boy, steady," whispered McDunn.

"It's impossible!" I said.

"No, Johnny, *we're* impossible. *It's* like it always was ten million years ago. *It* hasn't changed. It's *us* and the land that've changed, become impossible. *Us.*"

It swam slowly and with a great dark majesty out in the icy waters, far away. The fog came and went about it, momentarily erasing its shape. One of the monster's eyes caught and held and flashed back our immense light, red, white, red, white, like a dish held high and sending a message in primeval code. It was as silent as the fog through which it swam.

"It's a dinosaur of some sort!" I crouched down, holding to the stair rail.

"Yes, one of the tribe."

"But they died out!"

"No, only hid away in the Deeps. Deep, deep down in the deepest Deeps. Isn't *that* a word now, Johnny, a real word, it says so much: the Deeps. There's all the coldness and darkness and deepness in the world in a word like that."

"What'll we do?"

"Do? We got our job, we can't leave. Besides, we're safer here than in any boat trying to get to land. That thing's as big as a destroyer and almost as swift."

"But here, why does it come *here*?"

The next moment, I had my answer.

The Fog Horn blew.

And the monster answered.

A cry came across a million years of water and mist. A cry so anguished and alone that it shuddered in my head and my body. The monster cried out at the tower. The Fog Horn blew. The monster roared again. The Fog Horn blew. The monster opened its great toothed mouth and the sound that came from it was the sound of the Fog Horn itself. Lonely and vast and far away. The sound of isolation, a viewless sea, a cold night, apartness. That was the sound.

"Now," whispered McDunn, "do you know why it comes here?"

I nodded.

"All year long, Johnny, that poor monster there lying far out, a thousand miles at sea, and twenty miles deep maybe, biding his time, perhaps it's a million years old, this one creature. Think of it, waiting a million years; could *you* wait that long? Maybe it's the last of its kind. I sort of think that's true. Anyway, here come men on land and build this lighthouse, five years ago. And set up their Fog Horn and sound it and sound it, out toward the place where you bury yourself in sleep and sea memories of a world where there were thousands like yourself, but now you are alone, all alone in a world not made for you, a world where you have to hide.

"But the sound of the Fog Horn comes and goes, comes and goes, and you stir from the muddy bottom of the Deeps, and your eyes open like the lenses of two-foot cameras and you move slow, slow, for you have the ocean sea on your shoulders, heavy. But that Fog Horn comes through a thousand miles of water, faint and familiar, and the furnace in your belly stokes up, and you begin to rise, slow, slow. You feed yourself on great slakes of cod and minnow, on rivers of jellyfish, and you rise slow through the autumn months, through September when the fogs started, through October with more fog and the Horn still calling you on, and then, late in November, after pressurizing yourself day by day, a few feet higher every hour, you are near the surface and still alive. You have got to go slow; if you surfaced all at once, you'd explode. So it takes you all of three months to surface, and then a number of days to swim through the cold waters to the lighthouse. And there you are, out there, in the night, Johnny, the biggest damn monster in creation. And here is the lighthouse calling to you, with a long neck like your neck sticking way out of the water, and a body like your body, and, most important of all, a voice like your voice. Do you understand now, Johnny, do you understand?"

The Fog Horn blew.

The monster answered.

I saw it all. I knew it all—the million years of waiting alone, for someone to come back that never came back. The million years of isolation at the bottom of the sea, the insanity of time there, while the skies cleared of reptile-birds, the swamp dried on the continental lands, the sloths and sabertooths had their day and sank in tar pits, and men ran like white ants upon the hills.

The Fog Horn blew.

"Last year," said McDunn, "that creature swam round and round, round and round, all night. Not coming too near, puzzled, I'd say. Afraid, maybe. And a bit angry after coming all this way. But the next day, unexpectedly, the fog lifted, the sun came out fresh, the sky was as blue as a painting. And the monster swam off away from the heat and the silence and didn't come back. I suppose it's been brooding on it for a year now, thinking it over from every which way."

The monster was only a hundred yards off now, it and the Fog Horn crying at each other. As the lights hit them, the monster's eyes were fire and ice, fire and ice. "That's life for you," said McDunn. "Someone's always waiting for someone who never comes home. Always someone loving something more than the thing loves them. And after a while you want to destroy whatever the thing is, so it can't hurt you no more."

The monster was rushing at the lighthouse.

The Fog Horn blew.

"Let's see what happens," said McDunn.

He switched the Fog Horn off.

The ensuing minute of silence was so intense that we could hear our hearts pounding in the glassed area of the tower, could hear the slow greased turn of the light.

The monster stopped and froze. Its great lantern eyes blinked. Its mouth gaped. It gave a sort of rumble, like a volcano. It twitched its head this way and that, as if to seek the sound now dwindled off into the fog. It peered at the lighthouse. It rumbled again. Then its eyes caught fire. It reared up, threshed the water, and rushed at the tower, its eyes filled with angry torment.

"McDunn?" I cried. "Switch on the horn!"

McDunn fumbled with the switch. But even as he flicked it on, the monster was rearing up. I had a glimpse of its gigantic paws, fishskin glittering in webs between the fingerlike projections, clawing at the tower. The huge eye on the right side of its anguished head glittered before me like a cauldron into which I might drop, screaming. The tower shook. The Fog Horn cried; the monster cried. It seized the tower and gnashed at the glass, which shattered upon us.

McDunn seized my arm. "Downstairs!"

The tower rocked, trembled, and started to give. The Fog Horn and the monster roared. We stumbled and half fell down the stairs. "Quick!"

We reached the bottom as the tower buckled down toward us. We ducked under the stairs into the small stone cellar. There were a thousand concussions as the rocks rained down; the Fog Horn stopped abruptly. The monster crashed upon the tower. The tower fell. We knelt together, McDunn and I, holding tight, while our world exploded.

Then it was over, and there was nothing but darkness and the wash of the sea on the raw stones.

That, and the other sound.

"Listen," said McDunn quietly. "Listen."

We waited for a moment. And then I began to hear it. First a great vacuum sucking of air, and then the lament, the bewilderment, the loneliness of the great monster, folded over and upon us, above us, so that the sickening reek of its body filled the air, a stone thickness away from our cellar. The monster gasped and cried. The tower was gone. The thing that had called to it across a million years was gone. And the monster was opening its mouth and sending out great sounds. The sounds of a Fog Horn, again and again. And ships far at sea, not finding the light, not seeing anything, but passing and hearing late that night, must've thought: There it is, the lonely sound, the Lonesome Bay horn. All's well. We've rounded the cape.

And so it went for the rest of the night.

The sun was hot and yellow the next afternoon when the rescuers came out to dig us from our stoned-under cellar.

"It fell apart, is all." said McDunn gravely. "We had a few bad knocks from the waves and it just crumbled." He pinched my arm.

There was nothing to see. The ocean was calm, the sky blue. The only thing was a great algaic stink from the green matter that covered the fallen tower stones and the shore rocks. Flies buzzed about. The ocean washed empty on the shore.

The next year they built a new lighthouse, but by that time I had a job in the little town and a wife and a good small warm house that glowed yellow on autumn nights, the door locked, the chimney puffing smoke. As for McDunn, he was master of the new lighthouse, built to his specifications, out of steel-reinforced concrete. "Just in case," he said.

The new lighthouse was ready in November. I drove down alone one evening late and parked my car and looked across the gray waters and listened to the new horn sounding once, twice, three, four times a minute far out there, by itself.

The monster?

It never came back.

"It's gone away," said McDunn. "It's gone back to the Deeps. It's learned you can't love anything too much in this world. It's gone into the deepest Deeps to wait another million years. Ah, the poor thing! Waiting out there, and waiting out there, while man comes and goes on this pitiful little planet. Waiting and waiting."

I sat in my car, listening. I couldn't see the lighthouse or the light standing out in Lonesome Bay. I could only hear the Horn, the Horn, the Horn. It sounded like the monster calling.

I sat there wishing there was something I could say.

Summing Up

1. Why is the dinosaur attracted to the lighthouse?
2. Why does he become furious and destroy the tower?
3. Why weren't the men killed when the tower collapsed?
4. What happened to the dinosaur?

Appraising the Story

1. What is the general mood of the story, at the beginning?
2. How does Bradbury set the scene: what key words contribute to make the reader feel what it was like on that November night?
3. How does Bradbury feel about the dinosaur? Give examples.
4. What trick does he use (lines 50–65) to make the reader sympathize with the monster?
5. What points does Bradbury make, in the course of the narration, that have little to do with dinosaurs?
6. A science fiction author who admires Bradbury said that Bradbury's

stories were full of scientific inaccuracies. What is inaccurate or impossible in the story of the dinosaur?

In your opinion, do these inaccuracies ruin the story, make it less interesting, or do they have no effect?
7. In your opinion, what makes *The Fog Horn* a good, or a bad, story?
8. Why does the narrator say at the end: "I sat there wishing there was something I could say?" What would he say, and to whom?

Project

(Instructor: This exercise can be done in small groups, or individually. Then the results can be compared, and the two best projects chosen by the class.)

Find a subject for a science fiction story (a book, a film or a television series). Indicate the time (present, past or future); the location; and the main characters.

(If time allows, when the class has chosen the best project, the students might suggest a first episode for the story.)

Amelia Earhart
woman pilot

Introduction

The Vocabulary of Aviation

Aviation was still young when World War I broke out, and still looked upon as a daring adventure. The aviators who fought alone in the open cockpits of their small planes were regarded as romantic heroes. Some of them capitalized on their prestige after the war, using their expertise to entertain crowds at fairs and air meets. They performed all sorts of dangerous stunts, such as flying low, flying upside down, rolling over, spinning, making loops, stalling their engine to give the people below the impression that it was stopped for good, and flying under bridges or through the hangars and other large buildings of the airfield. On the ground, they looked dashing in leather coats and leather helmets, with large goggles protecting their eyes. Part of the regalia was a long white scarf that floated in the wind when the aviators were aloft (at least in the movies).

When Charles A. Lindbergh landed near Paris on May 20, 1927, after soloing from New York in a small plane that looks very frail nowadays, the thrill of aviation had not yet died down. Thousands of people were on the airfield waiting for him, ready to carry him to Paris in triumph—which they did. In New York, Lindbergh was given another enthusiastic welcome. He rode through Manhattan in what is known as a ticker-tape parade—riding in an open car while office employees showered him with pieces of tapes from the tickers (used to record stock prices) and all the paper they could put their hands on. Ticker-tape parades are still a tradition for returning heroes.

Looking Ahead

- How many different topics are covered in this chapter?
- In what way is Amelia Earhart related with the subject matter of the fourth section of this chapter?
- What do you think of women as aviators and astronauts?
- Have you heard of Amelia Earhart before? What does the piece below tell you about her?

Amelia's Last Flight

Amelia Earhart was thirty-eight, and probably the most acclaimed woman pilot in the world, when she decided to realize an old dream of hers—flying around the world "where it is fattest, at the equator." She prepared for the trip with infinite care. The plane that she bought for the purpose, a Lockheed twin-engine "Electra" airliner, was the most powerful nonmilitary flying machine of the day. On her instructions, it had been modified to carry extra-large gas tanks as well as a complete navigation room equipped with the most advanced instruments. Her navigator during the flight would be Captain Frederick Noonan, a man of great experience and formidable reputation.

Amelia and Noonan took off from Florida on May 29, 1937. They flew eastward as planned, to Puerto Rico, Venezuela, Brazil, then across the Atlantic to Africa, India, Burma, the East Indies and Australia; then from Australia to Lae in New Guinea. From Lae they still had to cover 7,000 miles over open water to their goal, which was California. There would be only one stop in that long stretch, on tiny Howland Island. Howland seemed a queer choice and, experienced as they were, Amelia and Noonan surely knew that it would be difficult to pinpoint that speck of land (two miles long and a half mile wide) in the immensity of the sea. Still, the Lockheed would carry plenty of gas, and furthermore three U.S. ships were positioned to assist. They were the U.S.S. *Ontario*, halfway between Lae and Howland; the *U.S.S. Swan*, between Howland and Honolulu; and the Coast Guard Ship *Itasca,* waiting just off Howland, ready to send and receive messages, to provide weather information, and to rush to the Lockheed's rescue if need be.

Amelia took off from Lae at 10:30 A.M. on July 2,[1] 1937, with considerable difficulty. The weather was not too bad, but the Electra, loaded with 900 gallons of oil and gas, almost failed to lift off the ground at the end of the runway. To the horror of the onlookers, it seemed for a moment that the plane would taxi into the ocean. It did lurch above sea level, however, climbed out of danger, and disappeared into an overcast sky. Aboard the *Itasca* a four-man watch was already in place waiting for the flyers' radio signals, which were expected to arrive every half hour, fifteen minutes before and fifteen minutes after the hour.

At 1:12 A.M., (Howland Time) Commander Thompson, skipper of the *Itasca*, signaled to his base in San Francisco that he had not heard from Amelia yet. But the plane was still about 1,000 miles away, and surely (he said) there was nothing to worry about.

At 2:45 A.M. the anxious operators of the *Itasca* finally heard Amelia's voice, barely audible:" Cloudy and overcast . . . headwinds." The next expected signal at 3:15 didn't come. At 3:30 *Itasca* radioed its weather report to the silent plane; there was no answer and the operators, deeply concerned now, kept calling the Electra and asking for its position.

When Amelia was heard again, faintly, at 3:45 A.M. she didn't mention the *Itasca*'s appeals nor its weather report. "*Itasca* from Earhart," came the distant voice. ". . . overcast . . . will listen in on hour and half-hour on 3105." The frustrated men on the ship didn't know what to make of the communication. Why was Amelia using a voice signal rather than key signals? Why was she not indicating her position and bearing? Was her radio

---

[1] 12:30 P.M., July 1, for the *Itasca* near Howland.

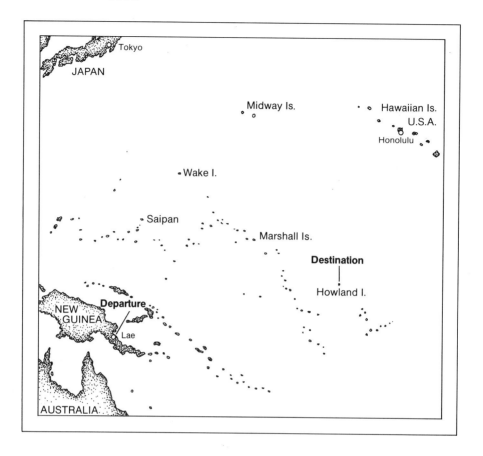

out of order? Was she flying in stormy weather with failing equipment? They couldn't believe that such an expert pilot would have left Lae if the plane was not in top shape. Fearing that Amelia might overshoot Howland, Commander Thompson had the island's runways cleared for emergency landing—just in case.

At 6:15 and 6:45 the operators, unable to hear Amelia distinctly, guessed that she was asking them to take her bearing, and she whistled to give them a chance to make an estimate. But the sound didn't last long enough to allow them to come up with a figure.

Not until 7:42 AM did the listeners hear Amelia's voice again; this time it was much stronger, a fact that they interpreted as proof that the Electra was not far from them. "We must be on you but we cannot see you," said Amelia. "Gas is running low. Only about thirty minutes left. Been unable to reach you by radio. We are flying at altitude of 1,000 feet."

There was another strong message fifteen minutes later: "We are circling but we cannot see you. Go ahead on 7500 either now or on schedule." Then at 8:45 AM: "We are in line of position 157-337 . . . will repeat the message at 6210 kilocycles . . . wait listening at 6210 kilocycles. We are running north and south." The voice sounded frightened and confused. *Itasca* waited anxiously, but there was no more communication.

From the meager information collected, Commander Thompson concluded that Amelia, having missed Howland, had kept flying northward, and was now probably down in a deserted area of the Pacific. Hopefully, the empty tanks of the Electra would keep the plane afloat for a time, if it was not damaged. Thompson gave the alert to San Francisco and plowed northward as fast as he could.

For ten days a fleet of U.S. vessels, including a battleship and an aircraft carrier, searched 262,281 square miles of ocean. No sign of the Lockheed or of its passengers was ever found. At the end of the ten days, Amelia's husband accepted the Navy's announcement that his wife and her navigator had been "lost at sea". His belief, as we shall see, was not shared by all.

Understanding the Text

Summarize in your own words, without unnecessary details, the story of Amelia Earhart's last flight:

1. Who was she?
2. What was she trying to do?
3. What did she still have to do to complete her flight?
4. What was the importance of Howland Island, and why was it a bad choice?
5. What happened after Lae?

Logical Reasoning Without Connectors

The logical relationship between clauses is not always indicated by a connector. In some cases, it is left to the reader or the listener to determine the link between the facts presented.

Consider the various groups of sentences below. Each group includes three sentences that may or may not present a cause and effect relationship. In some cases, the effect may have two causes. In which groups do you find a cause and effect relationship between two or all three of the statements? How would you make the relationship clear?

1. Amelia and her navigator missed Howland Island.
   They were flying very low.
   They had lost their way during the night.

2. Howland Island had been a queer choice anyway.
   If the aviators missed it, they would not find another possible landing spot nearby.
   The island was extremely small

3. The operators of the *Itasca* were dedicated and experienced.
   The *Itasca* kept a four-man watch around the clock.
   The operators couldn't hear Amelia's voice distinctly.

4. Amelia was lost and desperate.
   Amelia asked the operators of the *Itasca* to estimate her position.
   Amelia didn't whistle long enough.

5. It was well known that Fred Noonan was an alcoholic.
   Noonan was not an extremely good choice as a navigator.
   He had a great deal of flying experience and a good knowledge of the Pacific.

6. The captain of the *Itasca* had the decks of his ship cleared.
   He thought that Amelia might miss Howland Island.
   She could be short of fuel and in need of an emergency landing place.

7. "The gas is running low," said Amelia. "Only half an hour left."
   The operators thought that the plane was not far from the *Itasca*.
   The captain was waiting with them in the radio room.

Profile
Part One

Born July 24, 1898
Died July 2, 1937?

Skim the text to find out:
- What kind of a family Amelia Earhart belonged to;
- Whether or not she gained fame as a pilot in this first part of the profile;
- Where and when she learned to fly.

As you read the story, make a note of
any metaphors that you find.

Because of the manner of her disappearance, Amelia Earhart has become a figure of mystery. Even her personality remains elusive for those who did not know her personally and must therefore rely on conflicting testimony and documentation. Her friend Fay Gillis Wells, a flyer like herself, describes Amelia as "a really beautiful person, quiet, witty, concerned about the needs of others. . . . She had been caught up in the swirling interest in aviation long before Lindbergh's flight. Yet she shrivelled at the excesses of the press." Amelia's husband, for his part, emphasizes "her directness, simplicity, and lack of ostentation." But in his book *Among the Missing*, Jay Robert Nash makes mild fun of the delight Amelia found in appearing nearly everywhere in full flyer's regalia—"boots, khaki pants, leather helmet, and goggles." To him, her love of flying was "a passion that obsessed her with ambition and finally swallowed her with childhood's headstrong dreams of glory, which as an adult she refused to abandon."

Amelia Mary Earhart came from a family that was not merely respectable but distinguished. Grandfather Earhart, a Lutheran minister from Pennsylvania, was also a scholar who taught Hebrew and Greek at Midland College. His charming, handsome, and rather weak son married the daughter of Judge Alfred Otis, a wealthy and highly respected figure in Atchison, Kansas. For all their gentility, both families belonged to that hardy, enterprising generation of easterners who ventured into the rough and undeveloped western territories that were just becoming a part of the United States, and who adapted, endured, and prospered.

Amelia's father, Edwin Earhart, was a lawyer who had dreamed of ending his career as a member of the U.S. Supreme Court. But after marrying Amy Otis, who was used to luxury, Edwin found it necessary to secure a position that would be safer, perhaps, than finding a clientele. The job that he took as lawyer for a railroad company entailed much traveling away from his family and never satisfied his ambition. Edwin took to drowning his frustration in drink and eventually became an alcoholic. Amelia, who always loved her father, may well have learned from his example that happiness isn't necessarily found on the safest road, and that renouncing one's own aspirations for the sake of a loved one can lead to disaster for both. It seems that she sensed early that she should not make the same mistakes.

Both Edwin and Amy Earhart were brilliant, broadminded individuals with progressive ideas about child rearing. Amy held that anything unusual was bound to be educational. As a consequence, Amelia and her younger sister Muriel were brought up in a way that was unconventional for the period, and hardly proper for young ladies. They were allowed to stay up late at night and even to climb to the rooftop with their father to watch a comet or an eclipse of the moon. No effort was made to turn tomboy Amelia into a feminine little girl, and she had no trouble getting for Christmas the football and the popgun that she had requested. Amelia and Muriel were encouraged to be as inquisitive as they liked and to bring home all the fascinating odds and ends[1] that they found in the fields or the woods—be it red spiders or frog's eggs—and to keep their treasures in the room that had been set aside as their "museum."

Of the two, Amelia was the adventurer, bold and inventive. She was the one who designed and built a roller coaster with odd pieces of wood and rollerskate wheels. She nearly broke her neck testing the contraption[2] when it was completed. But defeat didn't discourage her—ever. If things didn't work out as expected, she launched into the next adventure without wasting her tears over the failure of the first one. She didn't raise a murmur when her parents dismantled the roller coaster to save her limbs and possibly her life.

Amelia's childhood was peopled with imaginary friends, and with animals—for which she had a great love. She rode horses, indeed took delight in all physical exercises, particularly swimming and rowing. Later in life she enjoyed driving automobiles very fast and experimenting with every mechanical device that came her way. She wanted, she said, to try all sorts of things at least once.

Although she took as much pleasure in mental challenges as in physical games, Amelia was not an altogether satisfactory student. She was bright, and particularly gifted in mathematics. But while she could find quickly the solution of a problem, she was not interested in explaining the reasons and the details of her operations, and as a result she never received the prizes that could have been hers with a little more patience. To the admonitions of her teacher she just replied that she didn't care for prizes and honors anyway. It doesn't seem that she had many friends at school, where she was known as "the girl in brown who walks alone."

Whenever possible Edwin took his family with him to travel in his special train car. Those occasions were a joy for Amelia, who claimed that she learned more there than in the classroom. But the greatest part of the girls' early life was spent in comfort and happiness at the home of their Otis grandparents—until tragedy struck in 1911. That year, Edwin lost his job, grandmother Otis died, and the house was sold. The Earharts moved to St. Paul, Minnesota. It was by no means their last move: in four years the uprooted Amelia attended six different high schools before graduating in 1916 from the Hyde Park School in Chicago. She was then sent to a finishing school in Philadelphia to acquire the social graces desirable for young ladies of good families who hoped to find a husband—social graces in which Amelia is said to have been totally lacking. It may be that she was still re-

---

[1] odds and ends—all sorts of small things of little value.
[2] a contraption is a machine that looks strange and is probably not very good.

taining some of her tomboy quality; although her friends claim that she was very feminine as an adult, she does look like a young boy on many of her photographs, even those taken shortly before her disappearance.

In the summer of 1917, Amelia paid a visit to her sister, who was in school in Toronto. As the war was still raging in France, many wounded Canadian soldiers were brought back from the European battlefields. The sight of hobbling or bandaged young men moved Amelia so much that she couldn't resist the impulse to "do something about it." She joined the Canadian Red Cross. Until the end of the war she worked as a nurse's aide in the hospital, "doing everything from scrubbing floors to playing tennis with convalescent patients." There were many dashing young Air Force officers around, all in great demand at social gatherings and air meets, where they would demonstrate their courage and their skills in hair-raising acrobatics. Amelia watched them, fascinated.

When she came back to the States, however, Amelia, convinced that her destiny was to attend the sick, enrolled in the Columbia School of Medicine. She also began to study French literature at Barnard College, and undertook for good measure to learn how to take care of automobiles and to play the banjo. It was a busy year, to say the least. Amelia's parents, meanwhile, had separated, and Edwin had moved alone to California, where he made an effort to stop drinking. In the spring of 1919, Amy and Amelia joined him in Los Angeles in the hope of a reconciliation.

That summer Edwin took his daughter to an air meet in Long Beach, and at the end of the show Amelia had her first flying experience with an ace pilot. She came down bewitched, her mind made up. Her father had to find out the price of flying lessons and the length of the usual training period. Since the cost of instruction was much too high for her resources, the only solution, as Amelia saw it, was to earn the thousand or so dollars that were needed. She promptly found a job with a telephone company. Her weekends were spent at the airfield taking instruction with Neta Snooks, the first woman to graduate from the Curtiss School of Aviation, and later from an ex-Army flyer who was giving advanced instruction. Amelia soloed for the first time in 1921.

Absorbed now in her passion for flying and anxious to look every inch like a seasoned "pro," she bought her first aviator's outfit. "I remember so well my first leather coat," she was to write later. "It was 1922. Somehow, I had contrived[3] to save twenty dollars. With it I bought—at a very special sale—an elegant leather coat. *Patent* leather! Shiny and lovely. But suddenly I saw that it looked too new. How were people to think I was a flyer if I was wearing a flying-coat that was brand-new? Wrinkles! That was it. There just had to be wrinkles. So—I slept in it for three nights to give my coat a properly veteran appearance. When I decided not to go to bed in it

---

[3] to contrive—to manage with difficulty.

any longer, I did give it a last going over[4]—rubbing the sheen off here and there."

Amelia's mother, who had caught some of the spirit of the adventure, helped her daughter buy a small secondhand plane to go with the coat. But even after Amelia had arranged to have the plane kept in a hangar free of charge, the gasoline and maintenance expenses far exceeded her possibilities. She then went through a series of jobs, most of them secretarial, and for a time she worked in a photographer's darkroom, learning to make portraits in the process. Whatever the situation, and even when she was only working to finance her true interest, Amelia always endeavored to give her best, as though she were starting the career of her life. She always aimed for perfection. And she enjoyed the variety of experiences. Ten years later she was to write: "I have had 28 different jobs in my life, and I hope I'll have 228 more. Experiment! Meet new people! That's better than any college education."

Still, her heart was in the cockpit of her plane. She spent all her spare time in the air, testing her skill and her machine, practicing stalls, spins, and forced landings—all the stunts that were then considered helpful to good pilots. She came very close to disaster more than once. But she was an excellent pilot, cool, fearless, and nerveless. In 1923 she set her first record by climbing to 14,000 feet, the highest altitude yet reached by a female flyer.

In 1924 Edwin and Amy Earhart were divorced. Amelia sadly sold her beloved plane and used the proceeds to buy a small car in which she and her mother drove across the continent to Medford, Mass., where they were reunited with Muriel. Amelia tried to go back to medicine, but after flunking her courses she gave up definitely in April 1925. "I didn't have the qualities to be an M.D.," she said. "I lacked the patience. I wanted to be doing something, not to be preparing for it." In the winter of 1927 she found employment as a social worker, teaching English to immigrant children in a poor section of Boston. It was an opportunity to do something useful— the sort of task into which she could throw herself completely. She did her work with enthusiasm, trying to give the children not only the language that could be their first step to achievement, but also the zest for life that she herself possessed. There was no time for flying. But she was "keeping in touch"—she had joined the National Aeronautics Association and had even invested a small sum in a modest aeronautical concern owned by a friend. Then out of the blue[5], on a fine spring day of 1928, came the chance that Amelia had not dreamed possible.

A British socialite, Mrs. Frederick Guest, had decided that she would be

---

[4] to give someone a thorough going over is to treat that person very roughly.
[5] "out of the blue"—unexpectedly.

the first woman to fly over the Atlantic as a passenger. For that purpose
she had bought a plane, the *Friendship*, and retained the services of a pilot
and a mechanic. At that point, Mrs. Guest's family raised such opposition
that she was forced to give up the idea of making the voyage; but she insisted that the flight would take place anyway with a woman aboard. Mrs,
Guest, an American by birth, charged some friends in the United States to
find an American lady for the trip, preferably with some experience of flying.
One of those friends was George G. Putnam, owner of the G. G. Putnam
& Sons publishing house. Putnam, searching around Boston, heard about
Amelia Earhart and after a few interviews, decided that she was the perfect choice for the flight. She could fly, she could also write—which was
desirable since she was expected to describe the flight in a book, to be
published by Putnam. At first, on being asked if she would be interested
in "doing something hazardous," Amelia had been overjoyed. She was less
thrilled when she understood that her role would be absolutely passive: she
was to ride along, while the pilot and the mechanic took care of things.
Amelia was rather irritated to be included in the flight only because she
was a woman, and to be no more than extra weight—"Just like a sack of
potatoes," she grumbled. She accepted nevertheless. It was still, after all,
an adventure.

The *Friendship* took off from Newfoundland on June 17, 1928 and landed
in Burry Port, Wales, 20 hours and 40 minutes later, having battled storms
almost all the way. Neither the pilot, the mechanic, nor Amelia were prepared for the exuberant reception that met them in England. The public
was not blasé[6] yet about aviation; it was still ready to explode with the same
genuine enthusiasm that had overwhelmed Charles Lindbergh in Paris in
1927. Now Amelia, "the first woman to fly over the Atlantic," was celebrated, pampered, paraded and treated for ten days, in the course of which
she danced and made friends with the then Prince of Wales, the future
King Edward VIII. When she was finally allowed to go home, she discovered with astonishment that she was front-page news. New York honored
her with a ticker-tape parade in an open car. Dozen of cities and towns
were clamoring for a visit, many of them claiming that they were Amelia's
birthplace. Offers of all kinds poured in—for lecture tours, radio interviews, magazine articles, and publicity endorsements. Since she was committed to write a book, Amelia set first to that task, which was completed
in 1929. As soon as she was free, she allowed herself some fun, like participating in the Women's Air Race from Santa Monica to Cleveland in a
small plane that she had bought from Mrs. Guest, and breaking the speed
record for women.

---

[6] blasé—(French) tired of something that has been repeated too often.

Understanding the Text

1. What do you remember of Amelia Earhart's family background?
2. Why is Amelia's father significant in the story of her life?
3. What was unusual about the kind of education she received at home?
4. How do you think a schoolmate would have described the tastes and character of twelve-year-old Amelia?
5. What seems to have been her main weakness, in school and again when she was studying medicine?
7. Amelia's friend Fay Gillis Wells says that Amelia was concerned with the needs of others. Does this part of her life reflect such concern?
8. Why was her first famous flight rather frustrating for her?
9. What kind of a flight was it?

Scanning for Details

A. 1. What kind of record did Amelia establish in 1923?
    2. When did Charles Lindbergh make his famous flight to Paris?
    3. Who wrote *Among the Missing*?
    4. How does Amelia describe her work as a nurse's aide?
    5. Where exactly did the *Friendship* land?
    6. When did George Putnam first approach Amelia about the *Friendship* project?
    7. What kind of offers did Amelia receive after returning to the United States?
    8. Amelia enjoyed sports, says the text. What examples are given?

B. *Choose in the list below the adjectives that, in your opinion, could be used to describe Amelia Earhart. Then scan the text to find as many facts as possible supporting your choices. As the teacher calls each adjective in the list, students will discuss reasons why it is or is not accurate for describing Earhart.*

ostentatious	independent	patient
coldhearted	impulsive	conscientious
warmhearted	adventurous	vain
a do-er	impatient	curious
modest	lazy	aloof
brave	frivolous	careless
selfish	timid	

Vocabulary

Choose in the list the word that can best replace the underlined word in each sentence. When called on by the teacher, read the whole statement with the new word. Be sure to make all necessary adjustments in articles, verbs, and nouns.

PROFILE 99

1. Charles A. Lindbergh was the first man to fly alone from New York to Paris in 1927.
2. People who see his small plane in the Smithsonian Museum in Washington can hardly believe that such an unsatisfactory machine could have crossed the Atlantic.
3. It looks like something that he could almost have built or taken apart himself.
4. Lindbergh never did dangerous tricks or athletic feats at air meets. But he piloted a mail plane between Saint Louis and Chicago in 1922, when he was 20 years old.
5. Lindbergh didn't particularly care to be seen in the special costume of the perfect aviator.
6. His wife Anne was a writer; both of them could have been prominent society figures. But they had little taste for the role. They lived in the country without display of wealth.

to stall	regalia	a stunt
ostentation	to solo	to dismantle
hangar	admonition	a device
acrobatics	a contraption	socialite

Did You Guess Right?

line 13 If you are headstrong, you are probably:
a) hesitant
b) determined
c) suffering from a headache

line 41 Amelia is described as a tomboy. From the rest of the story, what kind of girl qualifies as a tomboy?

line 68 Amelia's teacher's admonitions, when her lack of patience and care made her fail, must have been:
a) questions
b) scolding
c) congratulations

line 78 After the death of grandmother Otis and the sale of the house, the uprooted Amelia went through six high schools.
How do you uproot a plant? Why was Amelia "uprooted"?

line 141 When your car stalls, it
a) accelerates
b) stops running
c) falls apart

line 158 Amelia's zest for life was likely to be:
a) her enjoyment of life
b) her dislike for life
c) the plans that she was making for the future

line 199 Famous people are often asked to <u>endorse</u> products (particularly on television)
   a) they buy the product
   b) they criticize the product
   c) they praise the product.

The Main Idea

Check the statement in each group that best expresses the essential idea of the paragraph.

Par. 9 (line 90)
   a) In Canada Amelia saw many wounded soldiers from the battlefields of Europe.
   b) Amelia joined the Red Cross because she wanted to be useful in such a time of need.
   c) Amelia enjoyed watching the flyers doing stunts at air meets.

Par. 10
   a) Amelia's parents separated while she was in New York.
   b) In the spring of 1915, Amelia and her mother joined her father in California.
   c) Amelia undertook to study medicine and other subjects that excited her at the time.

Par. 11
   a) In the summer of 1919 Amelia began her flying career.
   b) Amelia learned to fly from another woman pilot.
   c) Since Amelia didn't have money for the lessons, she took a job in a telephone company.

Par. 12
   a) Amelia managed with difficulty to save $20 to buy her first leather coat.
   b) Amelia slept in her leather coat to make it look old and wrinkled.
   c) Amelia wanted to look like a professional flyer.

Par. 13
   a) Amelia wanted to have many jobs and experiences.
   b) Even when she had her own plane, Amelia had to work to pay for the expenses.
   c) Even though she liked to change jobs, Amelia always tried to do well in each one.

Par. 14
   a) Amelia almost killed herself several times in her plane.
   b) Amelia was not afraid to do dangerous stunts.
   c) Amelia kept practicing to perfect her skill as a pilot.

Topics for Discussion

1. Between 1903 (the first successful attempt to leave the ground) and 1932 (the first flight across the Atlantic by a woman) a number of pilots have risked their lives to be "the first" to do something—either fly over the sea, over a mountain, over a desert, over the North Pole, or to land on the deck of a ship, etc.

    Do such exploits serve a purpose?

    What motivates the men or women who undertake such ventures in spite of the danger:

    enthusiasm for something new?   the spirit of competition?
    hunger for publicity?   the need to be admired?
    love of danger?   any other motive?
    greed?

2. What do you think of the exploit that made Amelia Earhart famous?
3. Amelia Earhart thought that it was essential for the children of immigrants to learn early to speak English if they were to be American citizens. Some people now insist that immigrant children (and adults) should be instructed in their own language, vote in their own language, etc. What is your opinion?
4. Is "meeting people" or traveling (as Amelia Earhart did with her parents) really more profitable than a college education, as Amelia contended?

Profile
Part Two

What do you expect to happen now in the life of Amelia Earhart? Skim the text to answer the following questions:
- What did she do after the *Friendship* flight to deserve her fame as a pilot?
- What did she ever do besides flying?

After completing her book, *20 Hours 40 Minutes,* at the country house of George Putnam, Amelia dedicated the volume to Mrs. Putnam. George had been constantly at her side, helping with the preparation of the manuscript, protecting her from annoying strangers, and handling the mass of propositions that had been coming to her since her triumphant return from England. In 1929 the Putnams were divorced, and for the next two years Putnam did his best to persuade Amelia to marry him. She refused several times. He knew her well enough to understand that marriage frightened her as a threat to the total freedom that was essential to her happiness—freedom to live as she pleased, to fly and take risks without feeling restricted by somebody's concern, freedom even to be alone when she felt the need for solitude. She was determined to remain independent in every way; according to George Putnam, she wanted "to owe no one anything—any more spiritually than financially."

She did finally give in, against the admonitions of her family and friends, and they were married on February 8, 1931. Just before the ceremony, Amelia gave her husband-to-be a note in which she forthrightly stated her expectations. "In our life together," she had written, "I shall not hold you to any medieval code of faithfulness to me, nor shall I consider myself bound to you similarly. If we can be honest, I think, the difficulties which arise may be best avoided. Please let us not interfere with each other's work or play, nor let the world see our private joys or disagreements. In this connection I may have to keep some place where I can go to be by myself now and then, for I cannot guarantee to endure at all times the confinements of even an attractive cage. I must exact a cruel promise, and that is that you will let me go in a year if we find no happiness together." George Putnam accepted all her conditions, including her decision to keep her own name.

A variety of opinions have been expressed about George Putnam's character. A handsome, forceful businessman who knew how to push or charm people to have his way, he was respected but not generally liked. Those who are more sympathetic to Amelia than to her husband claim that he used his wife's celebrity to keep both of them in the limelight—that she agreed with reluctance to take part in the projects that he dreamed up for her. Newsmen who wanted to have a few words with Amelia complained that they had to spend much time listening to George first, and they accused him of including himself in the photos that they were trying to take of her. Other people, however, think that Putnam sacrificed his own interests to assist her in the various schemes that she initiated. Whatever the truth, George Putnam certainly did not object to his wife's career, and he devoted himself to the role of manager-advisor that he had been fulfilling since the Atlantic flight. To free himself from all other demands on his time he went so far as to relinquish his interest in the Putnam publishing house, which he sold to a relative.

Either to please George or of her own volition, Amelia did capitalize on her fame. She had agreed in 1929 to become an associate director for *Cosmopolitan* magazine, for which she had to write regular articles. She went on extensive lecture tours and made numerous personal appearances in which her only duty was to allow herself to be seen. She agreed to fly an autogyro[1] to publicize the Beechnut Packing Company, and endorsed a number of products—including a brand of cigarettes, despite the fact that she was a nonsmoker. She even undertook to design clothes, "for the woman who lives actively." Her most successful venture was a line of Amelia Ear-

---

[1] The autogiro is the forerunner of the helicopter.

hart Lightweight Airplane Luggage. She did refuse to star in a film, perhaps because she was intimidated by the cameras. But motion pictures intrigued her and for a while she played with the notion of writing a scenario in collaboration with Mary Pickford, one of the most beloved stars of the period. The two of them had much fun plotting the story, but since they were both extremely busy, they eventually had to abandon the project. Amelia, for whom writing had long been a favorite hobby, continued for a long time to write poems, short stories, and articles. She also wrote a second book, *For the Fun of It*.

Did she enter these various schemes and deals to please her husband or because of the not-inconsiderable financial returns that they procured? Amelia doesn't seem to have been interested in money *per se*[2] but, according to Putnam, she "wanted to pay her own way" and she may have welcomed the business deals as the only means "to owe no one anything." Flying, George Putnam explained sympathetically, was an expensive occupation. If we are to believe Jay Robert Nash, Putnam did finance his wife's flights, at least partly.

Ever since her return from England, Amelia had been dreaming of crossing the Atlantic again, but this time alone. Her friend Fay Wells believes that Amelia was eager to make up in that way for the unsatisfying role that she had been forced to play on the *Friendship*. Amelia took off from Newfoundland in May 1932 in her first important plane, a Lockheed Vega, built for long-distance flying. The crossing was a frightening ordeal all the way: the plane's altimeter failed during the night in the midst of a bad storm, the reserve tank developed a leak, and a fire started in the engine. With flames coming out of the plane's nose, and almost out of gas, Amelia had to make an emergency landing in the middle of a cow pasture in Ireland. The flight had lasted 14 hours and 36 minutes. Now finally, she had the right to feel that she had really accomplished something: she was the first woman to fly solo across the Atlantic.

The reception in Ireland and soon after in London was delirious. Amelia and her husband (who had promptly joined her) went through a whirlwind of celebrations in England, France, Italy, and Belgium, feted by kings, queens, presidents and ordinary mortals, and collecting medals and decorations. They finally came home to a quieter reception at the White House of President Herbert Hoover, who was soon to be replaced by Franklin D. Roosevelt. Amelia and George returned to the White House for dinner with the Roosevelts in April 1933. It was a dressy affair, with the women wearing long satin dresses and evening shoes. At one point in the conversation, Eleanor Roosevelt and Amelia began to discuss the joys of flying, and as Amelia was getting eloquent about the beauty of night flights, the First Lady expressed a desire to see for herself. Whereupon the two of them left

[2]*per se*—for itself (Latin).

for an impromptu air excursion—Amelia at the controls in long white evening gloves. They came back in high spirits and capped off the evening by taking a drive in Amelia's sporty little car. They had agreed together that Mrs. Roosevelt would take flying lessons from Amelia. But although she did obtain a beginner's permit, the First Lady did not pursue her project, which was perhaps considered too dangerous or too fanciful for the busy wife of the president.

A few months after her flight to Ireland, Amelia established a record for transcontinental flight for women, covering the distance between Los Angeles and Newark, N.J. in 19 hours and 5 minutes. She was to beat her own record the following year by two hours.

The public at large was treating Amelia like a movie star or a war hero, and acclaimed her lovingly wherever she appeared. But some discordant voices were being heard in the chorus of praises. Right after her trans-Atlantic flight she had been blamed for stating that she had made the flight just "because she wanted to." The reason was deemed frivolous, but Amelia stood by her words. "It's not," she said, "a reason to be apologized for by man or woman. It is the most honest motive for the majority of mankind's achievements. To want in one's own heart to do a thing for its own sake; to enjoy doing it; to concentrate all one's energies upon it—that is not only the surest guarantee of its success, it is also to be true to oneself."

Other criticisms came up later on. For some people, Amelia was too intent on being publicized and on collecting the rewards of her exploits. A former flyer turned journalist wrote that Amelia had accomplished nothing, that she was not even a good pilot, and that ocean flying was a racket[3] anyway. In 1935 Amelia was blamed again for the profits that she made that year from three spectacular flights. The first one, from Honolulu to Oakland, California, was the first solo crossing over the Pacific by a woman. It was suggested that Amelia had done it to attract attention to Hawaii and its sugar-and-pineapple economy, and perhaps to influence somehow a bill that was going through Congress to lower the tariff on sugar imports to the United States. The second trip had taken her from Los Angeles to Mexico City and set a time record of 14 hours and 19 minutes. The Mexican flight had been undertaken at the suggestion of the Mexican government, and the organizers had offered to reserve for Amelia a number of special postage stamps overprinted with her name and the date of her flight. It was understood that the sale of the stamps to collectors would defray the cost of the expedition. The operation didn't fail to bring unfriendly comments from the press. Nothing wrong could be found, however, about the financing of her third flight, which took her back from Mexico City to Newark and allowed her to break another record.

In the same year, 1935, that saw her speeding back and forth over North

---

[3] a racket is a dishonest way to acquire money.

America, Amelia was given an opportunity to enter a new career; the president of Purdue University asked her to join the faculty as counsellor of women students. The proposal delighted her for several reasons. In the first place she was not entirely fulfilled by the various activities and social obligations that took up her time when she was not in the air. To a woman who had always felt so keenly the need of being useful, most of her tasks appeared futile and uninteresting. Besides, she had enjoyed her position as children's instructor in Chicago and she had continued to describe herself as "a social worker whose hobby is flying." She accepted with pleasure Purdue's offer, and was even happier when it was decided that she would also be the university's Advisor on Aeronautics. Purdue was then the only American university with its own fully equipped airport.

Amelia launched eagerly into her counselling duties. She had much to say to her students—on education and on careers, as on most subjects that engaged her attention, she had very definite views. She thought, for instance, that children were not directed early enough toward the kind of activity in which they were naturally adept; the time would come—she hoped—when psychologists would be able to determine a child's special aptitude before he or she entered school. Moreover, she believed firmly that it was wrong to train young people only for the tasks traditionally assigned on the basis of sex: cooking and sewing for girls, woodworking and mechanics for boys. What of men who'd love to cook and would be good at it? What of women like herself who were fascinated by the insides of engines and cars? She was campaigning for a unisex education based on each young person's taste and talent. Most of all she deplored finding a student engaging in a life's career to please the aspirations of someone else—getting a degree in pharmacy, for example, "because Daddy wants me to be a pharmacist!"

The girls at Purdue soon found out that their new counsellor was an ardent feminist, concerned with the place of women in a man's world. For years Amelia had been a member of the National Association of Women; not that she favored separate political parties for women, but she thought that associations like NAW might be useful in eliminating discrimination in the job market. Women, Amelia maintained, should have access to any position that appealed to them—as long as they had the necessary qualifications. She was eager to help her students toward a fruitful and independent life, a life that they would enjoy as much as she was enjoying her own. Since it was impossible to meet individually the 800 girls attending the university, she addressed them in groups, and took great pains to provide them with useful information about the vocational opportunities opened to them.

On a list of "things to do" that Amelia had made for herself years earlier, there was one project that remained unchecked: a flight around the world. The president of Purdue, apprised of her dream, organized a fundraising compoaign—the Amelia Earhart Fund for Aeronautical Research—which collected $50,000 for the purchase of a long-distance plane. In the Lockheed Electra that she selected for the expedition, Amelia and Fred Noonan flew halfway around the world before disappearing over the Pacific on the 3rd or 4th of July 1937.

As is often the case when a charismatic figure disappears without a trace, all sorts of legends sprang up about Amelia Earhart's last flight—some of them still alive. Several books have been written about her disappearance, most of them to support a thesis. The fact that Amelia, an excellent and experienced pilot, had never given her position to the men on the *Itasca* puzzled many people as it had puzzled the radio operators. According to one thesis, Amelia *couldn't* give her position because she was not where she should have been if she had followed her official flight plan, and where the *Itasca* was expecting to see her. She had been (the story went) on a secret mission to fly over the Marshall Islands then occupied by the Japanese, and to photograph the war preparations that were in progress there. The version didn't take into account the fact that Amelia's voice had been heard clear and strong in her last messages, as indeed it would be when she was approaching Howland Island and the *Itasca*.

Self-appointed researchers traveled to the Marshalls after the war, and also to Saipan, which had been the location of the Japanese headquarters during the hostilities. They found natives who remembered seeing two American prisoners, a man and a woman, on their island. There was some disagreement about their fate afterwards: death due to disease, execution by the Japanese, or captivity in Japan. Some people came up with the idea that Amelia was the real Tokyo Rose[4]. But after listening to some of the Tokyo Rose broadcasts, George Putnam demolished the theory—the voice, he declared firmly, was not his wife's.

Since that time, other researchers have traced the Electra in Canada, then in the United States. According to them the plane has been used by several successive owners after Amelia's disappearance, until the last one, a stunt pilot, crashed in the mountains of northern California. Parts bearing the identification numbers of Amelia's plane were reportedly found there. One of the supporters of this last thesis wrote in the 1970s that Amelia was alive and well and living in New Jersey under an assumed name. The married woman alleged to be Amelia always refused to admit her "true" identity. The least that can be said is that she didn't look much like Amelia.

In every case the proof has remained elusive. Until he died in 1961, George Putnam affirmed that his wife had indeed been lost in the ocean, somewhere north of Howland Island. She wouldn't have minded such a death,

---

[4] *Tokyo Rose* was the nickname of one or several women who were heard on Japanese radio stations during World War II. They were broadcasting in perfect English, providing doctored news, playing American popular music, and teasing their American audience in order to demoralize the homesick soldiers in the Pacific.

he said; she didn't want to grow old, and she didn't believe that she would have a chance to grow old. She had often told him that she'd rather like to go in her plane, quickly. In the letter that she left to be opened if she'd ever fail to come back from a flight, she had affirmed again: "Please know that I am quite aware of the hazards. But I want to do it . . . because I want to do it!"

Understanding the Text

1. Amelia Earhart was accused of capitalizing on her fame. Was there a basis for such an accusation?
2. Why was she reluctant to marry?
3. What was George Putnam's attitude toward his wife's career?
4. Did Amelia Earhart have a hobby?
5. What was her second career?
6. What ideas did she have about the education of young children?
7. What did she have to say to the women students at Purdue?
8. What theories have been offered to explain her disappearance?

Scanning for Details

1. Why did Amelia fly an autogiro?
2. How old was she when she married George Putnam?
3. How long did it take Amelia to fly from Newfoundland to Ireland?
4. Amelia said that to do something to please oneself is "the most _____ achievements."
5. When did Amelia and George Putnam have dinner with President and Mrs. Roosevelt?
6. What kind of plane did Amelia fly to England in 1932?
7. When did George Putnam die?
8. What name did the president of Purdue University give his campaign to raise funds for Amelia's flight around the world?

Taking Notes

Suppose that you are Amelia Earhart. You have not been offered a position as counsellor of women at Purdue University, but you would like to apply for the job. Skimming both parts of the profile, note down the facts that you would include to show your good points and qualifications honestly. You would have to give the president of Purdue some idea of your education, your previous working experiences, and your opinion regarding women's education.

Write down a brief summary of your background (as Amelia), based on your notes.

Your Opinion

1. Do you find Amelia's efforts to make money objectionable? Was it "wrong" in some way to make lecture tours, write articles, endorse products, design clothes, and sell luggage?
2. Was she wrong in accepting the special stamps for her flight to Mexico in order to sell them at higher prices to collectors?
3. Do you think that Amelia flew from Hawaii to Oakland to be the first woman to accomplish such a feat, or did she fly to help pass the bill on sugar imports?
4. Do you think that Amelia Earhart came back from Lae in 1937 and lived afterwards in obscurity under an assumed name?
5. What opinion do you have of Amelia Earhart in general?

Facts, Inferences, Opinions.

The following text offers a combination of facts, inferences, and opinions. Read it carefully, trying to differentiate among the three, then answer the questions that follow. As always, some statements will be debatable.

Amelia Earhart had no fortune of her own. Perhaps she realized when she married George Putnam that he was in a position to finance all her future projects, but obviously she told him that she didn't want to owe him, or anybody, anything. Putnam was probably willing to help her; after all, he did prove that he was a devoted husband, ready to make sacrifices. At any rate, Amelia had to find some way to pay for her flights; and it would be absurd and uncharitable to blame her for the business arrangements that she had to enter to cover her expenses. Finding money must have been the least enjoyable part of her projects.

Amelia must have been a rather impressive person who struck people as being able to do much more than flying airplanes. She also seems to have been very likable. The president of Purdue apparently became a great friend and admirer of hers.

Amelia was a brave woman; and she had a kind heart. When she was getting ready for her last flight, Fred Noonan, whom she had known for several years, asked to be her navigator on the flight. She accepted immediately. But when her plans became known, friends warned her that it might be dangerous to rely on Noonan, who had a grave problem with alcohol. Amelia was in a difficult position, and she must have hesitated for a while. But Noonan was an experienced and skilled pilot who had flown many times over the Pacific; besides, he was an old friend that she didn't want to hurt. Perhaps she thought that she could help him regain his reputation. Anyway, she didn't change her mind and they took off together for that tragic last flight round the world. The ten days of search for the Electra must have been quite an ordeal for George Putnam. He never doubted that his wife had died in the Pacific, and he never believed that she was Tokyo Rose. The idea that Amelia could have been Tokyo Rose is ridiculous.

1. What opinions are expressed in the passage?
2. Which statements represent inferences from the Profile?
3. Did you find any sentences that could be understood as either fact or opinion; fact or inference; inference or opinion?
4. Can you infer from the passage the author's attitude about Amelia's business schemes?
5. Does the text suggest that Amelia may have known of Noonan's problem?
6. Does the text imply that Noonan could be of help to her at some stage of that flight?

Vocabulary: Did You Guess Right?

line 17   Amelia stated her expectations forthrightly. The note certainly was:
a) sweet
b) honest
c) extensive

line 33   They said that Putnam was using his wife's celebrity to keep them both in the limelight.
a) in full view
b) out of sight

line 45   Amelia took part in schemes and deals either to please George or of her own volition.
a) willingly
b) unwillingly.
Can you think of another word starting with vol that has to do with will and willingness?
Note: "schemes," which involve planning, and "deals," are not necessarily dishonest but they do imply careful preparations and business agreements. Scheme often has a connotation of dishonesty as in:"The police have just discovered a scheme to defraud elderly investors."

line 96   Mrs. Roosevelt and Amelia left the reception for an impromptu air excursion.
Does the context suggest that the excursion had been or had not been planned?

line 111 Amelia's remark was criticized as frivolous.
a) too serious
b) not serious enough

line 181 When the president of Purdue University was apprised of Amelia's dream, he tried to help her realize it.
How could you express the same thing in a different way?

Prefixes and Suffixes

The suffix meter indicates that something is being measured. A *dynamometer,* for example, is an instrument that is used to measure power. A *barometer,* which measures atmospheric pressure, gives an indication of the day's weather.

1. What is a *thermometer?*
2. What definition can you give for *chronometer?* What instruments deserve the name of chronometer, even though we call them by other names? (Actually, the name *chronometer* is usually applied to only the most accurate instruments of that kind.)
3. Why do we have *speedometers* in cars?
4. Why was Amelia Earhart unhappy when her *altimeter* failed?

The meaning of uni can usually be expressed by either of two different words. Which words might you use, for example, to express the meaning of uni in *uniform* and *unicorn?*

1. What did Amelia Earhart mean when she said that she favored *unisex* education?
2. It is considered dangerous for a country to start *unilateral* disarmament. Why?
3. What is a *unanimous* decision?
4. What shall we do to read this sentence in *unison?*
5. The *unicorn* is an imaginary animal; how many horns does it have?
6. What do you usually need to observe a *unicellular* organism?

Topics for Discussion

1. Amelia Earhart's husband said that the note she gave him before their marriage was "honest and touching." What do you think of it?
   Do you think that a marriage starting on such an agreement will work better, as well as, or not as well as an ordinary marriage?
   Would it be a good idea for people engaged to be married to let each other know what they wish and expect?
2. Do you think that aviation has the same kind of appeal now that it had at the time of Charles Lindbergh and Amelia Earhart? In what way is it comparable or different? Do astronauts have the kind of prestige that aviators used to have? Does anyone else? Would you want to be an astronaut, or simply to go up in the shuttle? Why?
3. Amelia believed that a boy should learn to sew and a girl to play football and weld metal if such are their interests. Do you agree? Should boys learn to sew and girls to repair automobiles whether they like it or not—just as general education? What should everyone learn?
   Do you think that many men and women are attracted by the activities of the other sex?
4. When Amelia Earhart disappeared, the cost of searching for her with ships and planes ran well over a million dollars. Do you think that it

was proper for the U.S. government to spend so much money for two individuals? Was the cost of having three ships in her flight path in the first place acceptable?

Reading

Skim around to see what this text is about.
- Does the article seem to say that women are doing extremely well, moderately well or not well at all?
- Does the article have anything to say about women in politics?

After reading the article, choose a title for it.

Amelia Earhart, who won fame in a field that was overwhelmingly masculine, was very eloquent on the matter of women's rights to live on an equal footing with men, and in particular to hold any job that appealed to them and for which they were fully qualified. She had no regard for women who demand a place that they do not deserve merely on the basis of their sex, and who expect special treatment at work.

There were already plenty of women working in the twenties and thirties, and some, like Rachel Carson, were indeed doing exactly what they enjoyed doing. But the great majority bowed to the fact that many fields were male preserves, had always been and therefore would always be. Having been encouraged since childhood to pursue her interests, however unconventional, Amelia Earhart was not prepared to subscribe to this belief, and she did her best to share her convictions, and her freedom, with the young women who consulted her at Purdue.

The situation has changed a great deal since the 1930s, and the last twenty years in particular have witnessed a large influx of women in all sorts of jobs, traditional or not. In the first place, more women are working; from nearly 38 percent in 1960, the proportion of employed women has increased to 53 percent in 1984. Among them are women truck drivers, Coast Guard captains, investors, and plumbers.

Yet it would be inaccurate to claim that the equality demanded by Amelia has been achieved and that women are accepted in all sectors on a par with their male colleagues and competitors. They have not been able to penetrate *all* professions. The resistance comes sometimes from employers, who balk at accepting women in blue-collar[1] jobs such as automobile repair, roofing, garbage collection, telephone line repair, and other categories of the same type in which women's gains have been slow. The wisdom of snatching such jobs from men may well seem debatable. There might

---

[1] Blue-collar jobs are factory or service jobs for which the workers wear either overalls or other practical clothes. White-collar jobs suggest the wearing of white shirt, coat and tie.

be women who would be geniuses at repairing a car engine, but garbage collecting, for instance, presents hardships that no amount of liberal thinking can ignore. In a suburb of Pittsburgh, the municipal clerks are bound by the terms of their contracts to replace any garbage collector who doesn't show up for work. The rule applies to all employees, male or female. A young woman from the tax department confessed to a newsman that doing the garbage route was almost more than she could live through. She always finished bruised and exhausted, she explained. "The bags hit you in the shin. You bend down to pick up the garbage bags and you feel like you are going to pass out[2] when it's hot. At the end of the day I am dead." Employers averse to hiring women for blue-collar jobs complain also that customers object to having certain types of work done by a woman—they are not sure that they can trust a lady roofer or electrician.

In many professions where qualified women can surely do as well as their male counterparts, they are not welcomed by their colleagues or by the public that they are expected to serve. This is particularly true in religion, where congregations look askance[3] at women pastors or rabbis; in medicine, where the number of women surgeons is very low, despite the fact that a third of all first-year medical students are women; and in aviation, where lady pilots and air-traffic controllers are a small, not entirely trusted minority. It is also still true in architecture and engineering, in the sciences and even, in some respects, in the arts—there are few women conductors of symphony orchestras for example. And it is true of the most exotic occupations—such as that of jungle explorer: "How could a woman," asked an educated gentleman once, "venture alone in a deep jungle and put up with the discomforts and the dangers?"—"How do we know that they can't stand its difficulties? There is no research on it! " retorted Amelia Earhart, who was an enthusiastic member of the Society of Women Geographers (another minority).

There are, as there have always been, exceptions in all categories. Isabelle Eberhart was exploring Africa alone in the 1880s and Margaret Mead lived alone in Borneo as an anthropologist. There are women astronauts. And in the world of music, Judith Somogi has conducted the orchestra of the famous Teatro Fenice in Venice, Sarah Caldwell founded and conducted the Boston Opera Orchestra, and Eve Queler is music director of the New York Opera Orchestra. Another woman, Beverley Sills, is director of the New York City Opera.

Even in fields where women have managed to be admitted in considerable number, they have cause to feel like second-class citizens. There is still a great disparity, they complain, in the level of responsibility that a woman can reach and in her chances for advancement. It is a rare woman who becomes chairman of the board, chief of police, senior partner in a

---

[2] to pass out—to faint.
[3] to look askance—to look with suspicion or disfavor.

law firm or a general in the Army. Only 5 percent of all top executives are women. And to get there, and stay there, they have to perform better than men, because they are constantly watched and constantly pressed to prove themselves anew.

Women who have gone up the ladder in the business world often feel that they are lost in a male club, never quite included in the club's activities. "You are not invited to many functions," says a lady executive, "not to the golf course or for drinks after work, where a lot of business gets transacted." The forty-year-old female treasurer of a manufacturing company says: "I am not 'one of the boys,'[4] I can't hook into the informal chain of communications. As a result, it's easy to be ignored."

Economists point out that women have been in business in significant members only since 1970, not yet long enough to be in line for the top positions. And a recent report from the Census Bureau notes that women's progress continues to be held down because a far greater number of women than men interrupt their careers for family reasons. Women find other explanations: when a male executive has to suggest his successor, he simply doesn't think of choosing anyone but another man, they contend.

Women's greatest cause of frustration and anger, the number one issue in their fight, remains the question of inequality of pay. Some progress has been made, but during the last three decades, women have averaged 62 cents for every dollar men make:

> Even in professional fields, the wage gap persists. A Columbia University study found that after ten years in business the average male with a master's degree in business administration was earning 20 percent more than his female counterpart: $49,356 compared with $40,022. In science and engineering, women's salaries range from 10 to 20 percent below men's. In computer programming, women make 81 percent of what men earn. (*U.S. News and World Report*, 29 October 1984)

But the picture is not as gray as these examples would seem to suggest. There are now many positions that guarantee equal pay to the worker, male or female.

Imperfect or slow as it may be, the march upward of women is bound to continue and possibly accelerate, partly through the pressure of women's groups and the goodwill of legislators, partly because of the growing importance of women in politics—both as voters (in 1984 women were making up 53 percent of the population) and as elected officials. There are lady governors, senators, mayors and chief justices. And not so long ago Geraldine Ferraro was the Democratic Party's choice as candidate for the Vice-presidency.

Betty Heitman, cochairperson of the Republican National Committee, says that there is an excellent chance of having a woman president by the end

---

[4] to be one of the boys—to be recognized as part of the group.

of the century. Is there such a chance? Even if one of the two parties had the courage to choose a woman as its candidate for the presidency, could she be elected? While most men agree now that women should get equal pay for equal work, and a large number pay at least lip service[5] to the fact that women are as intelligent and energetic as men, prejudices and traditions die hard. Quite a few men have a difficult time getting rid of the feeling that women are *naturally* unfit for all sorts of activities. But one also has to recognize that some women have the same prejudices against other women in positions of power or entering certain professions. Not all women would entrust their health to a female surgeon. And the ladies did not vote *en masse*[6] for Geraldine Ferraro.

Finding a Title

Which of the following titles do you consider best for the article?

Women's Victory in the Work Force
Women's Salaries Are Still Lower than Men's
Women Are Now on a Par with Men
Women in a Man's World
Some Women Are Conducting Symphony Orchestras
Blue-collar Jobs Are too Hard for Women
Women: The New Political Force

Understanding the Text

1. What makes women important in today's United States?
2. Did Amelia Earhart claim that a woman should be able to get the job she wanted?
3. Who objects to women in blue-collar jobs?
4. Did the young woman in Pittsburgh volunteer for the "garbage route"? What does her story tend to show?
5. Is it true that women's salaries are lower than men's?
6. What problems do women face in the business world when they have reasonably good positions?
7. Is it right to say that only men object to women in *all* occupations? Give an example.
8. Have women been successful in politics?
9. According to the text, is there a chance of having a woman president by the end of the century?

---

[5] to pay lip service—to express an opinion that is not really felt.
[6] en masse—in very large number.

Outlining

An outline is an orderly presentation of facts and other information. It is useful to make an outline of the topics you want to deal with before writing paper, as shown in the example below.

Title: Pesticides are beneficial and dangerous.
I. Benefits
   A. Health
      1. plentiful food
      2. control of epidemics
   B. Comfort
      1. pests (mosquitoes)
      2. weeds, excess vegetation
   C. Prosperity
      1. better crops
      2. tourism
      3. developers
II. Dangers
   A. Present time
      1. kills indiscriminately
      2. poisons through food.
   B. Future
      1. long lived
      2. immunity

You can make a full-sentence outline to keep a clear picture of the ideas presented in an article. The organization of the outline remains the same:

Title: Pesticides are beneficial to man but dangerous to all living creatures.

first idea	I.	<u>Pesticides are beneficial to man.</u>
first subtopic		A. They protect man's health.
examples		1. They assure a large amount of food.
		2. They eliminate pests that cause epidemics such as malaria and typhus.
2nd subtopic		B. They protect man's comfort by eliminating mosquitoes, etc.
3rd subtopic		C. They are beneficial to man's prosperity.
		1. They protect crops and allow better harvests.
		2. They make resorts attractive to tourists.
		3. They allow developers to offer pest-free homes.
second idea	II.	<u>Pesticides are dangerous.</u>
		A. At the present time
		1. They kill animals indiscriminately.

116 AMELIA EARHART

        2. Humans and animals can be poisoned by eating contaminated flesh or plants.
    B. In the future
        1. Because they remain indefinitely in soil, water, and flesh.
        2. Because some species develop an immunity to pesticides.

Make an outline, of the article about working women, that will show the two great reasons for women's dissatisfaction:
    a. not being accepted in all professions;
    b. having difficulties in the fields that they have entered.

Title:
Working Women Still Have Reasons to be Dissatisfied

```
(first reason)              I.   _____
(who resists?)                A. _____
(why do they resist?)            1. _____
                                 2. _____
(who resists?)                B. _____
                                 1. _____
                                 2. _____
(who resists?)                C. _____
    (why?)                       1. _____
                                 2. _____
                                 3. _____
(second reason)            II.   _____
    (complaint)                A. _____
    (complaint)                B. _____
    (complaint)                C. _____
```

Reading Graphs and Tables

Study the following graphs and table, then answer the questions that accompany them.

Figure A

1. Does this graph agree with the text?
2. Is the disparity getting larger or smaller?
3. Has the disparity been changing evenly?

Figure B

1. Has the percentage of working women increased evenly over those twenty-four years?
2. If it hasn't, what period(s) has or have been particularly good?
3. Does it seem that the progress is accelerating or slowing down?

FIGURE A

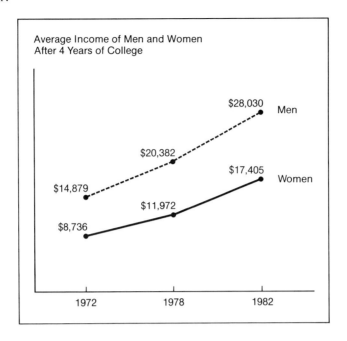

FIGURE B

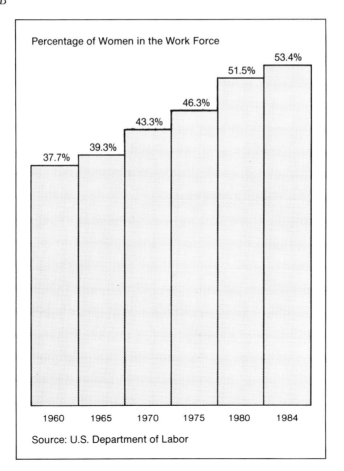

FIGURE C

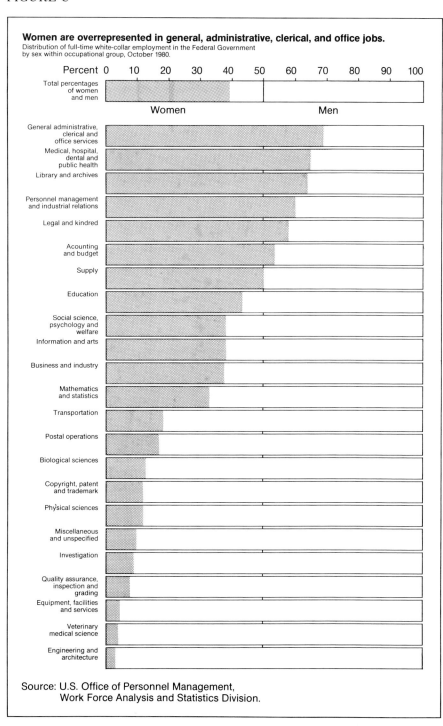

Figure C

1. In what kind of work are men and women in nearly equal numbers? Would you have expected something different?
2. What professions are the most overwhelmingly male?
3. The preceding table indicated that the percentage of women lawyers in 1980 was only 9.3. How do you account for the fact that in the graph in Figure C the percentage of women in legal jobs is given as 60 percent?
4. The percentage of women physicians in 1980 was 14. Why does the graph show about 70 percent under "medical, hospital, dental and public health"?
5. It has been said that parents and teachers are in part responsible for the poor showing of women in scientific professions, because they do not encourage girls to excel in mathematics and sciences. Does the graph reflect that failure? Do you think that boys and girls are equally gifted in those areas?
6. Do any of the facts on the graph surprise you? Which ones and why?

WHAT HAS CHANGED IN THE LAST FIVE YEARS?
(Percentage of women in professions)

Profession	in 1980	in 1985
Psychologist	48.1%	57.1%
Health Administrator	46.2	57.0
Designer	27.3	52.7
Economist	22.9	37.9
Chemist	14.4	23.3
Lawyer	9.3	15.3
Architect	5.8	12.7
Engineer	2.8	5.8

1. In what order is this list established? Is it in the order of professions in which women have made the most progress?
2. In what profession have women made the biggest gain? In what profession has the progress been the slowest?

Topics for Discussion

1. Women have always found it difficult to be accepted by employers, colleagues, and customers in certain jobs, such as those of auto mechanic, miner, sheriff, police investigator, or architect. Opponents offer various reasons, including the assertion that a woman's male co-work-

ers would have to watch their language and jokes. Do you think that they are right?

Are there jobs and sports that "are not for women"?

Should women force their way into jobs such as coal mining, that may not be very desirable, just to be recognized as equals?

Are there some occupations in which, as a customer, you would rather not find a woman?

2. Are there some occupations in which, as a customer, you'd be surprised and shocked to find a man?
3. What do you think of women in the armed services. Is it good for the services? Is it good for women? Should women be trained to fight? To pilot any sort of planes? Should women become generals and admirals?
4. Would it be good to have a woman as President of the United States? Why? Are you in favor of a woman as head of all, or some, of the various departments:

> Department of State
> Department of Defense
> Department of the Interior (natural resources, ecology)
> Department of Justice
> Department of Agriculture
> Department of Health and Welfare
> Department of Transportation (airlines, etc.)

Katharine Graham

newspaper publisher (Washington Post)
Watergate

Introduction

The Vocabulary of Journalism

While newspapers are usually published daily, magazines can be weekly, monthly, or bimonthly publications. Until about forty years ago, cities and towns had a choice of several dailies; but the rising cost of production and the loss of advertising to television have forced many dailies to merge or to disappear entirely. The *Washington Post* and the *Washington Times Herald*, for example, merged in 1954 to form one of the great newspapers in the country. The overall circulation of newspapers remains high (720,000 during the week and 997,000 on Sunday for the *Washington Post*), and the number of subscribers is growing.

The front page of newspapers announces in large headlines the great international, national, and local news. For analysis of the news, the readers turn to the editorial page, which presents in-depth articles by senior editors, or by well-known columnists who contribute regularly to the paper. The publisher, who sometimes owns the paper, is in charge of the overall production, but the content and the preparation of each issue are generally left in the care of the editor-in-chief, assisted by a number of editors who may be in charge of the different sections of the paper. The roles of publisher, editor-in-chief, and editor vary somewhat from paper to paper. One of the duties of the editors is to review the articles written by the reporters, and to decide which articles will be published. The layout editor is responsible for the arrangement of the articles and illustrations on the pages, and as a consequence, for the general appearance of the newspaper.

The paper is actually printed by the workers who run the presses and other machines and who are known—naturally—as "pressmen."

Looking Ahead

- Does this chapter discuss the press in general? What are the different sections about?
- Do you expect Katharine Graham to be a journalist? Why does she belong in this chapter?
- Are you familiar with any of the newspapers mentioned in the chapter? Does "Watergate" mean anything to you?

The American Press

At last count, there were 1,768 dailies in the United States, with a combined circulation of 64 million. About 60 percent of these papers belong to groups such as the Gannett chain, the Knight-Ridder chain, or the Newhouse chain, which include respectively 85, 34, and 30 newspapers, possibly more if they have made new acquisitions since these figures were published. Being financial operations largely concerned with profits, the chains usually leave a certain amount of editorial freedom to their publications. The remaining 40 percent of the dailies are owned by individuals or by various types of organizations. The small but respected *Christian Science Monitor* still belongs to the Church of Christ, Scientist, that founded it in 1908; the *Wall Street Journal* has been published since 1889 by its parent corporation, the Dow-Jones Company. Of the three leading American papers, the *New York Times* has been in the hands of the Ochs-Sulzberger family since 1896, the *Washington Post* has been published by the Meyer-Graham family since 1933 and the *Los Angeles Times* has belonged to the Chandlers since Otis Chandler acquired it in 1883.

The press' first and foremost mission is to report the news, or—as tradition has it—to provide answers to the six basic questions: *who, what, when, where, why,* and *how?* A good newspaper prides itself on relaying all the pertinent information quickly, truthfully, objectively, and in depth. Although a remarkable number of dailies, big and small, do a fine job of reporting what's new and what's significant, only a few achieve overall excellence. Even among the good ones, many have won respect for some particular feature, without rising above average for the rest of the publication. The *Baltimore Sun,* for instance, is famous for its excellent coverage of Canadian news, and the *Philadelphia Inquirer* is justly proud of its special reports, which have won several Pulitzer prizes.

With a circulation of over 2 million, the *Wall Street Journal* is the most widely consulted of the dailies. But in spite of an outstanding editorial page and numerous columns on social, cultural, and political events, it is above all a financial publication. Among the nonspecialized papers, the most prestigious is without contest the *New York Times* (daily circulation: 911,000). It is the most disciplined, the most impartial, and the most reliable of all. It has no comics, few pictures, and it is seldom guilty of amusing its readers. But they know that they will find in its pages honest and thorough reporting—very thorough in fact, for while other papers are content to print excerpts from lengthy speeches and documents, the *Times* provides the full texts. Whether or not they really desire to pore through all the material, its readers take the *Times* confidently, generally feeling that "if it's in the *Times,* it must be true."

The *Washington Post,* which became Number Two in the seventies, doesn't enjoy the same exalted reputation for integrity. It is more aggressive and more entertaining than the dignified *Times.* Despite its flaws—its occasional partisanship and inaccuracies—the *Post* is probably just as influential as the *Times,* partly because, being published in Washington, it appears every morning on the breakfast tables of very important people—diplomats, senators, congressmen, and other high officials, including the President. However annoying it can be at times, the *Post* can't be ignored. Needless to say, the competition is acute between the two papers, although the *Times* tends to look down its nose at its brilliant and brashy rival. "They are a long way from our class!" said the *Times'* managing editor.

The *Post* has had an uneven career. Founded in 1877 as a partisan paper devoted to the Democratic party, it was at first bold and successful. But as it changed hands, it became in turn conservative and good, then conservative and dull, then became a "sensational" sheet with flashy headlines, pink sports pages, and numerous cartoons. The quality grew steadily worse after 1916, with an emphasis on gory crimes, scandals, and society gossip. In 1933 the *Post* was declared bankrupt, and nobody believed that it could survive. But such as it was (and it was the worst of five Washington dailies), the paper found a buyer in the person of Eugene Meyer, a millionaire financier who nourished the ambition of running a serious publication where he could present his views on domestic and international affairs. Meyer bought the *Post* at the humiliating price of $850,000; although he did revive and improve it and made it respectable again, he never managed to make it financially successful. His son-in-law, Philip Graham, solved this problem brilliantly, and brought wealth to the *Post*. But it was Philip's widow, Meyer's daughter Katharine, who finally led the *Post* to greatness and who turned it into what journalist Tom Kelly calls "the most irritating and the most interesting paper in town."

What title could you give to each paragraph of the above text?

The Main Facts

1. Who owns U.S. newspapers?
2. When is a newspaper considered "good"?
3. Which are the most influential papers in the United States?
4. In what way do they differ?
5. Why is Katharine Graham's profile in this chapter?
6. Which are the six great questions of journalism?

Scanning the Text

1. Is there anything "tongue-in-cheek" in the description of the *New York Times*?
2. What is the attitude of the *Times* towards the *Post*? Give two examples.
3. Is there anything strange in the way the author expresses the *Times'* attitude? Is the expression the author uses to be taken literally? What is the tone of the paragraphs about the *Times* and the *Post:* very serious, serious, lighthearted, antagonistic, critical. . . ?
4. How much did Eugene Meyer pay for the *Washington Post*? Why is the price "humiliating"?

5. Is the circulation of the *Wall Street Journal* larger, equal, or smaller than the combined circulations of the *Times* and the *Post*? (You must scan both the text and the Vocabulary of Journalism.)
6. Which newspaper covers Canadian news particularly well?
7. Which great newspaper has been in the same family for the longest time?

Generalizations

Which of the following sentences express a generalization rather than a particular fact that could serve either as a supporting statement or an example of the generalization?

1. Most American journalists try conscientiously to be fair and accurate.
2. Of course it does happen that a newsman reports incorrect facts once in a while.
3. He probably did not have time to check his story properly.
4. Or perhaps he was misinformed by his source.
5. Reporters work under pressure, always anxious to meet the deadline.
6. Sometimes their only choice is to give the facts without checking or to drop a good story.
7. No journalist likes to drop a story.
8. He'd run the risk of facing a very irritated editor-in-chief if the story were published by the other papers.
9. In 1933 the bankrupt *Post* was hardly worth the $850,000 that Eugene Meyer paid for it.
10. Meyer probably thought that it was rather cheap.
11. Newspapers are worth millions of dollars.
12. Recently a small local paper in a town of 25,000 inhabitants changed hands for nearly $2 million.
13. The *Washington Post*, if it were sold now, would bring an enormous price.
14. Millionaires are not fond of losing money.
15. For years, however, Eugene Meyer had to pour $1 million of his own money to keep the *Washington Post* going.
16. He was rewarded for his patience.
17. Not only did his paper acquire great prestige, but it became wealthy also.
18. All important people nowadays read the *Washington Post*.

Cultural Notes for Profile, Part One

<u>Wire Services</u>

Newspapers, particularly those that do not have a large number of reporters, subscribe to wire services such as the Associated Press (AP) or the United Press (UP, or UPI for United Press International). The services provide them with articles on national and international news. AP and UP keep "bureaus" in numerous American cities and foreign capitals.

Pulitzer Prizes

Joseph Pulitzer, an American journalist of the turn of the century, gave $1 million to Columbia University in New York to found a school of journalism. In his will he also left money for the creation of several awards—the Pulitzer prizes—to be given each year for outstanding achievements in journalism. There are prizes in many categories, including "Reporting," "Commentary," "Feature Writing," "Criticism," "Photography," etc.

Profile
Part One

Born June 6, 1917

Skim the text to find out the answers to the following questions:
- Was Katharine Graham a journalist, or merely the daughter of the owner of the *Washington Post*?
- Was her husband a journalist?
- What kind of a person was Katharine Graham?
- As you read the text, make a note of metaphors and tongue-in-cheek statements.

Katharine Graham is a tall, elegant woman, still very much a member of the "in" circles of Washington society. Relaxed, among friends that she trusts, she jokes and laughs easily; as a matter of fact she says that laughing and learning are her two favorite activities. But she can look regal and quite forbidding to strangers—and to those of her employees who haven't acceded to the top of the company; and when she is not smiling, her most noticeable feature is a very determined chin. There is much steel in the character of Mrs. Graham, although few people were aware of the fact when she took charge of her father's newspaper.

At the peak of her career, Katharine Graham was described as the most powerful woman in the nation and it is true that she played a major role in the downfall of a President. As chairman of the board of the Washington Post Company, she controls not only the *Post* itself, but all the other holdings of the corporation, including *Newsweek* magazine, *Art News* and a string of radio and television stations. But even without the prestige of power, and even if we forgot that she must be credited with the *Post*'s present position of influence and affluence, she would still be noteworthy as a woman who, in mid-life, managed to transform herself from a shy, uncertain, and patronized wife into a triumphant tycoon.

There are still people in Washington who remember the Katharine of the old days, a quiet figure standing at the side of Philip Graham, too plump, too dowdy, and much too colorless, it seemed, to be the wife of such a dazzling man. Philip was brilliant, witty, and bold. Wherever he went he was the center of attention, admired and feted, while Katharine seemed only to be tolerated for his sake. Too shy to talk to the important people who surrounded them, she never volunteered an opinion, and no one had the curiosity to inquire if she had one. She was usually asked what Philip was thinking and what he was up to.[1] But until tragedy struck she was apparently happy to remain in his shadow and to play "dear old Mom" to their four children.

The main reason for Katharine's self-effacement was that she didn't have a very high opinion of herself. She still tends to make self-disparaging remarks, even now that she has proven to the world, and to herself, that she is more than a strong man's widow. At first glance, Katharine seems to have had every reason to be more confident: she belonged to a rich, successful family, and she was accustomed from childhood to the company of famous and talented people, beginning with her own parents. As it turned out, she was crushed by her own good fortune. Her parents, her husband, their friends, were all impressive and forceful. The quiet and uncompetitive Katharine, feeling inept and inarticulate in comparison, chose to withdraw within her shell rather than fight for recognition.

Katharine's parents, both prominent in their fields, expected superior achievements from their children. They hammered into them the belief that much is expected from those who have much, and that they should all distinguish themselves in some line of work. The mother was a formidable person who, long before her marriage, had been a friend of artists and intellectuals such as Matisse and Thomas Mann,[2] whose books she translated into English. She had been the first woman reporter of the *New York Sun* at a time when lady journalists were unheard of. She was an expert on Chinese art, which she collected (and lectured about) and a redoubtable supporter of causes. There was no gentleness in Agnes Meyer; she was a bully, totally self-centered and unable or unwilling to understand a daughter so different from her. She did a thorough job of destroying any shred of confidence that Katharine might have developed, never losing an opportunity to remind her that her sisters were either beautiful or witty, that the rest of the family was talented, and that she, Katharine, lacked all

---

[1] to be up to something—to be about to do something (connotation: something exciting and possibly naughty).
[2] Henri Matisse (1869–1954)—a famous French painter; Thomas Mann (1875–1955)—German writer, Nobel prize winner in 1929.

of those qualities. Although Mrs. Meyer lived long enough to see Katharine become the most admired publisher in Washington, she never gave any indication that she had changed her views. Once, at the top of Katharine's prestige, the two women had lunch with architect I. M. Pei. Pei explained to them a particular architectural problem. "Well," remarked Katharine, "I didn't know that."—"What's surprising about that?" interrupted Agnes, "You have never known anything!"

Undone by her mother, young Katharine couldn't find much support on her father's side. Not that he didn't love her, but he was too busy to devote much time and attention to his children. Eugene Meyer was not a self-made man: he had started life with wealth. But he had vastly enlarged his fortune in investment banking, railroads, and chemicals, and he had served with distinction in high level government posts. He had been governor of the Federal Reserve and was to be the first president of the World Bank. Katharine was his favorite daughter. He alone seemed to be aware of her intellectual depth and inner strength. He enjoyed the way she argued with him about politics. After he bought the *Washington Post* he made her work in various sections of the newspaper and took her along to management meetings, as though he were grooming her to succeed him. "You watch my little Kay," he said to a friend. "She'll surprise you." Yet when he decided to retire, it was not to her that he entrusted his paper, but to his brilliant son-in-law. Katharine didn't seem to mind; as long as Philip was happy, she never objected to anything.

Away from her family, Katharine could do very well indeed. She was an outstanding student in all her schools, at Vassar[3] and later at the University of Chicago, which was noted at the time for its liberal leanings and its tough curriculum. Not only was Katharine a brilliant student, but she also distinguished herself in non-academic activities. At Vassar, as editor of the college's publication, she earned her fellow students' respect for the quality of her articles. In Chicago she became a radical, and helped found a students' club promoting "Peace, Freedom, Security, and Equality." She made speeches and took part in demonstrations in support of the striking workers of a steel plant—an odd precedent for a woman who, in 1975, would crush the printers' union striking against her newspaper. All the while she was diligently studying economics, history, and philosophy.

Neither of her parents found time to attend her graduation in 1938, but her father did help her get a job with the *San Francisco News* where, as female reporters were still rare and unwelcomed, she was at first ridiculed by her male colleagues. They didn't laugh long, however, for Katharine, who had been assigned to cover a strike on the San Francisco waterfront, did such an excellent job that the editor proceeded to send her on more and more important stories. In no time at all she was the *News'* chief re-

---

[3] Vassar—a prestigious college originally for women, now co-educational.

porter on the strike. "Seldom," said a *News*' executive, "have I seen anyone take hold of a tough assignment as she did." Katharine, originally hired for two months, was still enjoying her work at the *News* seven and a half months later when her father sent for her, insisting that he needed her in Washington. Reluctantly, Katharine returned to the bosom of her family.[4]

For $25 a week, Katharine went to work in the letters-to-the-editor department of the *Post*. "She was tall," wrote Tom Kelly in the May 1981 issue of *The Washingtonian*, "earnest, competent, and self-conscious, and she worked in the editorial and Sunday departments rather than in the newsroom so she wouldn't feel too conspicuous." If Katharine had been lost as a child in the Meyers' social circles, she fitted even less as a young woman. Badly dressed in skirts and sweaters among her elegant sisters, she looked and behaved like an aggressive political activist, insisting on discussing serious matters with the young men attending the Meyers' parties. She felt "like a peasant in a drawing room." Even so, within six months she had captured the attention of the most sought-after bachelor in town—tall, handsome Philip Graham. Graham, born in 1915 in South Dakota, was the son of a farmer who had become rich in Florida and had eventually been elected senator in that state. After graduating from the Harvard Law School, Philip had gone to work for Supreme Court Justice Felix Frankfurter. There was no doubt in Frankfurter's mind nor in the mind of anyone who knew Philip, that the ambitious young lawyer would have a glorious career and eventually become a justice himself.

From their first meeting Philip Graham was fascinated by the awkward girl in sweaters, whom he found exciting and attractive. On their third date he told her that they would marry—and married they were in June 1940, to the delight of Eugene Meyer, who had fallen under Philip's spell like everyone else. Graham made it immediately clear that he would have nothing to do with his father-in-law's newspaper, and that furthermore he and his wife would live on his salary. Since they couldn't afford luxury, Katharine submitted happily to living in relatively modest surroundings. At that time, Philip had joined the team of bright young men collected by President Roosevelt to work on production problems, and he was already highly regarded for his effectiveness and his ability to get things done—and done well. After the entry of the United States into the war, he again made his mark as an intelligence officer in the Air Force. When he returned, more self-assured than ever, he was given the reception of a war hero.

While waiting for her husband in Washington, Katharine had been working as a columnist for the *Post*, and she too had performed well, although without attracting much notice. It didn't matter—she had no compelling desire to pursue a career, now that she was happily married; her

---

[4] the bosom of the family—the expression suggests warmth and love.

only reason for keeping up with her writing was to please Philip, who had told her from the start that he "didn't want to be married to a cook!"

When Graham came back from the war, Eugene Meyer, who had just been named director of the World Bank, declared himself too busy to be running a newspaper on the side. Although the *Post* had regained a measure of stability and respectability under his direction, it was still losing about $1 million a year. Except for a fine editorial page, it was still a mediocre paper. The staff was second-rate and Meyer, never interested in reporting the news, had been content to fill the front page with items from the wire services. Now he wanted out, and since his only son, studying to become a psychiatrist, adamantly refused to take over, the natural thing was to turn to his son-in-law. It does not seem to have occurred to Meyer that Katharine could be considered. Anyway, his first approach was not successful, for Philip, planning a political career in Florida, had no desire to turn journalist. After a brief struggle he did give in nonetheless, and officially became publisher of the *Post* in May 1946. Katharine stopped working to devote herself exclusively to the role of adoring wife and to the task of raising her growing family. She did all the things that were expected of a woman in her position—she sat on charitable boards, entertained, went to official parties, and followed Philip among the great and the famous whose friendships he was cultivating. She was still shy and socially inexpert—but conscientious. And for a time all went well enough.

Philip Graham was much more interested in politics and in social reforms than in journalism. Under him, the *Post* embarked upon crusade after crusade; it campaigned for the investigation of a public official suspected of corruption, for the building of a highway, for the renewal of a dilapidated section of Washington, for the racial integration of public restrooms, and for a number of other causes. Graham's *Washington Post* became an openly partisan paper, not always accurate in the presentation of facts and figures that could undermine its campaigns. It gained popularity despite its flaws because it was entertaining and because of its new editor's appealing personality. Besides, Philip was known to wield a certain amount of influence through his contacts with important people and his friendship with President John Kennedy and Vice-president Lyndon Johnson. In fact, Graham had been instrumental in the choice of Johnson as vice-presidential candidate in 1960. No doubt about it—Philip Graham was always in the thick of things.

At the same time, Philip had found a way of making Eugene Meyer's paper profitable. By acquiring (with his father-in-law's money) several radio and television stations and by binding them to the paper in a newly formed Washington Post Company, he definitely took the *Post* out of the red.[5] From then on, the profits from the stations would carry the paper. In

---

[5] to be "in the red" means to be in debt. In bookkeeping, debts and losses used to be written in red ink.

1954 Graham bought the *Post*'s only remaining competitor, the *Washington Times Herald*. The merger didn't improve the quality of the *Post*'s reporting, but it brought in the subscribers and the advertisers of the *Herald*. Philip went on to acquire two magazines, *Newsweek* and *Art News*, then a share of the *Paris Herald Tribune*. Finally he joined with the *Los Angeles Times* to create a common news service. Still second-rate, the *Washington Post* was nevertheless wealthy and secure.

But things were not going as well for Philip personally. Since 1957, it had become evident that Graham was suffering from manic depression; he would jump abruptly from periods of acute depression to periods of "ups" when he behaved in the most arrogant and bizarre fashion, insulting friends and strangers—and even President Kennedy, to whom he once shouted in the telephone: "Do you know who you are talking to?" When the crisis was over, a distressed Graham would apologize again and again to the people he had offended. During his bad cycles, Katharine took care of her husband and tried to hide his illness as best she could. But as the disease progressed it became increasingly difficult to conceal it. Besides, Philip was turning against her, making fun of her appearance, of her awkwardness, and doing his best to humiliate her in front of their friends and employees. In 1961 he left her to live with a young woman, a reporter named Robin, whom he introduced to all as his fiancee. Finally, he instructed a lawyer friend to start proceedings for a divorce and to draw a will that would leave most of his properties, including his shares of the *Post*, to Robin, and the rest to his children. The horrified lawyer tried to drag things out as long as possible, and managed to stall long enough to save Katharine from the effects of Philip's folly. In 1963, after a severe attack, Philip entered a clinic specializing in mental disorders. His condition improved rapidly, so much in fact that after a few months he was able to persuade his doctors to let him spend a weekend with Katharine in their country house. There, on August 3, 1963, while his wife was busy in another part of the house, Graham shot himself to death. Katharine was 46 and, ready or not, she was suddenly in charge of the *Washington Post* and its company.

Understanding the Text

1. Why is Katharine Graham an interesting subject for a profile?
2. Why was she so insecure?
3. Was Agnes Meyer right to judge her daughter stupid and unattractive?
4. Did Katharine Graham have any experience in journalism before she took over the *Post*?
5. Why did she have to take over?
6. In what way did Philip Graham help the *Post*?
7. What kind of disease is manic depression?

8. What happened to the Grahams' marriage when Philip became ill?
9. Why was Graham's lawyer so horrified?
10. What kind of newspaper did Graham leave for his successor?

Scanning for Details

A. You are a journalist who has to write Philip Graham's obituary—i.e., a brief account of his life (family, education, career, marriage) to appear in newspapers with the announcement of his death. Scan the text to collect all pertinent information, and write a brief article.

B.
1. How was Katharine Graham described in *The Washingtonian* of May 1981?
2. What did Philip Graham do in 1961?
3. For what newspaper did Agnes Meyer work as a reporter?
4. When did Katharine graduate from the University of Chicago?
5. What exactly did Eugene Meyer say to his friend about Katharine?
6. What examples are given of the *Washington Post*'s crusades under Philip Graham?
7. What is the name of the architect who had lunch with Katharine Graham and her mother?
8. How long was Philip Graham publisher of the *Post*?

Commenting on the Text

1. Did you find any metaphors or tongue-in-cheek statements?
2. What is the author's attitude toward Agnes Meyer?
3. Does the story support Mrs. Meyer's opinion of her daughter, as being unattractive, untalented, and ignorant?
4. Is it bad for a young girl to try to discuss serious matters with the young men at a party?
5. Can you understand why Philip Graham changed his mind and agreed to take over the *Washington Post*?

Vocabulary

A. *For each of the following, find the meaning of the underlined word.*

line 17 Philip Graham succeeded in giving the *Washington Post* power and affluence. The story shows that affluence means:
   a) excellence
   b) wealth

line 19 Philip and his friends treated Katharine in a patronizing way:
   a) as an inferior
   b) as a superior
   c) as an equal

line 22 She seemed too dowdy for her dazzling husband.
  a) bright
  b) rich
  c) dull

line 83 If a college is praised for its tough curriculum, "curriculum" must refer to:
  a) its students
  b) its buildings
  c) its courses

line 91 Katharine, a good student, worked diligently.
  a) with care
  b) without interest
  c) once in a while

B. *Complete each of the following statements with the most appropriate word from the list below, which includes more words than necessary. Be sure to make all needed adjustments in articles, nouns, and verbs.*

1. People who have been in high positions in Washington find it hard to retire somewhere else; they cannot stand not to be in _____ any more.
2. Agnes Meyer, a fighter for good and bad causes, was always ready to launch a _____.
3. The *Washington Post* was a _____ paper from the start since it had been founded as a Democratic paper.
4. In the first chapter of this book, Ray Kroc was put on a par with two famous _____.
5. Any ambitious young man dreams of making _____ in his field.
6. Some people thought that George Putnam had married Amelia Earhart out of ambition. But she had great charm, and it is possible that he found her _____.
7. Agnes Meyer, with her stern and domineering glare, must have looked quite _____ to her children.
8. Since Agnes and Philip were never short of words on any subjects, they found Katharine _____ by comparison.
9. Katharine, determined to stay away from her family, refused _____ to come home after her graduation.

noticeable   corruption   inarticulate
conspicuous   fascinating   the thick of things
formidable   partisan   tycoon
a clinic   a merger   crusade
adamantly   dilapidated   to humiliate
a mark

Prefixes

self

1. What *self-made* man have we studied in a previous chapter?
2. Agnes Meyer was a *self-styled* expert on Chinese art. What does that mean?
3. She was also a very *self-centered* person. What other word do you know that means almost the same thing?
4. Why is it uncomfortable for a *self-conscious* person to enter a room full of people, for example?
5. George Putnam was accused of having a passion for *self-aggrandizement* (a word related to "grand"); Katharine Graham, on the other hand, seemed to have had a passion for *self-effacement*. From her conduct, can you guess what this means, and how her behavior compares to George Putnam's?

Starting a Newspaper

[*Instructor's Note:* For this exercise, the class should be divided in discussion groups of four to six students. After the students have discussed the material in groups, the class as a whole can compare the different approaches taken.]

Suppose that you are planning a campus publication. What kind of paper do you want to have, in terms of:

appearance;
topics and sections to be included;
special topics to be covered occasionally;
type of illustration, if any;
financing;
staffing;
distribution?

What goals would your paper try to achieve, and what would it avoid doing?

Facts, Inferences, and Opinions

Which of the following statements express facts, which represent implications from the text, and which are the writer's opinions? As always, some statements might be debatable.

1. Agnes Meyer was an intellectual and an art collector.
2. She spoke several languages.
3. Once she told her daughter that she had never known anything.
4. She should not have humiliated her in public.
5. But Agnes was a cruel person.
6. Katharine would not have been so awkward if she had received some encouragement from her family.

7. Katharine Graham doesn't seem to be nice to all her employees.
8. Philip Graham bought several radio and television stations with his father-in-law's money.
9. Radio and television stations are good businesses.
10. Obviously Philip had not married Katharine because of her father's wealth and position.
11. Some farmers become rich in the United States.
12. I doubt that it happens often.
13. Philip Graham's father became rich as a dairy farmer and real estate businessman.
14. Eugene Meyer lost a great deal of money on his newspaper.

Topics for Discussion

1. What would, or could, have happened if Katharine Meyer had chosen to remain with the *San Francisco News* in 1939 instead of going back home?
2. Is it right for a newspaper to crusade against corruption, slums, racial discrimination, etc., or should they only report the news?
3. Should a newspaper publisher get as involved in politics as Philip Graham did?
4. Is it all right for a President to become a close friend of a newspaper publisher?
5. When a newspaper attacks an individual and prints false information about that person, do you feel that the person has a chance to do anything about it? Should a paper be held responsible when it publishes false information about a person? What can a person do when this happens?

Cultural Notes for Profile, Part Two

The Rand Corporation was initially a Research and Development organization devoted exclusively to the support of the Air Force. More recently, it has engaged in a broader range of research, but a major part of its work is still related to governmental activities and public policy.

Profile
Part Two

Skim the text to find the answers to the following questions:
- Is Katharine Graham still directly in charge of the *Washington Post*?
- What important events did Katharine Graham have to consider as publisher of the *Washington Post*?

> Why is there a note about the Rand Corporation at the beginning of this section?

As soon as the news of Philip's suicide spread around Washington, speculations began about the future of the *Post;* there were even a few offers to buy it. On the day of her husband's funeral, Katharine gathered the top executives of the paper and of the corporation to put a stop to the rumors. She would take over, she announced, until her son Donald, then in college, could succeed her. There was no question of letting the paper out of the family. However brave and confident she tried to appear, her uneasiness must have been obvious, for one of the editors remarked with a smile that she looked "like a shaky little doe coming in on wobbly legs out of the forest!" In all probability it was not so much the task ahead that scared her, since she already had some experience of the newspaper business. But she dreaded the prospect of facing her own employees—all men, and moreover men who had no great respect for her. She had never done anything of value that they could be aware of, and they had been used to seeing her treated lightly, even contemptuously, by her own husband. It was surely no comfort to Katharine to realize that every one in Washington shared the doubts of her staff about her ability to replace Philip. Worse still, she shared those doubts. But as Eugene Meyer had predicted, she was to surprise them all.

Many years later, remembering the first months of her takeover, Katharine Graham said : "I was paralyzed with fear at first. It was like being the new girl in school. You are disoriented. You don't know what your role is. The first time I asked a question at one of our private editorial meetings, I thought I'd die." She forced herself to overcome her shyness, and for once her lack of self-conceit turned out to be her salvation. She went for advice to the most experienced people she knew, among them the dean of columnists, Walter Lippman, who suggested that she read her paper carefully and talk with the men who wrote it. And so she did for about a year—listening, studying the *Post,* observing the staff and asking questions. Perhaps she remembered that her father had told her that the way to succeed was "to know everything there is to know, work harder than anybody and be absolutely honest."

It did not take Katharine long to understand that the *Post* was not as good as it could be. The news coverage was uneven and the writing dull in many sections—worse still, the direction was lacking in authority and boldness. A change was needed if she wanted to aim for quality. As she saw it, the first step had to be renovation of the editorial staff, starting at the top. Although she dreaded the thought of firing her editor-in-chief, she decided that it had to be done; her first outstanding action was to hire for the job Benjamin C. Bradlee, formerly on the staff of *Newsweek.* The choice was remarkable, considering that she had no reason to like Bradlee, who had been a good friend of Philip even during the last years, when Philip was trying to divorce and dispossess her. But after a few meetings with Bradlee, she felt that she had the right man for the task at hand; his ambition for the *Post* and his ideas about the best way to bring it to the level of the *New York Times* were in agreement with hers. Sure now that they were of one mind, she put him in charge, with a promise to let him run the paper without interference as long as they would agree on policies.

In many ways, Bradlee was like Philip Graham—dashing, quick-witted, overflowing with energy and ambition. But unlike Philip, who had been more of a politician than a newspaper man, Ben was pure journalist. One of his reporters once joked that the editor-in-chief didn't care who was elected President of the United States, as long as he could be the first to print the results of the elections. Later, the *Post*'s reporters in Vietnam complained that they couldn't figure out Bradlee's position about the war. His overriding interest was to bring the *Post* to excellence and to make it at least a strong competitor to the *Times*. And this he accomplished splendidly (recklessly at times), with the full agreement and support of his boss. Katharine never hesitated to provide the funds needed to bring to the paper outstanding writers such as David Broder, Haynes Johnson, or Meg Greenberg. Within two years, Bradlee had increased the editorial staff by 20 percent, and his reporters, encouraged to compete against each other and to be as bold as they pleased, were filling the pages of the *Post* with superior reporting. New sections were started—among them "Style," a sophisticated review of art news, local events, fashion, entertainment, and provocative columns. "Style" became so popular—despite outrageous columns from the editor in charge—that it was imitated by other papers throughout the country.

Katharine Graham carefully watched the developments; she often nagged Bradlee to improve the different features of "Style" and to be severe about the quality of the writing when she found it careless. Although she kept her word not to interfere in the running of the paper, she remained involved in all major decisions concerning the *Post*. At the same time, she was fulfilling what she considered her own task: the administration of the Washington Post Company and her public relations duties as publisher of a major newspaper. And she was becoming good at it. Having lost—little by little—her awe of celebrities and of men in general, she was now moving with increasing ease in the official and social circles of Washington, where she had been previously noticed for her shyness. She had learned to lunch confidently with leaders and politicians, and to speak her mind in front of large audiences. While her paper was gaining class[1], Katharine Graham herself was gaining authority. She needed it, for even with a forceful

---

[1] class—superior elegance.

editor-in-chief at the helm, she was the person who had ultimately to take responsibility for the paper's ventures, and the one who was called upon to make the hard decisions. The two most famous and dramatic of those decisions concerned the publication of the Pentagon Papers in 1971, and the investigation of the Watergate incident by two young and inexperienced reporters of the *Post* the following year.

The Pentagon Papers was a massive study of the U.S. operations in Vietnam, commissioned to the Rand Corporation in 1967 by Secretary of Defense Robert McNamara. The study, marked "Top Secret," was meant to be seen only by the president, the secretary of defense, and a few other senior members of the government. But a Rand employee who had grown dissatisfied with the war passed the papers to the *New York Times*, which began publishing them in June 1971. As soon as the first installment appeared, the government protested that it was illegal to print classified documents involving national security, and a court order enjoined the *Times* to stop publication until a decision could be reached by the court.

At that point the *Washington Post,* anxious not to be outdone by the *Times,* was getting ready to print the section of the papers that they had managed to obtain. By sheer coincidence, the Washington Post Company had just put its stock on the market; and of course any problem affecting the *Post* (such as a lawsuit) was bound to have a repercussion on the value of the shares. The decision to publish or not to publish the controversial material, risking a court injunction[2] and a fall in the price of stock, rested on Katharine Graham. Against the advice of her lawyers, she gave the order to print without waiting for the court's ruling on the legality of the action.[3] She commented afterwards that the paper had to publish important news, no matter what the consequence might be. She didn't add, but it was true, that she was ready to take great risks to prove that the *Post* was just as alert and just as brave as the *Times*.

The much more prolonged Watergate affair started as a minor incident; a small group of men had been caught burglarizing the offices of the Democratic Party, which was then busy with the coming presidential campaign of 1972. Two of the greenest reporters of the *Post* were assigned to cover this mildly interesting piece of local news. The young men, inexperienced but bright and ambitious, went to work as directed and soon discovered with keen interest that one of the break-in suspects was connected with a man who had worked, in a minor capacity, for the White House. From then on, the excited pair followed the trail in a stubborn, painstaking search that

---

[2] a court injunction is a written order from a court of justice to halt an action.
[3] On July 1, 1971, the Supreme Court lifted the first court order, declaring that the Papers could be published because they did not contain information essential to the security of the United States. The decision applied only to the Pentagon Papers, however; the Supreme Court didn't rule that newspapers always had the right to publish whatever classified documents they could find.

would lead to higher and higher members of President Nixon's entourage and finally to the president himself.

For a long time the press as a whole cautiously refrained from covering the story. At first it didn't seem to the publishers that the incident was as noteworthy as the *Post* wanted to make it look; the young men reporting it seemed overexcited, and the whole investigation resembled more a personal crusade of the giddy *Post* against President Nixon than it did legitimate reporting. But the search finally revealed not only the participation of members of the White House, but such a succession of lies, cover-up operations, abuse of power, and obstruction of justice by the president himself, that Nixon had to resign in the summer of 1974. By then the two heroes of the investigation, Carl Bernstein and Robert Woodward, were the most celebrated journalists in the country, and the *Post* was basking in a prestige that even Ben Bradlee had hardly believed possible. The *Post* received a Pulitzer prize for the reportage; another Pulitzer was to crown the book that Woodward and Bernstein wrote about their adventure,[4] and they were further glamorized by a film based on the book. As for Katharine Graham, who had staunchly supported her two reporters through the hard and the glorious times at the risk of losing her paper and possibly landing in jail, she had established herself as a fearless, high-minded, and altogether admirable publisher in the eyes of the nation.

A year after the end of the Watergate affair, Katharine Graham won a different kind of victory when she rid the *Washington Post* of a labor problem that had plagued the paper for years. Although well paid and enjoying good working conditions, the *Post*'s pressmen had long been aware that they could get any raise or improvement they wanted by threatening to start a strike that would make the paper lose days or weeks of publication. In the 1960s the workers had taken advantage of this situation several times, either for financial gains or to oppose the installation in the pressroom of ultramodern technology that would reduce the number of men needed.

In 1971 Katharine Graham began training office employees to run the presses, so as to have some skilled personnel available to keep the paper going in the event of a strike. The maneuver didn't go unnoticed by the unionized personnel, and in 1973 the printers renewed their contract without any fuss; they even accepted the acquisition of new machinery in return for a large cash bonus. But the following year, when the time came for the pressmen to renew their contract, the pressmen's union decided to strike for better terms. The strike soon turned ugly. Irritated by the administration's resistance, the pressmen forced their way inside the building, damaged the machines and set fire to the pressroom. It was a mistake; the pictures of the vandalized presses, liberally provided by the *Post*, turned

---

[4]*All the President's Men* (Simon and Schuster, 1974).

public opinion against the strikers, and the *Post*'s reporters, who had been considering striking also in support of the workers, changed their minds and stayed on the job. As long as her reporters provided her with news to print, Katharine Graham could keep the paper going—and she did. Non-striking employees went to work at unfamiliar tasks, with Katharine herself manning the telephone of the classified ads section. The previously trained employees (mainly advertising salesmen) prepared the paper, and helicopters took the material from the roof of the building to six non-union printing shops around Washington. All in all, the *Washington Post* missed only one day of publication. When the personnel department began to interview applicants for temporary replacement of the strikers, the union gave up. It was the first time in years that a newspaper had been able to fight a strike. The event didn't have on the nation the same impact as the Watergate affair, but for her fellow publishers Katharine Graham emerged as a heroine. She was certainly one for the board of directors of the Washington Post Corporation when they realized that the modernization of the pressroom (now unopposed by the defeated union) was saving $1.2 million annually in overtime alone, and doubling the *Post*'s profits for 1976.

The late seventies were years of glory for the *Washington Post,* years of confidence, and in many people's opinion years of arrogance. Katharine Graham, for her part, was enjoying a position of prominence in the highest Washington circles—at least equal to her husband's former status. She was showered with awards and honorary degrees, praised, courted—and feared. She was also, finally, very sure of herself. No "shaky little doe" any more, it was her turn to intimidate many of those who had to deal with her. The staff had come to admire her courage and the fact that she was at her best when the going was rough. But they didn't feel close to her—they found her cold, distant, dictatorial. There is no doubt that she enjoyed her power. Although she had announced in 1963 that she would retire as soon as Donald was able to take over, for many years after his graduation she didn't make any further mention of her original intention. Only in January 1979 did she relinquish the helm of the *Washington Post* to her son.

The change of direction has been slowly felt at the *Post*. While his mother had been primarily a businesswoman, Donald, a quiet, unassuming young man, seems more interested in the journalistic aspect of his job—gathering the facts, and conferring with the editors and reporters who seek, digest, and present them in the columns of his paper. He has made some changes in the personnel, and it seems that he is trying to tone down the voice of the *Post,* which a journalist had described as "matching Ben Bradlee's personality—daring, impulsive, unsecure, flashy, entertaining, and competitive." Donald is more interested in accuracy and fairness. While he is endeavoring to make his mark, Katharine presides over the board of directors, very much the Queen Mother. And she gives the impression that she is enjoying the part.

Understanding the Text

1. What major event really brought the *Washington Post* to its present prominence?
2. What was Katharine Graham's role in that event, and why was she admired?
3. Did Katharine Graham make changes immediately when she took over the *Post*?
4. What was remarkable in her choice of Ben Bradlee as editor-in-chief?
5. What was Katharine Graham's role while Bradlee was editor-in-chief?
6. What action taken by Katharine Graham was a main factor in her victory over the pressman's union?
7. Why did the pressmen lose the support of the reporters?
8. What was the effect of the *Post*'s victory on the pressroom and on the newspaper's health?

Scanning for Details

Decide whether each statement is completely true or completely false. If a statement is only partly true, give a reason why.

1. Ben Bradlee hired three outstanding journalists: Jack Broder, Meg Greenberg, and Haynes Johnson.
2. In 1968 Secretary of Defense McNamara commissioned a study of the Vietnam operations.
3. The editor said that Katharine Graham looked "like a shaky little doe coming in on wobbly legs out of the forest!"
4. Katharine Graham retired in June 1979.
5. Ben Bradlee had been editor-in-chief of *Newsweek* before becoming editor-in-chief of the *Post*.
6. Katharine Graham turned to William Lippman for advice.
7. Bradlee increased the editorial staff by 20 percent.

Key Words

Make a list of the key words in paragraphs four to seven that give an idea of the character of the *Washington Post* under Katharine Graham and Ben Bradlee. Compare your list with your neighbor's findings (and discuss it if necessary).

Write a brief description of the *Post* as the publisher and her editor wanted it to be (avoid using too many adjectives).

Vocabulary

For each of the following, find the meaning of the underlined word.

line 9   If a shaky, frightened person runs on <u>wobbly</u> legs, do you suppose that the legs are firm or not?

line 22 A newcomer at school (or anywhere) is always disoriented. From the context, the newcomer is surely:
a) confident
b) lost
c) excited

Newcomers at universities, business conventions, and large factories are often asked to attend an orientation class, meeting, or tour. What is the purpose of such meetings?
How can travelers orient themselves?

line 43 In writing his new will, Graham was trying to dispossess his wife. Is this likely to mean that he wanted to leave her or to deprive her of her property?

line 80 Katharine Graham was now bold enough to speak her mind in front of large audiences.
a) to dream aloud
b) to state her opinion
c) to talk to herself

line 83 Ben Bradlee was at the helm of the *Washington Post*.
a) in the office
b) on the top floor
c) in command

line 84 In difficult situations, the publisher is called upon to make the decision.
a) required
b) called on the phone
c) threatened

line 95 The *Times* published the first installment of the Pentagon Papers.
a) part
b) book
c) page

line 97 A court order enjoined the Times to stop publication.
a) advised
b) forbade
c) ordered

line 103 Any scandal would have a repercussion on the value of the stock.
a) an effect
b) an explanation
c) an improvement

line 127 The press in general considered the *Washington Post* giddy at the beginning of the Watergate investigation. Does the use of "giddy" imply
a) admiration for the *Post*?
b) criticism of the *Post*?

B. Prefixes

<u>out</u> and <u>over</u>

Consider the two sentences:

> Mrs. Meyer <u>outlived</u> her husband by many years.
> She never spent much time <u>outdoors</u>.

Is the meaning of <u>out</u> exactly the same in both words? How would you paraphrase these statements?

Paraphrase the following:

1. Ben Bradlee couldn't stand to see the *Post* <u>outdone</u> by the *Times*.
2. The pressmen who wanted to work could not get in because they were <u>outnumbered</u> by the strikers.
3. All nations are concerned about the <u>outflow</u> of their gold reserves.
4. At the *Post* the desire to be sensational often <u>outweighs</u> the respect for accuracy.
5. When Katharine Graham took over, most people thought that the <u>outlook</u> was grim for the paper.
6. Bradlee said that some machinery in the pressroom was <u>outdated</u>.
7. The striking pressmen thought that the paper couldn't be published without them. But Katharine Graham <u>outwitted</u> them.

Consider these two sentences:

> Although Katharine Graham was not slim, she was not really <u>overweight</u>.
> After the death of her husband, she spent several weeks <u>overseas</u>.

How would you paraphrase the above statements? What are the two meanings of prefix <u>over</u>?

1. Some people prefer fruits that are <u>overripe</u>. Do you?
2. What happens when you <u>oversleep</u>?
3. Can we say that Katharine Graham transformed the *Washington Post* <u>overnight</u>?
4. She of course had the right to <u>override</u> Ben Bradlee's decisions. Would he have been pleased? Why?
5. Can you think of a singer, an actor or any other personality who is <u>overrated</u>?
6. Can you think of words starting with <u>over</u> that can be applied to:
   a) a car?
   b) a government?
   c) a student?
   d) an object that you want to buy?
   e) a conversation?

The Main Idea

Which of the statements in each group best expresses the most essential idea in the paragraph?

Par. 1
a) Katharine was afraid of her own employees.
b) On the day of her husband's funeral, she held a meeting of the top executives.
c) After her husband's death, a very uncertain Katharine took over the direction of the paper.

Par. 2
a) She took time to ask for advice and to study her newspaper.
b) The first thing Katharine did was to ask Walter Lippman for advice.
c) Her father had advised her to work hard, know everything, and be honest.

Par. 3
a) It didn't take Katharine long to find that the *Post* was not as good as it could be.
b) Katharine realized that the *Post* needed a strong editor-in-chief and she hired one.
c) Ben Bradlee had been a friend of Philip Graham.

Par. 4
a) Bradlee concentrated on improving the *Washington Post*.
b) Bradlee hired a number of very good writers for the *Post*.
c) Bradlee was not interested in politics.

Par. 5
a) Katharine had been interested in perfecting the new "Style" section of the paper.
b) Katharine became a good representative and a strong administrator for her paper.
c) The two tough decisions that Katharine Graham had to make regarded the Pentagon Papers and the Watergate incident.

Par. 6   What is the main idea of the paragraph?

Outlining

With the facts provided in "The American Press" and in both parts of Katharine Graham's profile, make an outline of the career of the Washington Post. *The outline should show the different periods in the life of the paper since its foundation, and give some indication of what was right or wrong about the* Post *during each period.*

    I. From *(date)* to *(date)* the *Post* changed hands several times.
       A. Good success at first as Democratic paper
       B. Loss of quality, sensationalism leading to _____ in *(date)*
    II. _____ period, from *(date)* to *(date)*

A. Good Results: _____
B. Failures: _____
   1. _____
   2. _____
III. _____
   A. _____
      1. _____
      2. _____
      3. _____
   B. _____
      1. _____
      2. _____
IV. _____
   A. _____
      1. _____
      2. _____
      3. _____
      4. _____
         a) _____
         b) _____
         c) _____
V. _____
   A. _____
   B. _____

Topics for Discussion

1. Daniel Ellsberg, who gave the Pentagon Papers to the *New York Times* for publication, did so because he felt that the public had the right to know their government's decisions and actions in Vietnam. Although the government maintained that publishing the documents—which were classified as "Top Secret"—was endangering national security, Ellsberg said that, in his opinion, publishing them did not create such a danger.
   Do you think:

   a) that he had the right to decide whether or not he was endangering national security?
   b) that he had the right to steal the documents and give them to a newspaper for publication?
   c) that the public has a right to know everything that the government does?

By extension, do you think:

   a) that the public has the right to know everything about the financial status of a person running for office?

146   KATHARINE GRAHAM

    b) that the public should know the private life of public figures?
    c) that the public should know the physical condition of public figures?

2. Do you think that the *Times* should have accepted and published the Pentagon Papers?

Reading
The Press after Watergate

> What do you expect to find in an article with such a title? In what ways could the Watergate affair affect the press?
> Skim the text: What journalistic qualities are mentioned?
> What part of the article gives an anecdote to serve as example?

In the spring of 1974 a group of young Republican men and women came to the *Washington Post* for a tour of the building and a meeting with members of the Board. Katharine Graham, Ben Bradlee and a few other members were present. The visitors, obviously antagonistic, asked pointed questions and listened, unsmiling, to the answers (perhaps too complacent and self-assured) that were given to them. Before leaving the room, a young man remarked somberly: "I think you are very powerful." Katharine, after a brief moment of silence, answered slowly: "It may be that the press has too much power. Yes, Watergate brought down a president, and that was too much power."

A year or so later, speaking to the Magazine Publishers Association, Mrs. Graham went back to the subject and expressed to her colleagues her concern about the transformation of the role of the press. Watergate, she told them, had done great harm to the profession because "the manner in which the stories of corruption and misuse of power unfolded made the press too much a party of the events, too much an actor in the drama which was played out. Some individuals became celebrities, and the whole profession became regarded in some quarters as heroic. That is an unnatural role. . . . Our job is to relate what's happening, as fairly and completely as we can. . . . We may have acquired some tendency toward overinvolvement that we'd better overcome. . . . Nor should too much be asked of us. We are not prosecutors, judges, and legislators—or cheerleaders—and we should never be."

At about the same time, several months after President Nixon's resignation, some of the most thoughtful journalists had already reflected upon this matter of the changing role of the press. Many were concerned also about a topic that Katharine Graham had not addressed in her speech: the question of journalistic ethics—the qualities of integrity, fairness, and responsibility that had always been the basis of the public's trust in their newspapers. Except for scandal sheets and some gossip columns, the press has long recognized that it needs to be trusted by its readers and, generally speaking, it has done its best to deserve this trust. Occasionally a senior journalist, reminiscing, writes about the stern training that he received, as a young reporter, from his first editor; how strenuously he had to prove that he was reporting the truth and nothing but the truth, and how he had to give his boss the identity of his sources of information.

But in 1974 it seemed that Watergate had done away with these honorable traditions. Woodward and Bernstein had not stopped in their hot chase to consider if they were conducting it with all due fairness and objectivity. They were like sleuths tracking undoubted criminals. Neither did they bother to identify their informants to their editors. A great deal of their discoveries had been due to the assistance of a mysterious figure—known as "Deep Throat" because of his voice—who (they said) was providing them with precious hints and advice when they were in danger of losing the trail. It is generally suspected that even Bradlee was never told who Deep Throat was. Among the *Post*'s critics, it has been suggested that Deep Throat didn't exist at all and that he was only quoted when Woodward and Bernstein wanted to publish unverified stories.

Woodward and Bernstein were highly honored, however, for their uncovering of the scandal and for their relentless pursuit of subsequent wrongdoings. The sale of their book made millionaires of them. They were promoted and lionized. Young reporters in every newsroom were burning to follow in their footsteps—and to use their highhanded methods. It was even worse at the *Washington Post,* where competition had always been sharp among reporters, and where the editors goaded them to outdo each other, instead of keeping a critical eye on their production. Throughout the press there was a tendency to smell scandals everywhere and to denounce them, or suggest their existence, without worrying about proofs and without mentioning sources. Nothing much was heard about it until a scandal was discovered that humiliated the *Washington Post* and rocked the foundation of the whole American press.

In September 1980 the *Post* published on its front page the story of eight-year-old Jimmy, a black boy from the Washington ghetto, who (the story went) was being turned into a heroin addict by his mother and her boyfriend, a drug dealer. The author of the story, Janet Cooke, was a talented young reporter of the *Post*. The story of Jimmy not only upset the public, but it prompted the Washington Police Department to conduct a long, thorough, and expensive search for the little boy. When they failed to locate him, the mayor expressed doubt about the truth of Cooke's report. He knew his town, he said, and if Jimmy had existed he would have been found. Even at the *Post,* some members of the staff had reservations[1] about Janet's tale. She refused to give the identity or even the general address of Jimmy's family to anyone at the paper, insisting that the drug dealer had threatened to kill her if she did. When forced to lead an editor into the part of town where Jimmy was supposedly living, she seemed totally unfamiliar with the streets. And some colleagues couldn't help wondering what drug dealer would really inject a child with heroin in the presence of a chic young woman, a total stranger who was—of all things—a newspaper reporter.

The management of the *Post,* however, stood stubbornly by Janet and her sensational story. And nothing, perhaps, would have come of all the suspicions if Janet Cooke had not been awarded a Pulitzer prize for her piece. The publicity that followed was Janet's and the *Post*'s undoing. For she had to provide some biographical information about herself, and it was soon discovered that much of that information was fantasy. Miss Cooke didn't have the college degrees that she was claiming; she had not graduated from Vassar, she had not studied at the French Sorbonne. Faced with her lies, the *Post*'s editors became finally suspicious about the rest of her claims, and, questioned closely at last, Janet had to confess that neither Jimmy nor the dealer were real; she had fabricated the whole story.

Janet Cooke was fired; the *Post* returned the Pulitzer award and apologized to its readers. For several weeks, reporters and publishers across the nation agonized over the damage done to their profession. As they examined themselves, they had to admit some unpleasant truths. They recognized that, while few reporters would make up a false story, they were often guilty of stretching the truth in order to make a dull event more interesting; and when pressed for time, they often had to print facts that they had not checked with all desirable care. Since Watergate, too many newsmen had tended to put sensationalism or entertainment above truthfulness.

Most articles, and many signed by the great names of journalism, concluded with an appeal for a return to high standards and strict adherence to the rules. The press has been so thoroughly shaken that the policies are likely to be revised and the standards tightened in all newsrooms; and editors will again make it their business to scrutinize suspicious sources. Even so, it will probably take the public some time to regain complete trust in its newspapers.

Understanding the Text

1. What was Katharine Graham talking about when she said that Watergate had changed the role of the press?
2. What qualities have been traditional among serious journalists?

---

[1]to have reservations—to have unexpressed doubts.

3. What was wrong with the way Woodward and Bernstein conducted their investigation of the Watergate incident?
4. What was the repercussion of their success on other reporters?
5. Who was to blame in the Janet Cooke affair?
6. Would it be right to say that the Janet Cooke affair has had good and bad consequences?

Interpreting Public Opinion Polls

A survey made by the Gallup Organization for *Newsweek* appeared in the May 4, 1981 issue of that magazine. The poll listed the answers of 760 people to the following question:

A. *How much of what you can hear and read in news media can you believe?*

Answers:	I believe all of it	I believe most of it	I believe some of it	I believe very little of it
	5 %	35 %	52 %	9 %

1. Do most of the people questioned have a fairly good opinion of the press, or a rather bad opinion?
2. What percentage believes *at least* most of what they read?
3. Take a survey of the opinions of the classroom and put the percentage results under each figure in the table. How do they compare?*
4. Do you think that questioning 760 people gives a fair idea of the public's opinion?

The same survey also included the following question and results:

B. *How would you rate the honesty and ethical standards of people in these different fields?*

Percentage of People Who Say:	High	Average	Low
(Fields)	%	%	%
Clergy	71	22	4
Physicians	58	35	6
Police	52	37	9
Journalists	33	44	13
Business executives	31	49	15
Congressmen	16	44	34
Advertising executives	12	45	33

1. What do you think of the ranking of journalists in this survey? Is it better or worse than you expected?
2. According to the survey, how many people feel that journalist's standards are at least reasonably good?
3. What kind of opinion do most people have of their congressmen?
4. Are you surprised by the opinion that people have of advertising executives? Why? Find the percentage of answers to the same question ("How do you rate the people in the seven given fields?") among the students of the class.

A Summary (Scanning exercise)

On a separate sheet, write a brief but complete summary of the Janet Cooke story, including the few facts stated below. (Note: The lines do not necessarily indicate the number of facts needed to make the story understandable.)

Janet Cooke was a young reporter of the Washington Post.
In 1980, she _____

_____

Unfortunately, Janet was awarded a Pulitzer prize for her article.

The editors, becoming suspicious, _____

Topics for Discussion

1. Suppose that the story of Jimmy had been true; what should the journalist have done—write the story or alert the police to save the boy? Have you ever seen photos in newspapers that made you wonder what happened next to the person or the animal photographed?
2. If you were editor of a newspaper, would you hire Janet Cooke and give her another chance? If you were Janet Cooke, what would you do now?
3. After the Janet Cooke scandal, author James Michener (himself a Pulitzer prize-winner) wrote that "one of the most necessary professions in the world was made to look shoddy (bad)." Is journalism one of the most necessary professions in the world?
4. Should reporters be forced to reveal their sources, or should they be allowed to keep them confidential if that's the only way to get a story? Should the papers reveal their sources to the public or, in certain cases,

to the government or the police—or would this be an unacceptable limitation of the freedom of the press?
5. Is a journalist entitled to stretch the truth to make a dull story more exciting?
6. After reading this chapter, are you more, or less, interested in reading newspapers?

Walter Cronkite

Introduction

The Vocabulary of Television

Of the three media—press, radio and TV—television is not only the most recent but also the most influential and the most dangerous, because of the power of the image, and also because it reaches portions of the population—children, for instance—that are very impressionable.

Three large networks dominate U.S. television: the Columbia Broadcasting System (CBS), the National Broadcasting System (NBC) and the American Broadcasting System (ABC). NBC, which started in 1927 as a subsidiary of the Radio Corporation of America and enjoyed the financial backing of its parent company, established itself as the dominant network at first. It actually ran two networks until 1941, when the Justice Department enjoined it to sell one of them—which continued as an independent network under the name of ABC.

CBS, created in 1928, has been in fierce competition with NBC from the start.

All three networks rent or provide, at no cost, most of their programs to their affiliate local stations throughout the country. The foremost goal for any program is to attract the largest audience and therefore the largest number of advertisers willing to sponsor the show. The popularity of a show is judged by its ratings, that is, the percentage of the public that have watched it. Several organizations specialize in determining ratings, the most widely known being the A. C. Nielsen Company.

Each network presents several newscasts. Brief bulletins are read at fixed hours by an announcer, or sometimes by the top man of the news department, the anchorman in charge of the main news programs. The anchorman is an American institution. His role is to coordinate the work of the various members of the news department—reporters, writers, foreign correspondents, and photographers—and to pick out, among the events of the day, those that strike him as most important or interesting. Most anchormen do not limit their role to delivering the news, but analyze and comment on it. A good journalist like Walter Cronkite prepares the text that he wants to deliver to his public; but he is perfectly able to ad-lib without preparation at all if some last minute scoop arrives while he is in front of the cameras.

Looking Ahead

- A 1983 poll revealed that 64 percent of Americans cite television as their main source of news. Do you think that TV is a better information medium than the press? Which of the two media has the stronger impact?
- What do you think of the television news programs that you have seen?

- Are news programs different in countries other than the United States that you know?
- If you are not familiar with American television, describe the news programs that you see in your own country—what do you consider good, and bad, about them?
- Read the following two passages about Walter Cronkite's retirement in March 1981.

"Tonight, Walter Cronkite enters semi-retirement and leaves the CBS Evening News. The Republic may endure, but our national fabric will surely strain with the weight of the loss.

Farewell, avuncular Cronkite, Good night, sweet Uncle Walter.

Wait a minute, here. Who is this guy Cronkite and how did he come to be my uncle?

By being there, mostly. Oh, Cronkite is cooly professional, pleasant enough to behold, classically American in his values and sense of decency and right and all that. He's energetic, hardworking and he has a swell[1] voice.

But most of all, Cronkite is there.

Walter Cronkite's mustachioed mug[2] has been omnipresent during the entire lifetime of nearly half this country's population. Walter Cronkite has been before the nation as an anchor type, in one format or another, since 1951, when he hosted a show called "Open Hearing," a weekly CBS documentary series.

In these thirty years, America has been to war a couple of times, to the brink[3] a couple more, and has been jarred by social and technological revolution.

And Cronkite was always there, telling the survivors just what they had survived. Through some cosmic[4] connection having, I think as much to do with Cronkite's ubiquity[5] as anything else, America has just come to associate making it through another day with the fellow who stamped it "official" on the "Evening News."[6]"

"As it inevitably must, the time has come, and Walter Cronkite is retiring as the anchorman for the CBS Evening News—a position with which he has been identified in the public eye for many years. Although his replacement has been selected, no one will be able to fill the void created by the departure of this highly respected and beloved journalist who has reported so much of our national history for the last three decades.

Although he had been seen on a number of weekly television programs

---

[1] swell—colloquial for "fine," "nice."
[2] mug—slang for "face."
[3] the brink—the edge.
[4] cosmic—vast, universal.
[5] ubiquity—the faculty of being in many places at the same time.
[6] By Peter J. Boyer for the Associated Press, 1981.

previously and was already recognized as an eminent journalist, it is Cronkite's coverage of the 1952 conventions that brought him definitely to a national prominence in which he has remained through the years. With his fatherly appearance, his straightforward, undramatic delivery and his flat midwestern accent, he was a figure of integrity for his millions of viewers.

Cronkite had come through the hardest school of journalism—working long hours as a reporter for the United Press in Kansas City, when the pay was low and prestige nonexistent. To an almost unique degree he was admired by the public and by his colleagues in the press, the radio and the television—a remarkable achievement in that harshly critical profession."

Questions

1. What is the main idea of the first article?
2. Compare the tone of the two passages; are they equally friendly and serious? Which one is the most informal, and which words or expressions can you quote as examples of informality?
3. One of the articles was written "tongue-in-cheek." What jokes can you find in it?
4. What can you infer from "his flat midwestern accent" in the second article concerning (a) Cronkite, and (b) the American language?
5. Make two lists of the key words in the two articles and compare them; do they give you a different image of Walter Cronkite or the same one? Basically, what have you learned about Walter Cronkite from these two short passages?

Logical Reasoning—Connectors

Complete each of the sentences below with the most suitable connector from the list.

1. _____ he had been retired for over two years, Walter Cronkite was still an important figure in November 1983, _____ Linda Sanders interviewed him for the *Saturday Review*.
2. In the course of the interview, Cronkite said that he would not be successful _____ he were just starting his career now, _____ he was not pretty enough.
3. Cronkite obviously thought that a young journalist doesn't have a chance nowadays _____ he or she is attractive and young.
4. _____ to become an anchorman or anchorwoman, one also has to have "style," _____ in Cronkite's generation it was more important to have talent and experience.
5. Cronkite told Linda Sanders that years ago aspiring newsmen would have taken courses in journalism, history, and international affairs _____ to understand and analyze better the complex events that they would have to report.

6. They studied their trade, _____ today's aspiring journalists seem more eager to study "Make-up I and II" and "Trench Coat I and II."
7. _____ they start their career with no real feel for the world that they are about to report.
8. The new generation of journalists is only concerned about looking smart, _____ of course there are exceptions.

although	in order to	when
as a consequence	so as	whereas
because	unless	while
if		

Cultural Notes for Profile, Part Two

Before a <u>presidential election</u>, each of the two major political parties holds a convention, in the course of which the party delegates from the fifty states choose the candidate who seems to have the best chance of winning the election. The conventions are televised, one or two anchormen of each network following and explaining what is happening at the convention—and behind the scenes if they can.

The three networks strive to provide the best coverage and to get the best ratings. Election night is also the object of full coverage and of strong competition among the networks.

Profile
Part One

Born November 4, 1916

Skim the text to find out the answers to the following questions:
- What question does the first paragraph suggest?
- How much education and journalistic training did Walter Cronkite have when he went to work?
- Where was he during World War II?
- Did Cronkite go directly from wire-service journalism to television?

"Extraordinary!" remarked Eric Sevareid when Walter Cronkite retired in March of 1981. "Walter has more publicity and attention leaving the job than Carter had leaving the Presidency!" It was extraordinary perhaps, but hardly surprising, for in the last fifteen years of his long career Cronkite had come to enjoy an eminence and popularity seldom known before in the world of televised journalism. There had been other respected reporters, of course; Sevareid was one of them, and so was the elegant, scholarly, and outspoken Edward R. Murrow, for years the star commentator of CBS. Neither one, however, had ever been called "Uncle Eric" or "Uncle Ed" by their public.

"Uncle Walter!" How do you become the uncle of 235 million people? "By being there long enough," said Peter J. Boyer of Associated Press. Others have mentioned Cronkite's honest face, his unruffled, soothing manner, his deep mellow voice, or his distinguished white hair. But durability and appearance are not enough to explain the affectionate loyalty displayed by Cronkite's viewers. Surely one can't ignore the other factors that made Cronkite what he was—his years of experience as wire-service reporter, radio announcer, and war correspondent; his willingness to devote more time and effort than his competitors to any subject; his talent for clarifying the most complicated issue; and the flair he had for making his shows memorable and exciting, a flair born perhaps from his early experience in the theater. Uncle Walter was an accomplished actor. In her book *The Evening Stars,* Barbara Matusow describes Cronkite as he appeared at the beginning of his special on the Vietnam war in 1968. He was seen arriving in a Jeep, "his flak jacket unbuttoned at the neck, his helmet untied and slightly askew," and jumping off to start his presentation in a breathless voice. The audience couldn't help feeling that he had just left the scene of operations to talk to them. It was good acting, and Cronkite looked absolutely believable in a scene that might have been ridiculous with a less convincing performer. Needless to say, the report so dramatically introduced was thoroughly researched and masterfully delivered.

Someone said once that no matter how frightening the news may be on the evening newscast, Cronkite's viewers went to bed with the comfortable feeling that he would somehow keep the world turning and at peace until morning. It was Cronkite's great attribute to look completely trustworthy and reassuring to his enormous audience of Middle Americans, that great body of conservative, responsible, not-particularly-intellectual people who, from the Alleghenies to the Sierras, constitute the backbone of the nation. They loved and trusted him because he looked like one of them; and for all his worldly experience and knowledge, he was one of them indeed.

Cronkite's father, a dentist in St. Joseph, Missouri, had moved his family to Kansas City shortly after Walter was born. Ten years later the Cronkites moved to Houston, Texas. As described by Cronkite himself, his childhood was "absolutely normal. I dug caves, built tree houses, took piano lessons, did all the things an average kid[1] does." He was a good boy; he made good grades in school, played saxophone in the band and gave no problems to his parents. He stopped being an exemplary son when he went to college. The problem was that Walter, full of life and fun, found many things to do

---

[1] a kid—slang for "a boy."

that were more interesting than the courses at the University of Texas—
things like dancing, acting with the local theater group, writing articles for
the campus paper, and working part-time for the *Houston Post* and the
United Press bureau. Without planning for it, Cronkite had already discovered his lifework. There was something in the pressure and challenge of
news gathering that thrilled him, so much so that when he was offered a
full-time job with the *Houston Post* in his second year, he didn't have the
heart to pass up the opportunity. And since he was likely to flunk[2] the university exams, for which he had not had time to prepare, he chose the wisest
course of action—he left the university without taking them.

Cronkite never had cause to regret his decision. Journalism had clearly
been the right choice for him. From the *Houston Post* he went to work for
UP in 1937 and spent two happy years digging up stories, pursuing leads,
and writing capsule reports. Money being in short supply, he worked on
the side as sports announcer for a radio station. From both ventures he
gained the kind of experience that comes from trials and errors and occasional disasters—all painful at times, but infinitely valuable. It was a great
education and a happy one.

The only drawback to Cronkite's early years in journalism was the low
pay, a factor that he never overlooked. To improve his income, he made in
1938 his one and only incursion in a nonjournalistic field. That year he
agreed to leave UP to become regional traffic director and public relations
director of Braniff Airlines. The episode would have little interest if it were
not for the fact that Cronkite developed a lifelong passion for aviation and
for flying machines of any type.[3] The devotion eventually had an impact
on the American public when anchorman Cronkite, at the height of his
career, provided them with enthusiastic coverage of the U.S. Space Program, from the first manned flights of the 1960s to the missions of the
space shuttle in 1977. He spent so much time researching the subject at
Cape Canaveral that he was nicknamed "the eighth astronaut" by the personnel of the base.

Cronkite never liked the public relations part of his job at Braniff. He left
the company in 1939 to return to his old wire service, which in the interval
had become United Press International (UPI). In all his career, this was
the type of work that Cronkite liked best: collecting the facts—all the facts;
checking and rechecking them for perfect accuracy, and then having the
joy of breaking the story *before anyone else*. To the day he retired, Cronkite
was driven by a need to be first with the news—a need that seemed obsessive to his more relaxed colleagues. He usually succeeded, for he had a

---

[2] to flunk—slang for "to fail."
[3] Cronkite was strongly attracted by anything that involved adventure, speed and danger. For
years his favorite hobby was taking part in automobile races. He finally gave up racing for
the sake of his wife's peace of mind, and took up sailing instead—hardly an improvement
for Mrs. Cronkite, who felt obliged to sail with him in spite of her tendency to seasickness.

good nose for stories and pursued all leads, however weak, as long and as hard as was necessary to get to the core of the matter.

By 1942 Cronkite was so highly regarded at UPI that the company gave him the top assignment available at the time—covering the American Eighth Air Force in England. He made the most of it, flying risky missions and getting fresh interviews from returning pilots. Always intent on beating the competition, he contrived to be taken over Germany for a special night mission, from which he brought a first-hand report about bombing and air pursuits. "American Flying Fortresses have just come back from an assignment to hell," began one of his articles, "a hell 26,000 feet above Earth . . ." Some of his colleagues found the piece overly dramatic, but the public found it fascinating. It was later included in the anthology *A Treasury of Great War Reporting*.

By the end of the war, Cronkite had acquired a reputation for courage and professionalism that attracted the attention of Edward R. Murrow. Murrow offered Walter a place on his team of brilliant newsmen, with a weekly salary of $125, plus the payment of additional fees. Cronkite didn't know at the time that these fees could in fact triple his income, but since he was making a meager $67 at UPI, the offer was tempting anyway. He accepted on the spot, and was immediately confronted by a counteroffer from UPI—the true proof of his worth, since UPI was famous in the journalistic community for its reluctance to pay good salaries—and Cronkite, always loyal, chose to remain where he was.

UPI again gave him its choice assignments, first as observer at the Nuremberg trials of the Nazi leaders, and then as correspondent in Moscow. The Moscow position, although deficient in the matter of high living and even of simple comfort, was a most prestigious one. It proved disappointing, nevertheless, because of the parsimony of the company. Conkite had put up with the discomfort and the frustrations; but when UPI suggested that he buy a bicycle to replace the bureau's broken-down automobile, he rebelled and demanded to be brought home on leave. Although they granted his wish, the directors refused to raise Cronkite's salary on the ground that he was already at the top of their salary scale. He was good, they allowed, but they simply couldn't afford to pay more.

Fully conscious that he was indeed "very good," Cronkite concluded that the time had come to move on. The year was 1948. Since 1940, Walter had been married to a former reporter, Mary Elizabeth Maxwell, who was expecting their first child. While the Cronkites were quietly enjoying their leave in Kansas City, Walter took advantage of this visit to his hometown, and renewed old friendships. One of his friends, Karl Koerper, happened to be the owner of several radio stations, including Kansas City's KMCB, a CBS affiliate. Over lunch, Cronkite convinced Koerper that his radio news programs needed improvement in length as well as in content if they were to compete with the written press. The upshot of the conversation was that

Cronkite was hired as the station's correspondent in Washington, at the splendid salary of $200 a week.

It was a brave plunge into unfamiliar waters. Radio news was not taken seriously at the time. An insignificant item on the air (fifteen minutes or so in the evening), the news programs consisted of a brief summary, read by one of the announcers. It was a vicious circle: news programs couldn't attract adequate sponsors because of their small audience, and the stations couldn't make the programs more attractive for lack of funds. Radio reporters had no prestige whatsoever, and in the eyes of his colleagues of the written press, it was rather demeaning for a man of Cronkite's status and experience to accept such a position. Cronkite, however, was very happy with his new job. The pay was good, and he enjoyed the excitement of working in Washington, in the center of things. Furthermore, he was thinking with keen anticipation of the day when he might be able to return to Kansas City as Director of KMBC.

This reasonable and surprisingly modest dream for a man of Cronkite's drive and ambition collapsed in 1950 when Cronkite and television discovered each other. A war had started in Korea, and once again Edward Murrow appeared on the scene to ask Cronkite if he would be willing to cover it for CBS. Cronkite, delighted at the prospect of being a war correspondent again, accepted at once. But as he was idly waiting for transportation to Seoul, CBS, which had just acquired a television station in Washington, suggested that he take advantage of his temporary leisure to present a five-minute daily report about the Korean operations. For old UPI writer Cronkite, compressing the war news in brief capsules was child's play, but as usual he prepared his show thoroughly, finding his own good sources of information in the Pentagon, and producing an accurate, up-to-the-minute, and brilliant presentation. With no prepared script and nothing more complicated than a blackboard and a piece of chalk, he instantly established himself a master of televised reporting. He looked calm, benign, and commanding, and he exuded professionalism—a rare commodity in the world of television, which was still plagued with uncertainty and inexperience. After two days, CBS asked Cronkite to take over the six o'clock news at the Washington affiliate, and shortly afterwards he inherited the eleven o'clock newscast as well. Within a week the early news program had found a sponsor.

Cronkite never made it to Korea. Having done too good a job, he just remained in front of the CBS cameras. Besides the news about Korea, he started a documentary series in 1951, and found himself in 1952 in charge of the plum assignment of the year, the coverage of the presidential elections. Cronkite gave such a spectacular performance at the first convention that CBS's arch rival, NBC, which had always received the highest ratings, came in a poor second this time. Cronkite's television career was launched for good.

The 1952 presidential campaign, which gave the decisive impetus to Walter Cronkite's career, also marked the dawn of TV's coverage of news and public events. Except during World War II, when everyone was anxious to get the latest bit of news in a hurry, televised news programs had been neglected by the public and consequently by the networks. Both CBS and NBC waited until 1948 to launch their first evening news program, a fifteen-minute spot presented by a radio-newscaster reassigned to the new medium. The whole staff of the news department consisted of only one or two employees in addition to the announcer, who was not yet known as an anchorman, although he was occasionally described as "anchoring" the show. His role was merely to read the report that was given to him just before air time; to look calm under all circumstances; and to be able to ad-lib when part of the information had not arrived before the show—a frequent mishap, since the different offices of the network were scattered all over town, with the writers working in an office distant from the studio. Even the gathering of the news left much to be desired. NBC, the wealthiest and best organized network, had only three cameramen of its own; CBS made do with one man.

In the opinion of seasoned journalists, including the adventurous ones who, like Cronkite, had cast their lot with a network, the only serious way to report events was still through the printed press. Radio didn't measure up, and television was much too slow to compete. The cumbersome equipment couldn't be rushed to the scene of an event at a moment's notice or cover several distant happenings, trailing its cameras and cables behind its tiny crew. Besides, television didn't have the time to indulge in analysis and commentaries to compete with the newspaper's editorials.

The public, however, was getting excited about the entertaining new medium, and as the number of television sets reached 32 million, in 1954, the advertising agencies' interest grew in proportion. In the White House, President Eisenhower began to present his ideas to the nation via television. Then came the 1960 election campaign and the famous televised debates between candidates John F. Kennedy and Richard M. Nixon, which demonstrated to the last doubters the power of televised public affairs shows. That year the electorate followed the whole campaign on television screens, with passionate interest, and there is no doubt that Kennedy's victory was due in part to his superiority in front of the cameras. As president, Kennedy continued to make skillful use of television. The medium, meanwhile, had made tremendous technological progress; the equipment had improved, crews were larger, and the two great networks had hired a score of first-class reporters, experienced anchormen, and technicians. The members of the written press covering the White House were soon heard to complain that they were becoming second-class members of the profession. The young president, they thought, was finding television exciting.

So were his countrymen, who by 1960 owned 60 million sets, compared to 4 million in 1950. Television had come of age. And Walter Cronkite, already firmly established in the new medium, was on his way to becoming one of the dominant figures of televised journalism.

Understanding the Text

1. What has the career of Walter Cronkite taught you about the history of televised news programs:
   a) Why was it so remarkable that Cronkite's first news show found a sponsor?
   b) Why was it more difficult for television than for the press to cover the news?
   c) What factors contributed to making the late 1950s (and 1960 in particular) a turning point in the history of television?
   d) Why couldn't announcers analyze the news in the early programs?
2. What made Walter Cronkite so good?
3. Was he particularly well educated? How did he learn journalism?
4. Did Cronkite get all of his experience in the same medium?
5. How did he happen to start in television?
6. Who was Edward R. Murrow, and why is he mentioned several times?
7. What really established Cronkite at CBS in 1952?
8. Why is it interesting to note Cronkite's position at Braniff Airlines?

Scanning for Details

1. Did Cronkite go to England to cover the war in 1941, 1943, or 1942?
2. Was his wife's name Betty Maxwell, Betty Campbell or Betsy Maxwell?
3. Did Cronkite work for Kansas City's KMBC, KCMB, or KBMC?
4. Did he go to work for Braniff in 1936, 1938, or 1934?
5. What was the name of the director of the Kansas City radio station?
6. Who said that Cronkite became "Uncle Walter" by being on television for so long?
7. What did Cronkite write about the war mission: "American Flying Fortresses _____ above the Earth."
8. How many television sets were in the U.S. in 1954?
9. How does the author describe "Middle Americans"?

Vocabulary

Complete each of the following sentences with the best word from the list below (which includes more words than necessary). Be sure to make all necessary adjustments to articles, verbs, and nouns.

EDWARD R. MURROW, A _____ (BRIEF) PORTRAIT

Edward R. Murrow, the star reporter of CBS in the 1950s, didn't have the _____ (kind), _____ (uncle's) appearance that was one of Cronkite's appealing qualities for his public. Murrow's appeal was more difficult to define: although he was the son of a farmer in the Middle West, Murrow looked distinguished and _____ (worldly). He had a _____ (full of authority) presence. In the 1950s he was one of the few journalists who believed that televised _____ (news programs) would some day be the main source of information for Americans. He was not unaware of television's _____ (disadvantages): the lack of mobility, the difficulty of moving _____ (heavy and awkward) material, etc. Like Cronkite, Murrow could _____ (talk without preparation) easily. And like Cronkite he had a great _____ (natural ability) for the small details that add drama and interest to a report. Murrow was for years the _____ (main support) of the CBS news programs. A _____ (model) newsman himself, he was also a great discoverer of talents, and he gathered around him a group of young men who are the important _____ (news gatherers) and _____ (news explainers) of today, such as Eric Sevareid and Howard K. Smith.

newscast	benign	exemplary
accomplished	capsule	durability
to demean	backbone	to flunk
documentary	avuncular	commentator
debate	ad lib	cumbersome
flair	commanding	electorate
sophisticated	drawback	reporter

Did You Guess Right?

line 25　Cronkite's helmet was untied and slightly askew.
　　　　What is likely to be wrong with a helmet that is untied and worn in a fast-moving Jeep?
line 109　UPI was famous for its parsimony.
　　　　From the context, does it mean that it was
　　　　a) too generous
　　　　b) not generous enough?
line 113　Moscow was deficient in the matter of high living.
　　　　a) it had an excess of it
　　　　b) it didn't have enough of it
line 131　Cronkite met a friend and the upshot of their conversation was that Cronkite was hired as correspondent for the friend's radio station. Upshot must mean:
　　　　a) the main topic
　　　　b) the sad consequence
　　　　c) the result

PROFILE 165

line 162   Cronkite <u>exuded</u> professionalism.
    a) he lacked professionalism
    b) he showed professionalism
    c) he condemned professionalism

line 171   Cronkite was given the <u>plum assignment</u> of the year. From the context do you infer that the <u>plum assignment</u> is a good or a bad one?

line 176   The presidential campaign gave the decisive <u>impetus</u> to Cronkite's career.
    a) did it push it forward?
    b) did it stop it?

The Right Order

Put the following statements in the right chronological order to make a coherent story.

— As a young man, Walter Cronkite took a job as radio sports announcer in Oklahoma City.

— However, he was given a second chance.

— Unfortunately nothing worked.

— This time he did very well and later became a splendid sports reporter.

— He had been hired to announce Oklahoma University's football games.

— The electric board didn't work.

— Since he didn't even know the names of the players, he organized a system that he considered pretty good.

— But Cronkite had never covered a football game in his life.

— The watchers didn't follow the game.

— Cronkite expected to get fired.

— The system consisted in having "watchers" observe the game, pushing buttons on an electric board to indicate who had the ball, who was gaining, who was losing, etc.

— Cronkite, who didn't even have a list of players, made the most terrible report in the history of football.

The Main Idea

Check the statement in each group that best expresses the essential idea of each paragraph.

Par. 10   a) Moscow was a prestigious but not a pleasant assignment.

        b) Although he had the best assignment, Cronkite was so displeased with the working conditions that he went back home.
        c) After the war, Cronkite was sent to Nuremberg, then to Moscow.

Par. 11   a) Cronkite managed to get a fine job as a radio station correspondent.
        b) Cronkite knew the owner of Kansas City's radio station.
        c) In 1948 Cronkite and his wife were expecting their first child.

Par. 12   a) Radio news was not taken seriously at the time.
        b) Cronkite was hoping to end up director of KMCB.
        c) Although radio news had no prestige, Cronkite was pleased with his new job.

Par. 13   a) In 1951, CBS had just acquired a television station in Washington, D.C.
        b) As soon as he appeared on television, Cronkite proved so good that CBS kept him there.
        c) After accepting an assignment to cover the war in Korea, Cronkite waited for transportation to Seoul.

Par. 14   a) Cronkite covered the presidential election of 1952.
        b) Cronkite never made it to Korea.
        c) The coverage of the 1952 presidential elections was the real start of Cronkite's TV career.

Par. 15   What is the main idea of this paragraph?

Topics for Discussion

1. In what way has television transformed political campaigns? Is it good or bad?
2. What do you think of candidates debating the issues on television:
   a) Do such debates help the candidates present their ideas to the public?
   b) Can you judge the true worth of candidates by the way they perform on television?
   c) What would you think of a candidate who refused to appear on television?
   d) Do the debates serve the public interest?
3. The presidential elections are held every four years, and the campaign gets under way at least one year before the election's date. The president can serve only two terms.
       What are the advantages and disadvantages of four-year terms? Would it be better to elect a president for a longer but single term?

4. Would it be better not to replace certain important members of the Cabinet every time the president changes?
5. Are elections held differently in countries other than the United States that you know?

Profile
Part Two

What do we have left to learn about Walter Cronkite? What would you like to learn? Skim the text to find whether or not you are going to learn it.

Does the text give any information on Walter Cronkite's private life?

Will you find more information about Cronkite's Special about the war in Vietnam? Where?

Is Cronkite still alive and who is replacing him?

From 1952 to the early seventies, Cronkite remained in the eye of the public with a succession of documentaries, such as "Man of the Week" or "It's News to Me." Most of the shows turned around current events or historical scenes, with the exception of "Air Power," produced with the help of the Air Force and aired from 1956 to 1958, and a series devoted to the wonders of the modern world, "The Twentieth Century," which lasted until 1970, when Cronkite was reaching the top of his career.

The preparation of "It's News To Me," which was produced in New York, forced the Cronkites to move to the city in 1954. This was no hardship for Walter, who thoroughly enjoyed all the pleasures available in a big city, including jazz, dancing (he was a splendid dancer), and night life. In 1958 the Cronkites bought a house in upper Manhattan, and there their three children—Nancy, Kathleen and Walter, Jr.—were brought up. A devoted family man, Walter made a big effort to spend time with his son and daughters, an endeavor that became increasingly arduous as time went by and his obligations multiplied. His very celebrity was a source of concern. Once in a while, a letter would be found in the mail, threatening to kidnap one of the children. The young Cronkites were never told, but they were sharp enough to notice the men in trenchcoats who kept watch on the house and who followed them, not too discreetly, wherever they went.

By 1962, NBC was ahead of CBS in the ratings; this triumph was due to the tremendous popularity of a witty, exciting newscast coanchored by Chet Huntley and David Brinkley. CBS was, of course, intent on fighting back, and with this goal in mind, the network's directors decided to replace their own anchorman, the dependable but unspectacular Douglas Edwards. There was, however, some hesitation at the top about the choice of a replacement. To the directors, Cronkite seemed to be the perfect man to throw against the Huntley-Brinkley team; he had enough authority and wit to compete with them, and he was unlikely to get into controversial matters, as Ed Murrow and his friends were wont to do. But Murrow, still influential at CBS, had another candidate. Although he had been instrumental in bringing Cronkite to the network, the enormous success of his protege had been a bit of a surprise for him. To Murrow, who saw current events as matter for solemn reflection and occasionally for crusades, it was disturbing to watch an experienced newsman like Cronkite, solely concerned with reporting the news as he had learned to do it at UPI—promptly, simply, and accurately, without philosophizing about the state of the world. While he respected Cronkite's painstaking research of the facts and his ability to give his audience an intelligent, well-digested summary, Murrow never managed to regard Cronkite as a top-notch journalist. Nobody on his team had ever been satisfied with simply reporting the news.

Despite Murrow's recommendation to the contrary, Cronkite was chosen to replace Edwards. The future was to prove that the powers at CBS had made the right choice, but Cronkite didn't reach his position as Star of the News overnight. Neither was he given at the start the amount of control over the show that he would ultimately enjoy. There were ups and downs at first. Cronkite's darkest hour came at the Republican convention of 1964, when the ratings disclosed that Huntley-Brinkey had attracted 55 percent of the viewers, against 30 percent for Cronkite and 15 percent for ABC. After this disaster, the directors decided to have the Democratic convention covered by two of CBS's best reporters, Roger Mudd and Robert Trout. Cronkite, deeply wounded but ever-loyal, refrained from complaining publicly against his network, although he did entertain for a moment the notion of going over to the other side. Fortunately for him and for CBS, Mudd and Trout, excellent journalists but unused to convention coverage, failed entirely; the ratings showed that 86 percent of the audience had chosen to watch NBC. Cronkite, probably not too displeased with his network's discomfiture, was reinstated at his anchorman's desk in time to cover election night. Having regained his balance, he was able then to demonstrate afresh his superiority; this time, NBC didn't win, and there was no more question of replacing Cronkite in front of the cameras for an event of any magnitude. It must have been obvious to the directors of CBS that Cronkite was by far the news department's best asset—and also that he would never again put up with the kind of treatment that he had received after the Republican convention. From then on, he was treated like the star he was.

Walter Cronkite remained CBS's King of the News for the seventeen years that were to pass until his retirement, and during that time CBS overtook and definitely surpassed NBC in the ratings. Cronkite's stubborn perfectionism had much to do with the reversal of positions. Kind and avuncular as he may have appeared to his loving audience, Cronkite was a demanding taskmaster—they called him "The Boss" behind his back in the department. An overtime worker himself, he expected his staff to labor with the same passion that he devoted to his work. It was particularly trying for the writers who brought him a piece of copy; Cronkite would scrutinize it, demanding justification for each item until he was certain that it had been checked through, and that every corner of the topic had been covered. Although he seldom did any writing himself, he was the best editor in the business. To back him properly, CBS hired excellent writers, as well as a number of first-class reporters such as Dan Rather, Harry Reasoner, and Charles Kuralt.

For the last fifteen years of his career, Cronkite was very much in charge of the news department, with the final say on the choice of news stories and complete liberty to make any changes—even at the last minute—that he deemed necessary for the good of the show. Always eager to break the news before his competitors, he didn't hesitate to send his reporters running for a scoop or for clarification moments before air time. It was better to humor him than to bear his wrath if the other networks had a piece of news that he had failed to catch. He always watched NBC's newscast after finishing his own, and blew his top if the rival network came up with a good story. Says Joel Bernstein, a former producer of the news shows: "If NBC came up with something really good, you felt it. You felt the breathing down the hall, and you looked at your watch, knowing that in five seconds he would be there, demanding to know why *we* didn't have that."

The public learned over the years to trust him entirely and to look up to him with genuine affection. His prestige and popularity eventually reached the point of being embarrassing. Once he went to a meeting with presidential candidate John Anderson with the intent of interviewing the man. As soon as he appeared, Anderson's supporters forgot about their candidate—they flocked around Cronkite, chanting "Walter! Walter!" to the true star of the moment. Occasionally he used his prestige to bring a problem to the consciousness of his public. The enthusiasm that he felt for the space program stirred up the interest of his fellow Americans, and when he became concerned with the question of environment, his series "Can This World Be Saved?" had a strong impact, not only on his viewers, but on the legislators who launched the Environmental Protection Act in 1970. The organizers of the "Environment Awareness Day," April 22, 1972, made as much as they could of his support, for they could see the increase in the volume of their mail whenever Cronkite mentioned their efforts on the air.

A dramatic demonstration of his influence was given on a more momentous subject, the war in Vietnam. Cronkite was a moderately conservative man and, like most Americans of his age and background, a patriot, entirely supportive of his country and of his government. In the early days of the Vietnam involvement, his attitude remained firmly loyal to the president's policy, and he faithfully reported the data provided by the White House. By 1965 he had become disgusted with the young reporters based in Saigon, who were loudly critical of the American position and who refused to credit any information issued by Washington or by the official circles in Saigon. Cronkite had made a trip to Vietnam in 1962 to see for himself how things were going on, and upon his return he had made a fairly optimistic report of what he had seen. But as the operations dragged on, and the climate of opinion in the country turned from trust to unease, then to suspicion and to revolt, Cronkite became worried. Finally, in 1968, he took it upon himself to return to Saigon for a second look. After visits to the combat zones and a series of talks with soldiers, young officers, and with his old friend General Creighton Abrams, Deputy Commander of the American troops in Vietnam, he returned in a somber mood. His conclusion—that there was no hope for a rapid military solution—distressed him so much that he, always so cautious, so careful to preserve his reputation of impartiality, decided to present his views to the nation. He carefully prepared a special program describing what he had seen, and the appraisal he had been able to form of the situation. At the end of the show he announced gravely: "We should start thinking of getting out." It was the first time in Cronkite's career that his public had heard him express a personal opinion, and they were understandably shaken. David Halberstam wrote in *The Powers That Be*: "Cronkite's reporting did change the balance. It was the first time in American history that a war had been declared over by an anchorman. In Washington [President] Johnson watched and told his press secretary, George Christian, that it was a turning point, that if he had lost Walter Cronkite he had lost Mr. Average American. It solidified his decision not to run again."

Such was the power of Anchorman Walter Cronkite at this point of his career. Cronkite was too decent a man not to be concerned about the influence that his position was giving him. He was careful not to use it more than he had to, but he couldn't always foresee the effect of his actions. In 1972 he found himself making waves again, unintentionally and without pleasure. For some time the *Washington Post* had been publishing bits and pieces of information about the Watergate burglary. Nobody else in the press or in the public seemed to be paying much attention to the story, which was trivial and confusing. Cronkite, just as confused as anyone else, decided to put the fragments together as coherently as he could to give a clearer picture to his audience. The reports he gave on two consecutive nights didn't throw much light on the puzzle, but the mere fact that Walter Cronkite was interested gave the Watergate incident a brand new importance. Suddenly, just because Cronkite was talking about it, it was big news. At the Post, Ben Bradlee, delighted, expressed his gratitude. "After Walter's report . . . the story came out of page A-27 to the front page overnight. . . . It was as if the story had been blessed by the Great White Father." Cronkite was more startled than pleased with it all. But there was not much he could do about it. Like it or not, he had become an institution and a fount of wisdom; he was, according to several surveys, "the most trusted man in the land." Even Secretary of State Henry Kissinger felt that way. When Kissinger was passing through London after a visit to Southern Rhodesia, he didn't feel it improper to reveal to Cronkite the result of his talk to Rhodesia's leader Ian Smith *before* reporting to President Ford.

Some of his friends thought that Cronkite could do much better than reporting the news. Robert F. Kennedy advised him to run for the Senate, and others suggested him as a possible vice-president and running-mate of presidential candidate George McGovern in 1972. Politics, however, didn't attract Cronkite very much. He loved his profession, he loved his job, he enjoyed thoroughly being Walter Cronkite, boss of the CBS news department, with a pleasant $500,000 yearly salary.

Once in a while, he would make noises about his need to slow down, his desire to take time off once in a while to enjoy life and sail his boat. He could perhaps (he said) do the show three times a week and let a younger man take over the other shows in preparation for succeeding him eventually—Roger Mudd would be fine, or Dan Rather. The suggestion remained very vague, and since nobody at CBS was eager to see him go, he was never asked to be more precise. But a time came in 1980 when the new president of the network was faced with the possibility of losing Dan Rather, who was considered one of the most likely candidates to Cronkite's succession if Walter ever made up his mind to go. Rather was a first-class newsman; he had "star quality," and as his contract with CBS was about to expire, both NBC and ABC offered him an anchor job. Rather than losing Dan, the president of CBS went to Cronkite, now sixty-four, to explain the situation and ask Walter to clarify his own plans. Not too happily, Cronkite agreed to retire in a year's time—in early 1981. It was understood that he would remain a part of CBS as a "Special Correspondent," and would present a science series entitled "Universe."

As the deadline approached, Cronkite became increasingly depressed about a retirement that he had not really wished. But he did take leave of his public, on March 9, 1981, with his usual calm and benign dignity. As it turned out, the arrangement with CBS didn't work too well. The "Universe" series was cancelled after a year, much to Cronkite's disappointment, for he had been very keen about the show. Not that he needed an occupation; he was much busier than he had expected, what with narrating TV documentaries, making speeches, writing books about sailing, and granting interviews. His departure had been greeted with an enormous outpouring of love and sadness from his public, and of tributes of admira-

172 WALTER CRONKITE

tion from his colleagues. "For many years now," said Frank Reynolds of ABC, "Walter Cronkite has been a symbol of responsibility in a medium that grew in those years at a sensational pace and might have, except for people like Walter, succumbed to the temptation to be sensational in reporting the news." NBC's John Chancellor agreed. "Walter Cronkite," he said, "is the standard by which anchormen will probably always be measured." The last word about Cronkite's popularity came on the day after the presidential elections of 1984, which Ronald Reagan won overwhelmingly, with a majority of votes in forty-nine of the fifty states. "The only men who could have defeated Reagan," said a commentator, shaking his head, "are Robert Redford and Walter Cronkite."

Understanding the Text

1. What was the great difference between Ed Murrow and Walter Cronkite as newsmen?
2. Did Cronkite ever do poorly on television?
3. What kind of a person was he in private?
4. What was so remarkable about his report on the Vietnam war in 1968?
5. Was President Johnson concerned because he had lost the support of Walter Cronkite personally?
6. What was strange about Kissinger reporting the result of a meeting to Cronkite?
7. Why did Walter Cronkite retire?
8. Did he have political ambitions?

Scanning for Details

1. What important newsmen can you name, besides Walter Cronkite?
2. What did Cronkite say, exactly, about the Vietnam war in 1968?
3. When did George McGovern run for President?
4. What were the ratings for NBC, CBS, and ABC for the coverage of the Republican convention in 1964?
5. Who was George Christian?
6. Was Harry Reasoner at CBS, NBC, or ABC?
7. Whom did Cronkite replace as anchorman of CBS in 1962?
8. Who wrote *The Powers That Be*?

Outlining

Make an outline of Walter Cronkite's career, from his very first job to the last one. You must first skim the text, noting down the various fields in which Cronkite worked and the jobs he held in each field.

PROFILE   173

Walter Cronkite's Career

I. Newspapers _____ (first field)
        Houston Post _____
II. _____ (second field)
   A. _____ (assignments)
   B. _____
   C. _____
   D. _____
III. _____ (third field)
   A. _____ (assignments)
   B. _____
IV. _____ (fourth field)
   A. _____ (assignments)
   B. _____
   C. _____
   D. _____

Vocabulary

For each of the statements below, replace the underlined word or expression with the closest equivalent on the list, which includes more words than necessary. Be sure to make all needed adjustments in articles, nouns, and verbs.

1. In journalism, as in many other careers, the road to the top is very difficult.
2. The children never became seasick on their father's boat, as Mrs. Cronkite was in the habit of doing.
3. Two first-rate journalists were competing for Cronkite's job when he decided to retire.
4. CBS was surprised by Cronkite's embarassment at the Republican convention of 1964.
5. CBS was placed again at the top on election night.
6. To his fans, Cronkite looked like an uncle.
7. The remarks of the secretary of state indicated a complete change in the government's policies in the matter.
8. Most journalists will do almost anything to get a good piece of news.
9. Somebody had made a mistake, and they all knew that Cronkite would be furious.
10. Cronkite was not the kind of man who likes to create disturbances.
11. The president of CBS considered all the factors and made an important decision.
12. At the beginning, the Watergate incident seemed unimportant and confusing.
13. He said that he would like to start again in a new way.

14. The *Washington Post* was <u>partly responsible for</u> the downfall of President Nixon.
15. They did encounter problems of some <u>importance</u>.
16. He is a hard <u>man to work for</u>.

magnitude	arduous	reinstated
taskmaster	scoop	top-notch
deadline	wont	to humor
disturbing	to make waves	ratings
momentous	to blow one's top	discomfiture
trivial	instrumental (in)	reversal
afresh	avuncular	

Facts, Inferences, and Opinions

The text below presents a combination of facts and opinions. Read it carefully to differentiate between the two. As usual, some statements can be understood either way.

A NEW STAR

A few years ago, Kathleen Mary Sullivan was an obscure newscaster in Salt Lake City. She is now a six-figure* coanchor of ABC's "World News This Morning." She is also the most talked-about TV journalist, sometimes in glowing terms, sometimes with a touch of resentment, depending on the age and profession of the speakers. There is nothing there that should surprise her—or us. In any case, one thing is certain: for a young person with practically no reporting experience, her rise is most remarkable.

Ms. Sullivan was first noticed when she was cohosting a late-night report on the 1982 Olympics. Her fresh face and youthful enthusiasm made her look so sensational that she was promoted to some prime-time spots, then to the morning news. At the present time, rumor has it that she might end up coanchoring "World News Tonight" with Peter Jennings.

Ms. Sullivan is indeed a pleasure to watch. Although in her early thirties, she looks like a pretty coed on a California campus. This is not to say that she has no talent to go with her looks. The public has reacted warmly to her approach to the news. Says her producer: "You can relate to her [on the air]. She is able to translate what she is thinking into real communication with the viewer. It's a kind of magic."

Not surprisingly, Kathleen's success is distressing to many of her veteran colleagues. It must surely be irritating to see a lovely young woman climb in one great step to the top of the profession without having been a reporter or a network correspondent. She is neither a

---

*six-figure—in this context, a person with an income in "six figures"—at least $100,000 per year.

good reporter nor a good writer. But she looks good on camera and she is a first-class performer, who keeps cool under pressure.

In an interview given shortly after his retirement, Walter Cronkite deplored the fact that today's newsmen were merely actors without serious journalistic training. Apparently, he was right.

1. What opinions have you found in the text?
2. Did you find statements that could be understood as either facts or opinions?
3. Is there anything in the text that makes you think that:
   a) It was more difficult in the past to make one's way as a journalist?
   b) Ms Sullivan is not an exception in the profession?
4. What does the text suggest about the reasons that make a newscast appealing from the point of view of the public?
5. Which newscast is viewed as more important by the producers, the morning one or the evening one?
6. Has the author seen Kathleen Sullivan on the screen?
7. What can you infer from the story about the way network executives find and "try" their newscasters?

Topics for Discussion

1. Was it proper for Cronkite to make that report on the Vietnam war and to conclude by giving his opinion, as he did?
2. Should television show scenes of violence, combat scenes, and victims of accidents or crimes?
3. Cronkite was asked once not to report terrorist acts, in order to deny the terrorists the publicity that they want. Cronkite refused, offering the following reasons:
   a) If one piece of news is not reported, the public will come to suspect that many other news items are not given.
   b) Who should have the right to decide what is to be covered and what is to be hidden?
   c) On what grounds should the decision be made?
   What do you think of Cronkite's refusal: should terrorist acts be reported as the terrorists wish? Were Cronkite's reasons justified? How would you answer his questions?
4. Walter Cronkite was anxious to be the first to break a news story. "Being first" is almost an obsession with newspapers and television journalists.
   Do you usually notice what newspaper or which newsman has been the first to announce or publish an item of news? Is it important? Would you change newspaper or television station because it failed "to be first"? How do people choose their newspapers and their television news programs?
5. Because of the time difference between the East Coast and the West Coast of the United States (3 hours), it has happened that one of the two candidates for the presidency had obviously won the election be-

fore the Californians had finished voting. In 1984, the results were proclaimed by one of the networks—with the result that the California voters were discouraged from going to the polls, where their votes would have been important for the other candidates (senators, congressmen, etc.) that had to be elected on the same ballot.

Should the networks be forbidden to proclaim a winner before all voting polls are closed? Should there be a law to that effect? Or should the freedom of the press be respected?

6. What do you think of Walter Cronkite as vice-president or senator?

Selected Reading

To Have, To Have Not, Or To Have More

> *Excerpts from a speech delivered by James H. Rosenfield, Senior Executive President of CBS Broadcast Group, at the annual convention of the Maine Association of Broadcasters. September 23, 1983.*

Considering the identity of the speaker and of his audience, what do you expect to be the general topic of the speech? Will his attitude be surely positive? What could he have to say?

"The Haves and Have-nots" usually refer to the wealthy versus the poor. Skim the text to find whether or not Mr. Rosenfield uses the words to express the same meaning. What does his title seem to refer to?

Is Mr. Rosenfield concerned only about news programs?

As you read the text, pay particular attention to what he has to say about the various ways in which television is of social value, and about the qualities that make television such a valuable medium.

[*Mr. Rosenfield opened his remarks with the thought that we often fail, when we judge the value of a thing, to consider the whole picture.*]

Our critical faculties—by which we analyze and judge—at times totally blind us to seeing things in their entirety; we focus on trees, and miss the forest; perceive the parts, but not the whole. This flaw in critical perception, I think, is what is wrong with so much that is said and written about network television.

Those who write about our medium so often focus about what they don't like, or only upon what they don't want others to like. Whether it's commercial interruptions, or escapist situation comedy, these critics selectively settle on only what they see as negatives, failing to see or unwilling to see the whole of network television and its immense social value, particularly in this remarkable era of great change. That's why I so welcome the chance to be here to speak about the nature of television, what it is, and what it means to a society that values not only open competition and wide consumer choice, but which also cares deeply about equal opportunity for all.

As has been widely noted, we are entering an information age, a time in which technological advance in communications and the computer revolution are forcing us to redefine literacy, and rethink the ways in which people gain information and knowledge. Some have compared this period to the flowering of the industrial revolution in Victorian England, which through the emergence of machine-made paper and high-speed printing, made access to inexpensive books almost universal.

Yet, even as some Victorians tried to spread literacy and learning—through circulating libraries, cheap books, and public education—there were those who opposed the growing literacy of the people and the diffusion of information. Some feared that working people would waste their time reading novels and neglect their looms. Bitter battles were fought over the spread of libraries and coffee houses where common people would go to read and talk.

This foreshadows a similar tension in our own times, the concern that in this new age, this information age, we may be creating a split society, split between information haves and haves not. . . . It is a very pertinent issue for those of us gathered here: will our society be increasingly split between information haves and have-nots; between those who can afford personal computers and other emerging information technologies for their homes and schools and those who cannot; between those who can afford to pay for televised news, entertainment, and sports, and those who cannot?

As citizens, and as broadcasters, our task should be to strengthen the engines that can make our nation a society of information "have-mores," rather than being divided between haves and have-nots. Those three engines are: the advancing technologies of information and communications; quality public education for all; and a wise public policy that not only encourages diversity in mass communications, but also fosters communications media that reach the widest audience at the lowest cost. My aim here is not to address the educational and technological issues, but rather how "free, over-the-air" network broadcasting is a critical component in the process of guaranteeing that our nation will be a society of information have-mores.

And while the attributes of network television are well known to everyone in this room, sometimes it is important to restate and reexamine the obvious, because what's obvious, in this case, is too important to be overlooked.

To begin, network television is ubiquitous. It reaches just about every home that has a television set, reaching about 98 percent of all the people in the United States; that's a larger percentage than those who have telephones or full indoor plumbing.

And while it reaches just about everyone—in fact, in a typical day television reaches 88 percent of all adults—it does so for free, at virtually no cost for those reached. Advertisers, of course, support the medium and, largely because they do, it becomes universal. You don't have to subscribe to the service. You don't have to pay. It reaches all regardless of their ability to pay.

Though network television is primarily a medium of popular entertainment, it is the nation's leading information provider and most preferred source of news. It uniquely provides for instantaneous news coverage—national and local—whenever and wherever it happens. Now in the case of the CBS Television Network and most of its affiliates, that means 24 hours a day.

As a medium of national and local advertising, network television plays a crucial role in all of our commerce: introducing new products and services to the widest possible audience, differentiating them, driving the consumer economy.

Network television is also a unique force for cohesion in national life. You could call it a media melting pot. The experiences we shared through network television are as vivid and as universal as having seen [M.A.S.H.'s] Hawkeye's helicopter lift off in a final "goodbye, farewell, and amen"; as unforgettable as seeing the landing of a man on the moon, the Kennedy funeral, the capture of Kunte Kinte in "Roots," and seeing quarterback Ken Anderson comforting his son with a piggyback ride after a Super Bowl defeat.

Whether it's how we find out who won the Presidential election, or who shot J. R. [in *Dallas*], network television is the source of so much of our information, so much of our entertainment, so much of our shared experience.

Former Senator S. I. Hayakawa once observed that the civil rights movement was inevitable in America, given the presence of television. In order to maintain a caste system, Hayakawa noted, "members of different castes must not be permitted to communicate freely with each other and they must also be separated from each other by receiving their communication from different channels." But because of the unifying presence of television networks, he noted, such segregated communication was not possible in America. "The impact of nationwide networks," Hayakawa said, "enables white and negro, Jew and Gentile, Protestant and Catholic, to laugh simultaneously at the same jokes, thrill at the same adventures, admire and detest good guys and bad guys, yearn for the same automobiles, dream the same dreams and therefore develop ultimately the same value system."

You can also see this unifying effect powerfully at work in the presentation of information to a national audience. *60 Minutes* is a prime example. Its audience is not only huge, it is incredibly diverse. Not only is it the most watched popular prime-time program—with an average of 34 million people watching every Sunday—its huge audience is about equally split between women, men; young and old adults; high income, low income; among those who have never finished high school and those who have finished college. So, too, viewing by region is about the same in all parts of the country.

But there is another amazing fact about television networks, and that's the low cost to the consumer. Not only are the television networks and their affiliates the most preferred source of news, not only are they the most preferred source of entertainment—even in those homes that can afford all the new home entertainement technologies—the television networks are, by any measure, the least expensive medium of information and entertainment. Now, I know that when we speak of free, over-the-air television, we will get an argument from people who say there is no free lunch.[1] Well, broadcast television is about as close to a free lunch as you can get. In direct costs, the consumer spends about three cents for every hour he uses broadcast television. Cable television use per home costs up to eight times as much; newspaper use per hour is about four times higher. But even if you assume that the consumer, through his purchase of products and services, ultimately pays for the advertising that supports network television, you still find that it is a remarkable bargain.

Understanding the Text

Devise your own list of "Understanding the Text" questions. In doing so, you may find it useful to divide the text in six parts as follows:

"introductory" remarks   (lines 1–13)
part A   (lines 14–30)
part B   (lines 31–40)
part C   (lines 41–51)
part D   (lines 52–81)
part E   (lines 88 to end)

Appraising the Text

1. What do you think of Mr. Rosenfield's arguments:
   a) That television is practically free, as it costs only 3 cents per hour to operate, and that it is cheaper than all other information media?

---

[1] a reference to the popular saying—"There is no such thing as a free lunch."

    b) That television plays a useful role by advertising new products. Is advertising good for the consumers?
    c) That television acts as a melting pot. Are people "unified" by watching the same programs? Do people develop the same value system by watching the same shows?
2. Do you agree with Mr. Rosenfield's implied idea that, in spite of possible flaws, the impact of television is of positive value? Can you think of some reasons that he has not mentioned?
3. How do you interpret the saying: "There is no such thing as a free lunch?" Do you know a non-American way of expressing the same idea?

A Survey

A survey conducted among 1,917 youths and adults in forty-one states to find out what they want to see more often, gave the following results:

Want more comedy	51.9%
more movies	51.3%
more drama	35.3%
more music	33.1%
more sports	17.2%
more news	9.1%
more religious programs	6.9%

1. What does the low percentage of people asking for more news indicate?
2. Does the demand for any of the categories mentioned surprise you?
3. Conduct your own survey, including more types of programs if you want, and compare the result to the survey given by the National Telemedia Council, Inc.

Topics for Discussion

1. What are your main criticisms of American television or of the television in the country where you live?
2. Is television good or bad for children, or is it both good and bad? Explain your answer.
3. Can you compare the importance of television in the United States (where the average watching time per household is over seven hours per day) to that in some other countries?
    a) Are the programs different?
    b) Are people watching television as much?
    c) Is television expensive?
4. Do you think we would all be happier without television? What would be better, or worse?
5. In some countries, people who own a television set pay a yearly tax to support TV, which presents little or no advertising. Is this a better system?

Imogen Cunningham

Introduction

Looking Ahead

- What different parts do you find in this chapter; what are they about?
- What plans should you make now for the fourth section of the chapter?
- What kinds of photographers seem to be considered in this chapter: reporters, war correspondents, portrait photographers, amateurs, professionals, technicians (medicine, astronomy, etc.), fashion photographers . . . ?
- Are you interested in taking photographs? In developing your own photographs? Why?
- What do you consider a good photo?
- What careers are open to a good photographer?

Photography and the Vocabulary of Photography

Skim the text below to find out what it is about. Is it:
- A series of instructions for taking good photos?
- An article on the technical aspects of photography?
- an essay on photography as art?
- Information about careers in photography?
- History of photography?
- A mixture of the above?

Photography is by no means a modern invention. It has been known for centuries that a ray of light entering a dark room through a tiny hole projects on the opposite surface an inverted image of the objects that the light has hit before shooting through the hole. Leonardo da Vinci and other Italian painters of the sixteenth century observed the phenomenon and tried to make something of it. But it was to take a long time before a practical way could be found to put this old piece of knowledge to use. The first experiments involved rooms ("camera" in Italian) so large that the photographer could sit inside. The real breakthrough came in the nineteenth century; it is generally agreed that photography made its official debut in 1837 when a French painter by the name of Louis-Jacques Daguerre produced a clear picture of a corner of his studio, carefully arranged in artistic disorder for the occasion.

The basic principle used at that time is the same as in today's most advanced cameras: a light-tight container, a circular opening (the diaphragm) behind which the image is focused by a glass lens on the receiving surface. This surface, nowadays, is usually a small section of film. The process used by Daguerre and his contemporaries was messy and the equipment cumbersome. The first cameras, large and heavy, had to be set on sturdy tripods, and the receiving surfaces were fragile glass plates that had to be dipped in liquid chemicals just before use. Until 1880, the shutter controlling the opening and closing of the diaphragm was too slow to allow photography of moving objects.

Neither the clumsy operation nor its limitations discouraged the early photographers or their patrons. For the general public, the advent of photography was a miracle: for the first time people of modest means could afford to have their faces and the main events of their lives recorded for posterity—a privilege that had been hitherto reserved for the wealthy, who could have themselves painted and displayed in gold frames. Photography was quick and cheap. It was well worth sitting motionless, unblinking and preferably without breathing for thirty or forty seconds, to be captured in one's Sunday best, leaning solemnly against a half-column of fake marble. There is no question, when one sees a portrait taken at the turn of the century or before, that both photographer and sitter took the matter seriously and even reverently.

The very difficulty of the photographic process spurred the researchers on. Means were found to get several prints from the same negative. The bothersome wet glass plates were replaced by wet metal plates, then by dry plates coated with gelatin. Faster shutters made it possible to catch moving objects. A new era began in 1883 when George Eastman invented the small, portable, box camera, which he named *Kodak* because "it seemed a good name, pronounceable in any language and easy to remember." Eastman was also responsible for the invention of roll film, originally made of gelatin-coated paper, that the least skillful amateur could handle. At first, there was nothing to handle: the original Kodak was sold already loaded with a roll of film sufficient for a hundred pictures. When the roll was finished, the owner of the camera had to return his box to the Kodak factory where the film was removed, cut into strips of twelve exposures, and individually developed. Camera, film, and developing cost $25. One had to pay an additional $10 to have the camera reloaded.

From the beginning, professional photographers were divided into two camps: on one side the realists, primarily interested in showing the world as it is; on the other side the artists, determined to create beauty with their black boxes.

Before the notion of artistic photography could blossom, the early photographers had realized the documentary value of their craft. While some concentrated on making portraits of their most famous contemporaries, others went forth to capture images of war or sights of faraway places, which held great fascination in that un-touristy era. The first war reporters followed the troops in the Crimean War in the 1850s and in the American Civil War ten years later. They brought back pictures that surprised and shocked a public that had never been confronted with such realities. The effect continues in our time, through still photos and televised images that turn viewers against the horrors of war and violence in general. Among the "sightseeing" photographs, the first good picture of the Kremlin under a blanket of snow dates from 1840—and an excellent one it is.

The work of those pioneers was no child's play. It is difficult not to be awed by the fortitude of William Henry Jackson, who explored the West, and climbed up and down the Rockies with several large cameras, a tripod, a large tent to be used as a darkroom, a provision of chemicals for developing, and a number of crates containing the big breakable glass plates that he had to use, since the enlarging process was still in its infancy. Not only did Jackson survive the expedition, but he brought back safely a collection of fine pictures of the still unexplored territories. The hardy Jackson died in 1942 at the age of ninety-nine, in his bed.

Another group of realistic photographers turned to social action. Lewis W. Hies, a trained sociologist, took over 5,000 photos of small children employed in cotton mills, and turned them over to the National Child Labor Committee, which was to produce the first laws limiting child labor in 1910.

The "artists," meanwhile, attempted to develop photography as an art form. There was plenty of confusion at first, since nobody had a clear idea of what kind of art it could be. For some time, it was felt that photography's only artistic aspirations should be to imitate painting as closely as possible. Unlike the reporters, who considered that most of their work was done when they had picked a good subject and clicked their shutter, the "artists" not only prepared their scenes with the utmost care (as Daguerre had done), but they did considerable work on the negatives—correcting, redrawing, retouching, and painting to their heart's content in order to give their photos the appearance of "real" pictures in oils or watercolor.

Not unnaturally, those early partisans of artistic photography shared the taste of their time for romantic or edifying scenes, called "scenes de genre," like the much admired "Fading Away" (1858), for example. "Fading Away" depicts a dying girl surrounded by apparently grief-stricken figures, all of whom had been posed separately by models, the various negatives being pieced together for the final effect. Another famous photo of the same period, "The Two Paths of Life," was concocted from thirty separate negatives.

Toward the end of the nineteenth century, some photographers began to criticize and to ridicule the artificiality of these stiffly posed and heavily retouched pictures. Although they didn't all see eye to eye about the methods to be used or even about the place of photography among the arts, the "naturalists" supported the notion of "honest" photography, without tricks or camouflage. In America the cause of straight photography was pioneered by Alfred Stieglitz of New York, who maintained that photography was an art in its own right, independent from painting in every way—style, goals, and execution. Stieglitz founded a movement that he called Photo-Secession, and organized innovative exhibitions of his own work and of the work of other photographers. He also demonstrated that pictures of great aesthetic value could be made with the simplest equipment, such as the portable Kodak, which was looked upon with contempt by the professionals of the period.

While Stieglitz was thus conducting his revolution in New York and winning to his ideas the East Coast photographers, a young woman photographer was following his crusade with keen interest. Her name was Imogen Cunningham; she was practicing her craft in northern California, and she is the subject of the profile in this chapter.

Understanding the Text

1. What is the main idea of the first paragraph? Give a supporting statement (in your own words).
2. What is the main idea of the second paragraph? Name a few differences.
3. What is the main idea of the third paragraph? Give one supporting explanation (in your own words).
4. What is the main idea of the fourth paragraph? Give several examples.
5. What do you remember about the first Kodak?

Outline

Scanning the text if necessary, make an outline showing the two main camps, or schools, of photographers, and the various types of work and of opinions in each camp. Give examples whenever possible.

I. The realists, who wanted to show the world as it is. (main group)
   A. Portraitists _____ (subgroup)
      1. ordinary people _____ (examples)
      2. _____
   B. _____ (subgroup)
      1. _____ (examples)
      2. _____
   C. _____ (subgroup)
      1. _____
      2. _____
   D. _____ (subgroup)
II. _____ (main group)
   A. _____ (subgroup)
      1. _____ (examples)
      2. _____
   B. _____ (subgroup)
      1. _____ (examples)
      2. _____

Logical Reasoning: cause and effect vs. restriction

Some of the groups of two sentences below express a *cause* and its *effect*, to be indicated by using either <u>because</u> or <u>since</u>. The other groups present a *restriction*, to be indicated by either <u>but</u> or <u>although</u>. Combine the two statements in each group, using the connector that expresses their relationship, as shown in the examples.

<u>Examples</u>: A. The early shutters were too slow.
It was impossible to photograph people in motion.

These two sentences, showing a cause and its effect, could become:

Since the early shutters were too slow, it was impossible to photograph people in motion.

Or:

It was impossible to photograph people in motion *because* the early shutters were too slow.

B. The first Kodak was not as convenient as our present cameras.
It was a great improvement on the bulky cameras.

These two sentences, showing a contrast, could become:

Although the first Kodak was not as convenient as our present cameras, it was a great improvement on the bulky cameras.

Or:

The first Kodak was not as convenient as our present cameras, *but* it was a great improvement on the bulky cameras.

1. The basic principle of photography has always remained the same.
   The equipment and processes have changed enormously.

2. We call our Kodaks and Rolleiflexes "cameras."
   "Camera obscura" means "dark room" in Italian.

3. The name of our "dark rooms" (or "dark boxes") is Italian.
   The principle of photography was first applied by Italian artists.

4. They didn't find a way to use the principle they knew.
   They were brilliant and talented men.

5. The film was ruined.
   I unrolled it in full daylight.

6. The early photographers were excellent technicians.
   They didn't know how to get several prints from the same negative.

7. The enlarging method had not been perfected.
   Johnson had to use large plates to make large pictures.

8. "The Two Paths of Life" looks extremely ridiculous to us.
   Queen Victoria admired and bought it.

9. The noncombatants had never seen the results of a battle.
   They didn't feel about war as people do now.

10. Stieglitz could take artistic photographs with a Kodak.
    The art is in the photographer's eye, not in his camera.

Cultural Notes for Profile, Part One

<u>Hippies</u>. The word *hippie* was used in the late 1960s to refer to men and women who had chosen to reject conventions and authority. As a sign of independence of mind, they usually wore their hair and beards long, wore unusual or very casual clothes, and generally tried to give the impression that, seeing human worth and beauty as an internal matter, they didn't wish to look externally attractive, or even clean.

The so-called "flower children" earned their name by offering flowers to the members of the police force or of the Army confronting them, so displaying their love of nature, sweetness, and beauty as opposed to the brutality of officialdom.

The peace symbol, devised by those against the Vietnam war and war in general, also made its appearance in the 1960s.

<u>Communes</u>. A commune is a group of people who have the same interests or the same religious beliefs, and who live together, sharing their properties and responsibilities. Although some hippies chose to live in communes, the notion was not new in the 1960s. There had been religious communes long before that time, as the text will show. Many communes are located in the country, but there are some in towns.

Profile
Part One

Born April 12, 1883
Died June 24, 1976

As you read the text, keep in mind that you want to discover:
- the personality of Imogen Cunningham;
- the kind of training that a photographer like her receives;
- the kind of work for which she is noted.

She was a familiar sight in the streets of San Francisco, the little old lady in a black cape, topped with an outlandish hat, a camera dangling from her neck amidst the peace symbols decorating her dress. She could be seen trotting around, alert and brisk, until she saw something that caught her fancy. Then she'd stop and aim the camera at her subject—a couple of "flower children" lounging on the sidewalk, a striking face in the crowd, or her own reflection in a store window—anything that caught her practiced eye. Passersby who did not know her took her for one of those celebrated San Francisco characters[1] (which in truth she was); those who recognized her smiled and promptly got out of the way so as not to interfere with a great photographer's work. For the old lady was an outstanding artist and one of the pioneers in the art of photography, revered as such by professionals and serious amateurs alike throughout the country. But the San Franciscans didn't only revere her—they loved her. A friend of hers, who once drove her to an assignment, recalls that every time they had to wait at a red light, someone in another car or on the sidewalk would point, smiling broadly, and exclaim: "Look! Here's Imogen!" Everyone called her Imogen.

Imogen was not a native San Franciscan. She had been born in Portland, Oregon. Her father, a widower with three small children, had left Texas after the death of his wife to seek a new life in the north, where he remarried. Imogen was the first of six children born of the second marriage, and obviously his favorite. Father and daughter were alike in many ways—both smart, spirited, and fiercely independent. Imogen's own son Rondal had this to say to Judy Dater, author of *Imogen Cunningham, A Portrait*: "Basically, Imogen was an early hippie. That came from her father. His name was, I think, Isaac Burns Cunningham. Imogen's father grew up on what his family called a plantation in Kentucky, with maybe four slaves, and they were rather poor. . . . My grandfather was a mystic, a seeker of the real truth, and he studied every religion he could find. When Imogen was fifteen or so her father took her to a religious commune in Port Angeles, Washington, where they cut down trees, prayed, and practiced vegetarianism. Her father had a gentle nature; he never drank or swore, and was so horrified when he saw a horse being beaten that he'd buy the horse—so naturally he ended up pretty poor. In Seattle he had a contract for leveling the streets, and before that he was a grocery clerk in Portland. The experience of vegetarianism at the commune affected Imogen all her life. She was in every food fad—tiger's milk, wheat germ—and milk. She thrust quarts and quarts of milk on her children. . . . Her father's attitude influenced Imogen but sometimes in a negative way. Her stance that she was liberated and that she could do whatever she wanted was mostly a reaction

---

[1] A "character" is an unconventional person.

to the way her father treated her mother: friendly and pleasant, but as if she were a slave-child."

With this passive, submissive, and nearly illiterate mother, Imogen doesn't seem to have had much rapport, although she made loving portraits of her. Two of her most beautiful portraits are those of her mother and father in their nineties. Imogen's quick, inquisitive mind came from Isaac, and she demonstrated early that she was neither passive nor submissive. She was not even gentle; her wits were sharp, her tongue even sharper, and all her friends agree on her acid quality, although some believe that it was a cover-up for a sensitive and essentially loving nature.

Even as a young girl, Imogen made it clear that she could, and would, do as she pleased in any circumstance. Her schooling and her choice of a career exemplified this. Her father had wanted her, alone of all his children, to have the good education that her intelligence deserved. Isaac himself was entirely self-educated, and always eager to know more; he started learning advanced mathematics at the age of seventy from a correspondence school. His ambition was to see Imogen become a teacher. Imogen, however, had been impressed by the work of some photographers when she was still in high school, and she announced promptly that she was planning to become a photographer of the same class. Isaac had too much respect for individual liberty to oppose her wish, although he did sigh that photography was "a dirty business," hardly fit for a lady. But he let her order a small camera and book of instructions from the International Correspondence School in Scranton, Pennsylvania. He even went so far as to build her a dark room in the woodshed behind their house, and carefully lined the walls with tarpaper to make it lightproof.

As she was about to enroll at the University of Washington, with the intention of majoring in art and art history, Imogen discovered with dismay that the university had no art department. With her usual determination, she adjusted her plans to reach her goal in spite of the difficulty: if she couldn't get into photography as an art scholar, she would as a chemist. Undaunted by the fact that chemistry was still considered a male preserve, Imogen went ahead with her program and got her degree in three and a half years instead of the usual four. Right after graduation, she found work in the studio of Edward S. Curtis in Seattle where, for the next two years, she practiced the difficult process of platinum printing. In 1909, having learned that a scholarship was being offered for a photographer to study photochemistry in Dresden, Germany, she submitted a portfolio of photographs to the committee. She won the award by unanimous vote over fifty candidates.

At that point of her budding career—and despite the fact that she had been for some time producing drawings and paintings of some merit—Imogen was only interested in the technical aspects of her work. Most of her time in Dresden was accordingly devoted to scientific studies and to experiments with various mediums. She invented a method of coating printing paper with salts of lead, much less expensive than the platinum generally used. The process, published in a German magazine, was later pirated by an English firm.

Although fully dedicated to her work, Imogen availed herself of the pleasures that Dresden had to offer to a young and curious mind. She went to concerts and operas; she spent long hours in museums, studying the masterpieces of great painters who had been only names in art books. Fascinated as she was by paintings, it is remarkable that she never wavered from her determination to make photography her exclusive occupation. During that year, Imogen learned to speak German well—she was to use the language almost fluently to the end of her life. By the time she was to come home, she had also made an important discovery: she was not as interested in the chemistry of photography now as she was in the artistic potential of the craft. And she was eager to put her ideas into practice. She hadn't taken many photographs in Germany, however, and she didn't take many in England during the week that she spent there on her way home. The reason was less a lack of interest, probably, than the prosaic fact that she couldn't afford to pay for plates and printing. The few pictures that she brought back had been taken with a small folding Kodak—a going-away present from her friends at the Curtis Studio.

Back in America in 1910, Imogen promptly went about opening her own portrait studio in Seattle. The notion of a woman earning a living in such a line of business was unheard-of, and rather shocking. And the unusual decor of the studio, with simple draperies and framed photos, struck the visitors as just as odd as the young woman's choice of occupation. Even so, it didn't take long for the society of Seattle to recognize that Imogen Cunningham was a superior portrait photographer, and to provide her with all the work that she could handle.

"From the very beginning," says her friend, photographer Margaretta Mitchell, "Imogen's portraits reflected her respect for the individuality of each sitter; while she didn't want to endow her subject with a phony 'heroic' quality, she strove to reach the inner person and to bring out that person's quality in the portrait." After Imogen's death, another friend and fellow photographer added: "Imogen was a complete humanist, and a complete believer in the integrity of every individual human being. She has never photographed crowds of people. She has always selected one or two people and made them memorable. She has never photographed expanses of ocean or mountains or forests. She has always photographed individual plants and has given them the same concentrated attention that she has given her people."

In her spare time, Imogen read and read and indulged in a different kind of photography to please herself. While in Germany she had particularly admired the work of Gertrude Kasebier, a German artist who made soft-focus photographs, often on religious or symbolic subjects. The use of soft focus, which results in hazy, ill-defined pictures not unlike the paintings of famous artists of the period, was very much in favor among professional photographers. Like her contemporaries, Imogen liked the mysterious quality of soft-focus pictures, and the sentimental art work done by Kasebier and others. She was anxious to find out what she could achieve in that vein, while expressing her own personality and feelings. She began to photograph her friends draped in decorative silks and transparent veils, producing photographs entitled "The Dream," "Conscience," and "A Veiled Woman." Most were highly symbolic. One of her first noted photos, "Eve Repentant," represents two nude figures, Adam and a contrite Eve who, with her hand on his shoulder, seems to beg forgiveness while he turns away. The print, published by a local magazine, made quite a sensation in the Seattle of 1910.

Imogen's work attracted considerable attention in the 1910s; wherever they were exhibited they won high praise from art critics on both coasts. Meanwhile, she was being courted by a handsome, talented etcher[1] named Roi Partridge. Since Partridge lived in Paris, the courtship was conducted exclusively by correspondence. Even at that time, in her youth, Imogen was no beauty. A devoted friend of hers described her as "plain as a mud fence," with bright red hair which, he conceded, was "part of her charm." But neither Roi nor Imogen's circle of friends felt that she needed beauty, being all enthralled by her intelligence, her tart wit, her vivacity, and her absolute honesty.

Roi and Imogen were married in 1915 and for a time they worked side by side in adjoining studios in Seattle. Their first son, Gryffyd, was born a year later, followed by twin boys—Padraic and Rondal—after Roi and Imogen moved to San Francisco in 1918. In 1920, Roi accepted a position as art teacher at Mills College, near Oakland, and the young family settled in a house near the campus.

There Imogen undertook to handle wifely duties, motherhood, and photography all at once. On the whole, she managed very well. She ran a happy, lively house. A splendid cook and an enthusiastic hostess, she entertained the faculty members and the visitors with whom Roi was involved; she helped him organize exhibits for the art department; she somehow kept the three wild boys under reasonable control; she went camping with them and Roi; she took care of the garden. She never stopped. If her housekeeping left something to be desired, it was simply due to the fact that she was more interested in the important elements of life—people, ideas, books, poetry, and plants—than in the tedious task of keeping the most orderly kitchen in the block. As they grew up, the boys learned to give a hand with clean-

---

[1] etcher—an artist who engraves drawings with acid on metal plates.

ing chores and even to cook. It was an informal, exciting, and stimulating household to grow up in.

Imogen was also busy taking and printing photographs. She made portraits of the Mills College girls, and some publicity pictures. But most of her work was done for her own pleasure. Since she couldn't drive (and never learned), she had to find her inspiration in her immediate surroundings: the flowers of her garden, the college buildings, and the things that the boys brought her—a live snake in a bucket, a magnolia blossom, a few interesting blades of grass. From that period of confinement date some of Imogen's superb studies of plants.

Imogen was not really isolated. She was keeping in touch with her photographer friends, among whom were Edward Weston and Ansel Adams. Like them, she was following with keen interest the battle waged by Alfred Stieglitz and the other proponents of "pure" photography. Independently from Stieglitz and from each other, Imogen, Weston, and Adams had become convinced that photography had its own expressive possibilities, and all had now rejected the soft-focus method of their early work. Imogen herself had moved far from the romanticism and the symbolism of "The Dream" or "Eve Repentant" (she referred to them as her "poetic period") and was now intent on catching the appearances of the world as it is.

Although they were working in very different directions, Imogen, Ansel Adams, Edward Weston, Wynn Bullock, and a few of their friends decided to form an organization to spread their ideas. They called it "The f-64 Group," f-64 being the small lens aperture that gives the sharpest pictures. The common exhibition that the group held in San Francisco in 1932 was a revelation—and a revolution—for the photographers of the West Coast. The group, which had been informal and loose from the outset, dispersed three days after the exhibit, but it left its mark on the work of other photographers. Its impact is still felt today in the work of a new generation of artists, including Weston's sons Bret and Cole. The members of the group had not entirely realized the importance of their manifesto. Imogen was quite surprised, many years after the San Francisco exhibit, to read that it was considered a turning point in the history of photography.

Understanding the Text

1. Imogen's son Rondal says that she was "an early hippie." Does her photo and the facts in the text explain his description?
2. Why does the author spend so much time on Imogen's father?
3. In your own words, why is she considered such a fine portrait photographer?
4. What other kind of photography is she renowned for?
5. Was she always a revolutionary photographer?
6. What is the great technical difference between the pictures of the "poetic period" and the photographs of the f-64 Group?

7. Why is the f-64 Group important in the history of photography, since Stieglitz had already done exhibits and expressed the same general ideas?
8. What kind of training did Imogen receive as an aspiring photographer?

Appraising the Text

1. What is the general attitude of the author toward Imogen: neutral, antagonistic, friendly, serious, amused, ironic, critical . . . ?
2. What do you think of the way Rondal refers to his mother?
3. Why did "Eve Repentant" make such a sensation in Seattle in 1910?
4. What does the text imply about Imogen's house in Oakland? About the intelligence of Imogen's brothers and sisters? About San Francisco? Do we have reasons to believe that, however tart and acid, Imogen was a likable person?
5. Can Imogen be compared to any of the other women portrayed in this book?
6. If you had to make a guess about Imogen Cunningham's political position, what would you say?

Scanning for Details

1. What is the name of the famous German photographer that Imogen admired so much?
2. Which members of the f-64 Group are mentioned in the text?
3. What did Margaretta Mitchell say, exactly: "Imogen's portraits reflect _____ sitter"?
4. In what year did Isaac and Imogen join a commune in Port Angeles?
5. How many children did Isaac Cunningham have?
6. What are the names of Imogen's sons?
7. Who wrote: *Imogen Cunningham, A Portrait*?

Vocabulary

A. 1. From the context, can you tell what a <u>mystic</u> is interested in?
   2. What well-known word, related to them, explains the meaning of:
      a) budding
      b) prosaic
      c) vegetarianism

B. *Complete each sentence of the story below with the most appropriate word from the list, which includes more words than necessary. Be sure to make all needed adjustments for articles, nouns, and verbs.*

   1. Imogen met Roi Partridge when she was in Europe. They didn't meet often since she was in Dresden and Roi in Paris most of the time.

194 IMOGEN CUNNINGHAM

2. Roi was not at all a _____ artist; he had already earned a great reputation.
3. The plain-looking girl with the bright red hair _____ (attracted him) because she was intelligent, original, and full of life.
4. For a while his friends didn't think that his infatuation was serious. One of his friends mentioned once that Imogen was ugly, but felt _____ (very sorry) afterwards and apologized.
5. Roi kept writing to Imogen, sometimes about art, sometimes about such _____ (ordinary) matters as his difficulties with his landlord and the price of drawing paper.
6. Imogen, who was working hard in Seattle, sent him a _____ of photographs of which she was particularly proud.
7. So far the idea of getting married had always seemed _____ (most extraordinary) to Roi. But he did ask Imogen to marry him, and joined her in Seattle.

prosaic	portfolio	contrite
outlandish	to catch someone's fancy	mystic
etcher	budding	to endow
to revere	humanist	

Taking Notes for a Summary

Skim the text and note down the facts that you will need to sum up briefly, without details, what you know about the early life of Imogen Cunningham, including her origin, training, professional establishment, and marriage. The summary should have no more than sixty words.

Facts, Inferences, and Opinions

Which of the following statements express a fact? Which express an inference? Which express an opinion? Which statements are debatable?

1. While she was studying in Germany, Imogen Cunningham invented a cheaper method of coating printing paper.
2. An English firm stole the method.
3. Apparently Imogen didn't know how to protect her inventions.
4. Isaac obviously thought that Imogen was the most intelligent of his children.
5. This is probably why she was his favorite.
6. Imogen majored in chemistry because she couldn't study art or photography at the University of Washington.
7. It is strange that an important university should have no art department.
8. Around the turn of the century, painters as well as photographers produced symbolic or anecdotal pictures.

9. They look too sentimental nowadays—and often ridiculous.
10. Even when they were young, Imogen's sons tried to please and help her.
11. Imogen's friend shouldn't have compared her to a mud fence.
12. The San Franciscans seem to like "characters."
13. Isaac was good at working with his hands.
14. Imogen's portrait of her father at ninety shows him as a handsome old man with a flowing white beard.

Topics for Discussion

1. You surely have seen many tourists loaded with cameras and sophisticated photographic equipment. Do you think that it is a good idea to take many pictures when you travel? What are the best pictures to take?
2. It has been said that one picture is worth a thousand words. In what aspects of everyday life can you verify that photography is a powerful means of communication? Do photographs influence people's lives? Is that influence good or bad?
3. Would you like to live in a commune? What are the advantages and the disadvantages of such an arrangement? Are there cases when it is better for people not to live in a commune but to share an apartment or a house? Does it work?
4. Do you approve of vegetarianism? Is it healthy? Would you give up meat and fish in order to avoid the killing of animals? Is there a food fad or a diet that you consider good?

Profile
Part Two

Skim the text to find the answers to the following questions:
- What happened in Imogen's personal life?
- What happened to her sons?
- What did she do on television?

While reading the text, note down the words and expressions that, in your opinion, must not be taken literally.

A year or so before the San Francisco exhibit, Imogen had begun to work occasionally for *Vanity Fair*, a high-society magazine which would be absorbed by *Vogue* in the late 1930s. She was thrilled by this first opportunity to venture into a different professional world. In the spring of 1934 she accepted happily an invitation from the editors of the magazine to come and see them in New York, and perhaps make some pictures there. Roi did not approve of the trip, however, and he told Imogen that their marriage would be over if she went. Either to prove her independence or because she didn't believe him, Imogen went to New York. When she came back, Roi was in Reno starting proceedings for a divorce.

If one relies on their friends' reaction to the break-up, the most surprising fact is that Roi and Imogen could have remained married as long as nineteen years, considering the complete incompatibility of their characters. Roi, the only child in a solid middle-class family, was used to having his own way in all things; he liked the comfort, the tidiness, and the peaceful atmosphere of a well-run home. None of this could be expected from Imogen the bohemian, despite her honest efforts to maintain what she considered an acceptable standard. She was gay, mischievous, and people-oriented, with little regard for money. Roi was serious, scholarly, reserved, and remarkably tight-fisted.[1] Their son Rondal describes the relationship: "My father and my mother never got along one day in their lives. They loved each other very much, but they never got along. Roi was absolutely dogmatic and sometimes crabby,[2] so Imogen would invite people for dinner because at least he couldn't be crabby with people there. He'd become pleasant then. Imogen was very gregarious anyway, so all the visiting artists and art historians and professors, people like that, would come and there was never a week without a dozen or maybe twenty people coming for dinner."

After the divorce, Roi and Imogen remained excellent friends and kept in touch—visiting each other, going to the same parties and admiring each other's work. Roi remarried, but Imogen never did and never showed any desire to do so. She remained in the house in Oakland with the three boys, who were now of high-school and college age. All three were close to their unorthodox mother. "It was interesting, having Imogen as a mother," says Gryffyd, "because she could answer any kind of question, be it on art, literature, chemistry, or the latest news about the neighborhood. . . . There was nothing that Imogen was not interested in, with the possible exception of automobiles and sports. She was interested in everything that she was doing, in everything that we were doing, and in the world at large, so we had a very lively time. . . . Music was very important to her. One of her early friends, in the twenties, was Henry Cowell, the avant-garde[3] composer. I don't think she read music, but she subscribed to *Modern Music*, a journal with scores by people like Cowell and Charles Ives. I have gone with her to concerts in which John Cage was beating out a non-tune on an old suitcase, or Henry Cowell was playing—with surprising melody—what he called 'tone-clusters,' hitting the piano with his forearm. And she really enjoyed it."

Imogen's sons remember her as a friend—supportive, understanding, and

---

[1] tight-fisted—reluctant to open his hands, figuratively, to give money.
[2] *crabby* is an informal word meaning "cross and complaining."
[3] avant-garde artists are the radical ones who are ahead of their contemporaries in time.

concerned. She influenced them strongly, but more through her example and the very strength of her personality than by any conscious effort on her part to mold their lives. She did try to instill in them the same independence of spirit that her own father had encouraged in her, and to help them follow their own bent. Gryffyd, the eldest and most conventional of the three, who is now an architect, remembers that from the day he indicated his interest in buildings, she never gave him any present that was not a book on architecture. Of the "wild" twins, Padraic has become a mining engineer and geologist; Rondal is a photographer who specializes in "action" photographs of the West.

Although Roi had left the house to his wife, and probably a certain amount of money for the education of the boys, life after the divorce was difficult for Imogen, both financially and emotionally. She had to work hard to make ends meet. She made a series of superb portraits of important people and movie stars for *Vanity Fair*. The magazine's editors, based in New York and perhaps unaware of California distances, didn't hesitate to send her on assignment in Hollywood as though it had been next door. Until the portable Rolleiflex became available, tiny Imogen somehow had to drag her heavy and cumbersome equipment over the 400 miles from Oakland to Los Angeles. Between trips, she pursued her own work, photographing whatever attracted her because it was beautiful or provocative: the hands of a sculptor, the shapes of a human body, the swirling sheets on an unmade bed, or a bunch of vegetables—all things of beauty as caught by her camera.

In 1947 Imogen moved to a small house on Green Street in San Francisco, the only one on the street that had a garden in front. Gardens were important to Imogen; she loved to take care of hers and she knew the names of all the plants. On Green Street she made many studies of flowers and leaves. No one had done flowers quite in the same way before, in a precise, quasi-scientific manner that revealed the inner structure of the blossom without losing its beauty.

But, admired as she was on the West Coast, Imogen was by no means famous in the rest of the country, as were Weston and Ansel Adams, both of whom enjoyed national recognition. Even in California, despite the admiration bestowed on her, Imogen was still making only a meager living, partly because she never charged enough for her work. It embarrassed her to raise her prices as her colleagues did. She lived simply, by taste as much as by necessity. "The amount of money she survived on astonished me," said photographer Stephen Goldstine, who knew her in San Francisco. "It was regularly under $2,000 a year. In those days in the 1950s her price for a sitting and five prints was $100, and $5 apiece for extra prints—mounted 8 by 10! It struck me as remarkable that she obviously didn't want for things. And she didn't acquire stuff, she was not acquisitive. She eschewed her father's spiritualism, but on the other hand she was as unmaterialistic as anyone could be. She didn't want junk around. That didn't mean that she had to wear crummy clothes or whatever, but she bought only what she needed, in a very modest way, and craved nothing."

She may have owned few possessions, but what she did own was either beautiful or striking in some way; it had been chosen with discrimination. A friend who visited her often in the Green Street house remarks that it was "a very good nest. It was original, totally Imogen. Everything—her house, her garden, her clothes, the colors and textures, the food she prepared—everything was simple and yet very refined; everywhere there were arrangements[4]. Even the clutter had character. Everything was of an artist, you would see that she followed where her eyes and mind led her; it was a kind of beauty that was not conventional." Another friend has more to say on the same subject. "One of the most striking things about Imogen was her incredible good taste. Every time I saw her, everything she was wearing was related. Even when she was very old, even when she was lying on that bed and couldn't get up much, she'd wear a pretty scarf every day. She was incredibly attuned aesthetically, and I am sure it bothered her a great deal that she was not gorgeous. She didn't talk about it, but I felt that her aesthetic sensibility was offended by her own looks. But taste is everything and Imogen through her taste became someone beautiful."

There was much of the actress in Imogen. She loved acting—particularly when she could hold center stage. As a child she had written and performed "scenes" with a friend whose house offered an enormous attic suitable for their performances. Toward the end of her life, Imogen expressed some regret that she had not taken advantage of her years in Hollywood; she thought that she might have had a career there—perhaps as an actress. Actually, she did have an acting career of sorts. In 1952 she appeared in a televised documentary, and in the 1960s she was the subject—the star!—of two films about her work. She also acted a part in a film entitled *The Bed*, enjoying herself hugely. As she grew old, she took to playing more and more in real life the role of the eccentric old lady, outrageous and biting, that she knew was expected of her. At that time she began to wear her famous black cape, and those eye-catching hats decorated with embroidery and bits of mirror.

Imogen enjoyed upstaging the conceited people who, in her views, needed to be deflated. "She likes to put a pin in people's balloons when it seems appropriate," said her friend Jack Welpott, who had himself been pricked a few times. She was particularly fond of playing with the considerable ego of her old friend and colleague Ansel Adams, whose overconfidence and tremendous success—artistic and financial—amused and irritated her. Imogen once went to an exhibition of photography where Adams was present. The tall and bulky Adams was as usual holding court, basking in his admirers' adulations and looking, as his irreverent students were wont to

---

[4] An "arrangement" is a group of objects disposed to look beautiful together.

say, like God the Father visiting his worshipers. Adams's star status lasted until Imogen made her entrance, which she no doubt had carefully planned. All in black, from the top of her large hat to her flat shoes, a thick black veil falling from her head to her shoulders, she trotted around the room from photograph to photograph, pausing and lifting her veil to study them in turn, and of course diverting everyone's attention—as she had fully expected to do.

In 1967 Imogen had the honor of being elected a Fellow of the American Academy of Arts and Sciences. But it was only in the 1970s, when she was already eighty years old, that her celebrity spread from coast to coast. Amateurs began collecting her work in New York and in the eastern states as they had been doing for years on the West Coast, and museums too bought her photographs. The irrepressible Imogen couldn't refrain from chuckling: "Why didn't they discover me years ago? I was just as good then!" Even so, financial success didn't come to her until the last six or seven years of her life. At eighty-one she had applied in vain for a Guggenheim Fellowship grant that would allow her to go to England to photograph famous women artists and authors, a project that was dear to her. The Fellowship was eventually awarded to her six years later, much too late for the eighty-seven-year-old Imogen, who had to admit that her traveling days were over. She asked for permission to use the money to publish some of her earlier work, which was granted. Three years later she had to decline, regretfully, an invitation from the officials of the Winter Olympics in Tokyo to come and photograph the athletes.

Imogen at ninety was still pretty much what she had been all her life, "a sharp-tongued person with a point of view," interested in everything that went on—music, books, sewing, politics, and new babies—and involved in more activities than she should have contemplated. Money was now coming to her in bewildering amounts. All of a sudden, as life was running out, she was rich, famous, and hailed as one of the great photographers of all time. She enjoyed to the full the attention that she was getting, but it was not in her character to rest on past laurels.[5] In 1972, at ninety-two, she decided that it was time to realize a project that had been in the back of her mind for some time, a book of portraits of elderly people, which she planned to entitle *After Ninety*. She worked steadily at it, seeking out old people (preferably those with active creative minds like herself), photographing them, supervising the printing of the portraits, and sending copies to the sitters. It would have been an exhausting work even for a young person, but she refused to concede that it might be too much for her.

While she was thus engaged, in April 1976, Johnny Carson, host of NBC's *Tonight Show* invited her to be his guest on one of the shows. Carson surely

---

[5] to rest on one's laurels—to be content with past success and rest. The ancient Greeks and Romans gave crowns of laurel leaves to victorious athletes or generals, or other distinguished citizens, as a reward for their achievements.

had no idea of what he was exposing himself to. The story of what happened that night has been related by photographer Tom Eckstrom, Imogen's assistant, who drove her to the studio and remained in the wings while Imogen, in splended form, proceeded to upstage the experienced Carson in his own show:

> At first [Imogen] refused any make-up, but finally she said: "My nose does get a little red," and she let the make-up artist powder her nose— but that was it. Then we went to the green room, where all the guests sit and watch the monitors,[6] waiting their turn. Imogen was the last one to go on. It was a typical Johnny Carson show, and she sat there, her hands on her cane, stoney-faced. Carson would make one of his silly cracks,[7] and she'd turn to me and say in a really loud voice: "What are they laughing at? That's not funny!" And I am trying to get her to lower her voice. Then, part way along, the producer came in and asked her what she thought of the show. "The most ridiculous thing I have ever seen!" she snapped. . . . Then Carson said: "IMOGEN CUNNINGHAM!" and I gave her a little nudge out between the curtains and ran back to the green room to watch.
>
> Well, it had been a pretty ho-hum[8] night until then, but suddenly everyone in the green room was glued to the monitor, and everyone started going nuts![9] I mean EVERYONE—the technicians, the sound guys and the cameramen backstage were all screaming with laughter. The producer was running around saying: "Why haven't we had her before? We must have her back!" Everyone was just going crazy. And they fell in love with her. After the show everyone usually leaves right away, but the guests all stayed around, Carson leaning over his desk. And Robert Blake [the star of the show "Baretta"] said: "Can I give you a kiss?" "No," said Imogen, "I don't want any of your germs." But he bent over and gave her a quick peck on the cheek anyway, and she picked up her cane and screeched: "You wretch!" as he went running out. Then a lot of the audience came down to the stage to talk with her too. When we finally left, she was cool as though she had just been to the drugstore. "Well, how do you think I did?" she said. She knew exactly how she had done. It was quite an evening. [From Judy Dater, ed., *Imogen Cunningham: A Portrait*]

After that sensational debut, Imogen was asked to appear in a half-hour documentary about her career. But it was to be the last appearance on television. Imogen's health had been failing for months and dizzy spells were forcing her to keep to her bed much of the time. She was still working on the final stages of *After Ninety* when she died, on June 24, 1976. She had been involved to the last day, as she wanted to be. During the

---

[6] monitors—the television sets used backstage to follow the show.
[7] crack—slang for "joke."
[8] a ho-hum night—an ordinary, boring night.
[9] going nuts, going crazy—slang, for someone getting extremely excited, or furious, or amused.

preparation of her book, she had expressed much sadness to find many of her elderly sitters unoccupied, separated from the mainstream of life—a situation in which she would have never allowed herself to fall. "Her presence among us," said Margaretta Mitchell, editor of *After Ninety*, "proved that life could be lived fully, savored even, until late old age. She wore many hats,[10] real and symbolic, including among them: cottage queen, comic-opera witch, hippy grandmother, curious child, researcher, gossip, intellectual, horticulturist, gardener, cook, worker, comedienne, and—last but first—artist."

Understanding the Text

1. Was Imogen Cunningham very successful as a photographer?
2. To your knowledge, what kind of photographs did she take?
3. What reasons are given for the collapse of her marriage?
4. Why was she so interesting to her sons and to her friends?
5. Which were her outstanding qualities?
6. What examples can you give of her sense of fun and mischief?
7. Did she ever know financial success?
8. What was her last project?

Appraising the Text

1. Did you find words or expressions in the text that are not meant to be taken literally?
2. What do you think of Imogen's appearance at the exhibition (lines 131–140) where Ansel Adams was upstaged? What impression do you have of Ansel Adams? How do you think that Imogen felt about Ansel Adams?
3. Consider the behavior of Imogen Cunningham just before she went on stage on the Johnny Carson Show (lines 180–192). Could it be explained in different ways?
4. What is the tone of Tom Eckstrom's narration of the Carson Show: formal, informal, light-hearted, serious, conversational, amused, concerned, critical?

Vocabulary

Complete the definitions with the right word from the list below, which includes more words than necessary. Be sure to make the necessary adjustments in articles, nouns, and verbs.

1. A _____ is a television set that allows people to follow a show even if they can't see it directly.
2. A person's _____ is that person's inclination or preference.
3. A _____ person cannot be stopped or hushed.

[10] to wear many hats—to have many occupations.

4. A _____ person enjoys the company of others.
5. A _____ artist is one whose tastes are ahead of his contemporaries.
6. _____ clothes look cheap and in bad condition.
7. A _____ is a gentle push, usually with the elbow.
8. A _____ person does not like to be parted with his/her money.
9. A _____ person doesn't care to accumulate possessions.
10. _____ is the inability to get along together.

supportive	to eschew	bent
monitor	crummy	geologist
provocative	incompatibility	irrepressible
gregarious	nudge	unmaterialistic
tight-fisted	prick	
avant-garde	score	

Scanning for Details

1. Johnny Carson's show is known as:
   a) The Evening Show
   b) The Tonight Show
   c) The Today Show
2. The son of Imogen Cunningham who is a geologist is:
   a) Padraic
   b) Rondal
   c) Gryffyd
3. Imogen moved to San Francisco
   a) in 1947
   b) in 1957
   c) in 1944
4. The friend who said that Imogen liked to put a pin in people's balloon was:
   a) Tom Eckstrom
   b) Harry Cowell
   c) Jack Welpott
   d) Stephen Goldstine
5. Imogen made her first television documentary:
   a) in 1963
   b) in 1957
   c) in 1952
6. The musician who played on an old suitcase was:
   a) John Cage
   b) Charles Ives
   c) Henry Cowell
7. Imogen's friend said that Imogen was:
   a) extraordinarily attuned aesthetically

b) singularly attuned aesthetically
c) beautifully attuned aesthetically
d) incredibly attuned aesthetically

What Is Important?

Check the six statements, among the fifteen listed below, that express the most important facts to remember about Imogen Cunningham.

1. Imogen and her husband had incompatible personalities.
2. Imogen Cunningham's work consists mostly of portraits, plant and flower studies, and some pictures taken in the streets of San Francisco.
3. Imogen, although greatly admired on the West Coast, achieved national fame very late in life.
4. Imogen did receive a Guggenheim grant when she was eighty-seven years old.
5. Of her three sons, Gryffyd, who was the eldest and the most conventional, is now an architect.
6. Imogen was much more interested in people and ideas than in material possessions.
7. *Vanity Fair* was an elegant magazine that merged with *Vogue* in 1935.
8. Imogen never photographed crowds or large expanses of nature—just individual human beings and plants.
9. Toward the end of her life, she began to wear her famous black capes and outrageous hats.
10. The eccentric way in which she dressed revealed her individualism, her sense of fun and her joy in playing a part.
11. After nineteen years of marriage, Imogen found herself alone with three sons in high school and college.
12. She made extraordinary portraits because she understood and loved her sitters.
13. Although she couldn't read music, Imogen had a subscription to *Modern Music*.
14. Imogen was a free spirit with a lively interest in the world.
15. Imogen Cunningham moved to San Francisco in 1947.

Topics for Discussion

1. Has this chapter given you a new attitude about photography? In what way? What have you learned about photography that you consider interesting?
2. What makes a better marriage: identical tastes and interests, or contrasting personalities?
3. Is it possible for people of very different backgrounds, or people with opposite tastes and personalities, to be very good friends? Do you know cases that illustrate this question one way or another?

4. What defects are the most difficult to put up with in marriage or friendship: lack of kindness, untidiness, wastefulness, parsimony, unfaithfulness, bad temper, irony, or any others?

Selected Readings

About Imogen Cunningham and Ansel Adams

Read the following quotations, paying particular attention to the words and phrases that show the qualities and weaknesses of Imogen Cunningham. Take note also of the differences between Imogen and Ansel Adams that can be inferred from these brief passages.

Most of my life I didn't think of Imogen as more than just a good photographer and a great personality. At least that was my estimation of her until her show at Stanford in 1967, her first big retrospective. I walked into that show and saw the whole circle of my mother's work, and I stood there and I said: "Wow! I have been underestimating her all my life." At that moment I understood what Imo was all about.[1] Imogen didn't know anything about technique, and she didn't seem concerned about it. She used any developer anybody told her to use. . . . Almost every negative she ever printed has a yellow stain on it. She'd rub a print between her palms to bring the highlights down, she'd wipe her hands off on a towel, and then—with her hands still full of developer—take the negative out of the enlarger and put it in an envelope. All those yellow spots!"

Rondal Partridge

To me, Imogen was not a great artist but a great personality, one of the most unforgettable people I have known. . . . She and Roi and my father too were very "artistic," and bohemian, part of that artistic era of the twenties. And she remained so. . . . Imogen has been a definite force and stimulus in the world of photography on the West Coast. . . . But I think her major contribution was in stimulating young people in the way that Stieglitz did. I don't think either of them, Imogen or Stieglitz, is of the stature of Strand or my father. No way. I think they were both catalysts.

Bret Weston
(photographer, son of Edward Weston)

I hated saying this while she was alive, but at first I was not particularly drawn to her photographs. I liked the *Magnolia Blossoms* and the early flowers things very much, but until I had seen a lot of the portraits I couldn't understand why she liked the ones she showed so often. They

---

[1] what she was all about—what she meant, what she represented.

seemed very offbeat.[2] I wondered why she didn't do things more in keeping with the fact that she was an old lady. Of course that was not Imogen at all—she still had such a young spirit. . . . I had a delayed reaction to the photograph of Morris Graves.[3] I knew Graves' work fairly well and when I first saw Imogen's picture of him, the early one, I couldn't understand how it could be taken as a definitive[4] portrait. Now I admit openly, was I wrong! The more I found out about Morris Graves, and I found out a great deal about him over the years, the more I realized what a tremendous portrait it is. It has a feeling of mystery in it, it evokes the kind of atmosphere that you find in Graves' work—his birds have that sense of mystery. I don't know if that's his own garden or some place Imogen found in the forest, but she got a light, a perspective, a scale between his figure and the background that has a kind of mystery, an oriental quality that recalls his work rather than just define his features. That picture

Morris Graves, Painter, 1950, by Imogen Cunningham

[2] offbeat—unusual, unconventional.
[3] Morris Graves is a West Coast painter.
[4] definitive—final, making all others unnecessary.

made me realize what tremendous insight Imogen had about people and what they stood for.

Morley Bauer
(photographer)

To me, Imogen is one of the giants of photography. . . . The portrait of Morris Graves—that to me is one of the great landmarks[5] of portraiture. She didn't just take someone out into the woods and photograph him. She welded the whole thing—the setting, and who he is, and what he is—and so it all works beautifully together.

Arnold Newman
(photographer)

Imogen was the most prolific[6] and broad-ranging of anyone. She was a superb artist, always creatively oriented, with a warm sense of people.

Ansel Adams

[Ansel Adams'] technical capability went far beyond what most photographers ever realize. To my knowledge, no gallery museum or exhibition ever got sloppy[7] work from Ansel Adams. He had meticulous standards and that is not true of photographers any more.

Morley Bauer
(photographer)

I have always had the feeling that Imogen's final print never quite achieved what she had intended. Her printing was extremely uneven. Some had a perfectly gorgeous quality but some made me feel: "What a great pianist! but the piano is not very good!" You know in the early days she was thrown together with painters a lot, and painters don't worry about photography, especially about photographic technique. So Imogen was not exacting about the way she made photographs. She was inclined to be a little sloppy[7] . . . We never talked about technical matters much, though. She did ask me once what bromide did in the developer—she knew it did *something*. She'd ask simple questions and expect simple answers.

Her *Magnolia Blossoms* is one of the most beautiful photographs I have ever owned.

Ansel Adams

[Adams'] technique was straightforward. He was meticulous. He knew exactly what he wanted and how to get it.

James Allinder
(photographer)

---

[5] landmarks—important points.
[6] prolific—productive.
[7] sloppy—careless, dirty.

Discrimination at a Rummage Sale, by Imogen Cunningham

Questions

1. From the various opinions expressed in these passages, what seem to be Imogen Cunningham's great qualities as a photographer? What were her weak points?
2. What is the great difference between Imogen Cunningham and Ansel Adams, as photographers?
3. What does Ansel Adams have to say about Imogen as a technician? Does he think she was knowledgeable about such things as developers? Why is this surprising?
4. Besides the interest of comparing Adams' and Imogen's qualities, what was the purpose of including some opinions *about* Ansel Adams?
5. Based on the remarks of Morley Bauer and Arnold Newman, what makes a superior portrait?
6. As a conclusion, what did these various comments add to what you already knew about Imogen Cunningham—good or bad?

Project: Judging Photographs

Bring to class a photograph—to be judged by the whole class—that you consider either beautiful or interesting; it can be either a photograph that you have taken, a professional portrait, or a picture from a publication or a book.

Instructor's Note: It would be best to limit the selections to one or two types of photographs, for example portraits and plants; or portraits and advertisements, or any other types that the students have agreed upon]

The class will judge the entries, taking into account the following points:

Is the photo clear and sharp?
Is the composition well planned?
If it's a portrait, does it reveal something of the person's character, or feelings, or interests?
If it is an ad, is it simple and effective?

Each student will vote for the two photographs that he/she considers best. The class will poll the votes and discuss the choices.

The same project can be done with "the worst" or "the most ridiculous" pictures.

Jackie Robinson

Introduction

The Vocabulary of Baseball

A baseball team includes nine players, who come to bat in rotation. The pitcher throws the ball to the batter of the opposite team. The batter's job is to hit the ball with his bat within the limits of the playing field in such a way that he (hopefully) will have time to run to first base, or further, before the opposite team can retrieve the ball.

The batting average of a player is determined by dividing the player's number of hits by the total number of times he batted. When a player has a batting average of .350, it means that he has hit the ball at least once out of every three times at the bat. Anything above .300 is considered a good average.

Spikes, which will be mentioned in the story of Jackie Robinson, are sharp pieces of metal attached to the soles of running shoes or baseball shoes, to give the athletes a better grip on the ground while running.

The field is diamond-shaped, and therefore known as the diamond.

The umpire sees to it that the rules of the game are respected.

The term farm club is applied to a minor league team that is used as a testing ground by a major league team, which hopes to hire the minor league's better players.

Teams frequently trade their players, either because of personal difficulty with a player, to improve the team at a particular playing position, or for financial gain. A team might trade one of its good players for two players from another team, or for one player plus a certain sum of money.

Looking Ahead

Look quickly through the chapter.
- Is baseball the general theme?
- Who is Jackie Robinson likely to be? Do you know anything else about him?
- Do you think that baseball is, presently, the most popular game in the United States? Can you think of other games that are widely played or watched on television?
- What is the most popular game in the country where you live or where your family has lived? How is it played and who plays it?

Baseball

No sport, surely, would be considered more genuinely American than baseball. Yet the Great National Game appears to have originated not in the United States, but in Great Britain, sometime around the beginning of the eighteenth century. It was a simpler game then, with uncertain rules, but it did involve the use of a ball, a stick or bat, and a circle of stations already called "bases" that the players had to touch in order to score. In England it evolved into several games, one of which is cricket. On the other side of the Atlantic it became popular under the name of base ball—in two words—among boys who played it on empty lots and other places sufficiently distant from breakable windows. It was a schoolboy's great pastime, "the only thing," according to baseball historian Robert Smith, "outside the stern discipline of home chores and schoolroom studies, that gave a boy's life any goal." Baseball was not restricted to schoolboys, however; young gentlemen were enjoying it in their free time and even girls played a gentle form of it known as softball.

The game spread rapidly. Teams and baseball clubs multiplied, and in 1845 the founder of the Knickerbocker Club of New York, Alexander J. Cartwright, wrote down the first set of rules, prescribing the use of four evenly spaced bases, of a bat instead of an ordinary stick, and of two teams of nine players each. In 1857 the National Association of Baseball Players was formed for the purpose of standardizing the rules further, and two years later the Association formally forbade players to accept any remuneration for their participation in the game.

This last rule was meant to protect the amateur status of the game. In fact, some players had already received money for playing, but the practice remained a secret until 1869, when the Cincinnati Red Stockings admitted that they had indeed been receiving a regular salary. The notion of baseball as a professional game was received at first with considerable skepticism: could a man really expect to make a living playing that still-confused game? Could a "professional" team expect to attract enough paying spectators to defray its expenses and cover its payroll? Who would pay good money to watch a handful of men "hit a little ball with a big stick and then run and kick a sandbag"? It seemed absurd! But obviously baseball had many fans willing to do just that, and "pro" baseball flourished, developing over the years all sorts of complications, tricks, and refinements that made it increasingly exciting to watch for enlightened devotees, and increasingly confusing for the rest of humanity.

1876 saw the creation of the National Association of Baseball Clubs, which grouped a number of clubs from New York, Boston, Philadelphia, Saint Louis, Cincinnati, and Louisville. Another association, the American League, came into being in 1900, and brought together other teams from Boston, Chicago, Milwaukee, Cleveland, Detroit, Washington and Philadelphia. Today these organizations are known as the major leagues, which include only big cities' teams. Teams located in smaller towns are members of the minor leagues.

Each of the major leagues includes twelve teams that compete exclusively among themselves. During the baseball season, from April to September or early October, each team plays 162 games. The two teams that win the greatest number of games during the season play against each other for the league's championship. Whichever team wins four of the seven games is declared the league's champion. In the World Series that follows, the champions of the National League compete against the champions of the American League, and the team that wins four of seven games is declared World Champion.

Why did baseball become the favorite American game, to the point of being dubbed the Great American Game? Possibly it is because the game is less brutal and bloody than some other team sports, such as football. But it seems more likely that the game came to interest the whole nation because practically everyone, including women, played it as a child, belonged to a Little League team, and tried to show off for a sympathetic public of Moms and Dads. Even in the hearts of those who never played afterwards as adults, the cheerful memories linger.

In *The American Diamond,* Branch Rickey, former President of the Brooklyn Dodgers and a man who has spent his life playing or managing baseball, has this to say about the beauty, the meaning, and the value of his beloved sport: "With a ball and a bat and his imagination, a boy is a complete team. He can swing at the ball, chop at it, golf at it. He can run after it, use the trees for bases, or throw the ball against the side of the house to catch it. This is how the game begins, how the boy discovers it. To hit a ball, to throw it, to catch it, are exhilarating successes that he attempts again and again. Baseball is a romance that begins when a boy is very young. It starts his dreaming and teaches him to hope. It brings a diamond into his vision where the bases are fixed and the outfield is endless, and he begins to care about playing, about hitting the ball past everyone and rounding the bases, touching them and sliding home. He finds accomplishment in the diamond, something he can measure. It gives him direction and becomes a vital part of his summer. Hitting a ball and scoring a run are in a way what all of us try to do all our lives. Baseball becomes a symbol, win or lose, and the romance never really ends."

Understanding the Text

1. What is the difference between amateur sports and professional sports?
2. What do you remember about the difference between major and minor leagues?
3. Do major league and minor league teams compete against each other?
4. Who competes in the World Series?
5. How many games are played in the World Series?
6. How many teams does each major league include?

Your Opinion

1. Sports are supposed to teach fairness and many other qualities. Do you agree? What qualities can they teach?
2. Do you agree with Branch Rickey that the goals of baseball and the

goals of life are comparable? Does baseball give more to a little boy than reading or hearing stories, for example, or playing with friends, or any other activity?
3. Of all the sports you know, which do you think is the most interesting to play? To watch? Are "spectator sports" interesting?

What Is Important?

Choose among the following statements those that seem to be the most significant and most interesting to remember.

1. Baseball originated in Great Britain.
2. At the beginning baseball was written in two words.
3. The game was played by boys and girls and men and women.
4. The boys played baseball in places where there was no risk to break windows.
5. The first set of rules was written in 1845.
6. It was written by the founder of the Knickerbocker Club of New York.
7. The rules prescribe two teams of nine players each, four evenly spaced bases, and the use of a bat.
8. In 1857 the rules forbade players to accept payment for participation in the game.
9. Almost from the beginning, players were willing to be paid to play.
10. "Pro" baseball has flourished since the early 1870s.
11. In 1869 the Cincinnati Red Stockings admitted that they were receiving salaries.
12. The two major leagues have been in existence for a century or so.
13. Major league teams compete only among themselves.
14. The National Association of Baseball Clubs included teams from New York, Boston, Philadelphia, Saint Louis, Cincinnati, and Louisville.
15. The baseball season extends from April to September or early October.
16. Each team plays 162 games.
17. The World Series determine whether the World Champion for the year is a team from the National League or from the American League.
18. Little League teams seem to play mostly for the parents of the players.
19. People who have played baseball as children remember their games with pleasure.
20. Milwaukee has a team in the American League.
21. The National League is fourteen years older than the American League.

Cultural Notes for Profile, Part One

The Baseball Hall of Fame is a memorial institution located in Cooperstown, New York. It includes a library and a museum where photographs of early teams, and relics that belonged to famous players (uniforms, bats, trophies, etc.) are displayed. The names of the best players and of those who have contributed to the advancement of the game are inscribed on bronze plaques in the Hall of Fame. Those names are chosen by a committee of people prominent in the field of baseball, including sportswriters.

In schools and colleges, athletes who become members of their school's best team are frequently authorized to wear the initials or first letter of the school's name on their sweaters; they are said to have earned their <u>letters</u> for excellence in their sports.

Profile
Part One

Born January 31, 1919
Died October 24, 1972

> From the photograph of Jackie Robinson, can you guess what kind of a problem Robinson had to face during his career in baseball?
> Is the problem presented anywhere in this part of the profile?
> Did Robinson face the same difficulty in an organization other than baseball?

Only a baseball fan is likely to remember that Jackie Robinson's batting average for his whole career was a beautiful .342, that he had sometimes hit .400 in a season, and even an extraordinary .625 in a minor league. A few devoted admirers may also be aware that Robinson was the first Negro admitted to the Baseball Hall of Fame. But those would have to be people blessed with a superior memory. On the other hand, it's a rare American—even among people not interested in the Great National Game—who doesn't know that Robinson was the first black man ever allowed to play in a major league team, and that his first appearance on the diamond was seen by many spectators and players as one of those revolutions that threaten the order of the universe.

It's not that the excellence of black athletes was ever in doubt. For a long time Negroes had been competing with their white peers in boxing, racing, jumping, swimming, and other sports; and all-black baseball teams had occasionally played against all-white teams in the minor leagues. But no white team had ever included a black member. The reason had less to do with the game, perhaps, than with the fact that in team sports, the players live as one family, sharing locker rooms, team buses, and hotel rooms. Most white players had never slept or showered close to a black person. Even those who didn't object to the proximity were not quite sure of the attitude they were expected to take toward a black teammate. There was, furthermore, the all-important question of the feelings of people back home, and how they would treat the native son who had agreed to share a black man's room. Finally, the reaction of the public to baseball's integration had to be considered. What if the majority of white fans stayed away from the stadium rather than watch a mixed-race game? All these questions were answered in 1946 when the president of the Brooklyn Dodgers, Branch Rickey, decided that the time had come for what is now called "the noble experiment." The man he selected to break precedent was a superb athlete and an intelligent, articulate college-educated Negro whose full name was John Roosevelt Robinson, better known as "Jackie."

Jackie Robinson was the grandson of a slave and the son of a Georgia sharecropper, an occupation that Jackie described bitterly as "a newer and more sophisticated form of slavery." Jackie was six months old when his father ran away with a neighbor's wife, never to be seen again. Left with five small children and no job prospect in Georgia, Mrs. Robinson took her family to Pasadena, California, where she had a brother willing to give her a helping hand. Mollie Robinson promptly found work as a domestic servant for several white families, and rented a place of her own to avoid being a burden to her brother. The jobs didn't pay enough to feed the children properly, even with some assistance from Welfare, but the leftovers that she brought home from the kitchens of her employers kept the family from going hungry.

A courageous and determined woman, Mollie Robinson knew exactly what she wanted to do for her children. In the first place, she obstinately refused to move to an all-black section of town, despite the hostility of her white neighbors. And although she had little time to spend with her children, she did her best to impress them with the importance of religion and family togetherness. Most of all, she insisted that they take their education seriously. She saw to it that they all went to school while she worked. Since Jackie was too young to be accepted anywhere, his older sister Willa Mae took him along and dropped him at the nursery school's sandbox, where he played by himself until she could trot him back home. It was a great day for Jackie when he was finally old enough to pass from the sandbox to his first classroom.

As early as grammar school the boy showed great athletic abilities, and did well in the classroom also. His great cause of worry in those years was that he couldn't help his mother, for whom he felt—and would always feel—the deepest admiration. The best he could do at his age was to run errands for the neighbors, cut grass, and deliver newspapers. Then he began to steal small things, mostly food. In his early teens he joined a street gang. "Hardly a week went by," he was to write later in his autobiography, "that I didn't have to report to Captain Morgan, the policeman who was in charge of the Youth Division." Although the gang never committed any real crimes, it was risky business. Two men helped Jackie out of his dangerous association. The first one was a car mechanic named Carl, a kind man who explained to Jackie that he was bound to hurt his mother badly if he remained in the gang; Carl urged him to disengage himself from the group of mischief makers and to make his own decisions on what he wanted to do instead of following orders—in other words, to be his own man. Jackie's second mentor, Reverend Karl Downs, helped him further by giving him a place to spend his free time productively. In an effort to attract the idle youngsters of the neighborhood, the clergyman had organized a program of sports and games, peppering volleyball and badminton with spiritual and practical guidance. Jackie so admired Karl Downs that when he was in college, he volunteered to teach Sunday School. The decision was nothing short of heroic, considering that Jackie, who was playing football on Saturdays, had some difficulty dragging himself out of bed and to church next morning, when he was still stiff and sore. This worthy sacrifice was proof of his devotion to Karl Downs, who remained Jackie's friend to the end of his life.

At John Muir Technical School, Jackie earned letters in football, basketball, baseball, and track. In college he broke the record for the broadjump established by his own brother Mack, who had finished second at the Olympic Games of 1936 behind the famed Jesse Owens. With that background, Jackie could choose among the various colleges and universities eager to offer him a scholarship. He decided in favor of UCLA (the University of California at Los Angeles), where he established himself in no time as one of the best all-around athletes in the country; he won twenty-four letters in two years. A star in basketball and football, a record-breaking jumper, he could also play any position in baseball. The fact that he was pigeon-toed[1] doesn't seem to have interfered with his running, although it did give an individual touch to his gait when he was trotting around the field. As he was also a bright student, Robinson could easily have been one of the best-loved campus heroes, if it had not been for his belligerent character and his sharp tongue. According to San Francisco columnist Will Connolly, Jackie always had "a genius for getting into extra-curricular scrapes."

Jackie didn't finish college. After two years at UCLA, he came to the conclusion that no amount of education would help a black man get a decent job, and that he'd better give up the notion of getting a degree. With luck, perhaps he could become athletic director of some school. He did in fact find that kind of work with the National Youth Administration Youth Camp at Atascadero. But in that summer, 1939, the war was just about to begin in Europe, and when it did the Youth Administration closed its camps. Finding nothing better to do, Robinson joined a football team, the Honolulu Bears; he spent a year playing with them in Hawaii. When he came

---

[1] pigeon-toed—Jackie walked with his toes turned inwards.

back, the United States had entered the war, and Jackie willingly joined the Army.

At UCLA, Robinson had met a young woman named Rachel Isum, who had made quite an impression on him. But to Jackie's immense surprise and distress, Rachel had shown no inclination to warm up to him because, as she explained frankly, she suspected the campus football hero of being cocky, conceited, and self-centered. It took Robinson some time to improve his image; but he succeeded well enough to keep the relationship going while he was in Hawaii, and later at the Army's Fort Riley, Kansas. After Jackie was commissioned a second lieutenant in January 1943, they became formally engaged; the marriage would take place as soon as Rachel was through nursing school.

But the year 1943 didn't go smoothly for Robinson. To begin with, a quarrel with Rachel resulted in a break-off of their engagement. Then Jackie got in trouble at Fort Riley for sitting in the front section of a bus, next to a white woman, the wife of a fellow officer with whom he had started a conversation while waiting for the bus. When the driver ordered Jackie to move to the back of the bus, he refused to do so. The driver appealed to his superiors when they arrived at the terminal, and the fracas caused Robinson to be court-martialed. The court dismissed the charges against Robinson, and he was allowed to leave the Army with an honorable discharge at the beginning of 1945.

As soon as he was out of uniform, Robinson joined the Kansas City Monarchs, a professional black baseball team belonging to the Negro American League. His salary of $400 a month seemed pretty good at the time, but Jackie never adjusted to his team. It was a lively group, rather on the noisy side when they were happy with their game, and Jackie—a nondrinking, nonsmoking Methodist—didn't like to participate in their celebrations. Besides, he resented being a member of a segregated team, and was shocked by the lack of organization in the scheduling, the finances, and the promotion of the games. What irked him most of all was the narrow prospects open to a black player. What kind of a future could he plan on? At this point, Branch Rickey entered Robinson's life, to change it utterly and forever.

Branch Rickey was an eminent and respected figure in baseball. Nothing in his life up to that time had indicated that he was not a conservative in racial matters, presumably as opposed as any man to mixing colors in baseball teams. But this was not the case. Having given much thought to the matter, Rickey had felt for some time that segregation, which deprived white teams of excellent players, was absurd. He was enough of a realist not to try to oppose the general feelings as long as there was no chance of winning. But in 1943, he began to think that the time was ripe for a first step toward integration and that he could risk a cautious move. There would be stiff opposition, and possibly some ugly incidents—he knew that. But he believed that a slight change of attitude had already occurred. On the battlefields, blacks and whites had gotten used to fighting—and living—alongside one another; and the returning black veterans would be in a mood to stand up for their rights, to include the right to watch their favorite ball game with the white crowd, and perhaps even to play ball with white teammates.

Rickey didn't try to rush things. For almost two years, under one pretense or another (such as putting together a black team) he sent scouts to watch black teams and gather information about the best players. By the end of the summer of 1945, a careful study of the reports and of the personalities of the men under consideration led Rickey to decide in favor of Jackie Robinson. The man seemed to answer all his requirements: an immaculate private life, an honorable military career (marred only by a refusal to be humiliated), some college education and, obviously, a strong character. From the details collected by Rickey's scouts in California, it was evident that Jackie Robinson was a proud young man who keenly resented racial slurs and who didn't hesitate to talk back when insulted. At the same time, it seemed that he was intelligent and disciplined enough to play the role that Rickey had in mind for him.

The two men met for the first time in August 1945, and Rickey carefully explained to Jackie what the plan could be: Robinson would join the Montreal Royals, a minor league team that served as the top farm club for the Dodgers. Later on, he would be transferred quietly to the major league team. Then they'd wait for the reaction. Rickey didn't hide the fact that it would probably be rather unpleasant, but—he added—Robinson would have to bear whatever abuses, insults, and even bodily attacks that might greet his first appearances in the white team. "They'll be awful!" he warned. And to make clear that he knew what he was talking about, for three hours he proceeded to abuse the startled Jackie, as a sample of what was in store for him. Under the taunting of Rickey, who had imagination and a rich vocabulary, the young man began to have second thoughts about the whole idea. "I was twenty-six years old," he wrote later, "and all my life, back to the age of eight when a little neighbor girl called me a nigger, I had believed in pay-back, retaliation. The most luxurious possession, the richest treasure anyone has, is his personal dignity!" The reward, however, would be so great that after more discussion about the possible consequences of his decision, Robinson agreed to give it a try. He would be patient; he would be silent; he would—as Rickey requested—"be a ball player with guts[2] enough not to fight back." The contract was signed, to be kept secret until the beginning of the next training season.

The first question that Branch Rickey had asked Jackie was whether he

---

[2] guts—slang for "courage."

had a wife or a girlfriend to provide moral support during the hard time ahead. It was a rhetorical question, since Rickey already had the answer, having thoroughly investigated every aspect of his candidate's life before engaging in his "experiment." He knew that Robinson had made his peace with Rachel, and he knew also that the young woman was a perfect choice. It was therefore with Rickey's blessing that Jackie and Rachel were married in April 1946. A few weeks after the wedding, they left for Florida, where Robinson was to report for training with the Royals.

As Rickey had predicted, it was an unpleasant experience. In the first place, the trip to Daytona Beach, Florida, had been a nightmare: the newlyweds were only able to fly as far as Pensacola, where they were forced to de-plane to make room for two white passengers. When they reached Jacksonville, their destination, after sixteen hours in the crowded back section of a bus, they couldn't find a place to stay, or even to eat. Two black newsmen finally came from Daytona Beach to take them to the training camp. The problem of finding accommodations was to remain a serious one for years, particularly for Rachel, who always had the utmost difficulties in finding taxis, beauty parlors, and other conveniences when she accompanied her husband.

On the team itself, Robinson was at first given the cold shoulder by the majority of his fellow players, until they found out that he could indeed hit the ball. But although overt hostility disappeared fast enough, the players didn't become really friendly, and Jackie lived and traveled alone from game to game. The reactions of opposite teams, on the other hand, were violently antagonistic, and so were those of the southern municipalities and of the white baseball fans. In Florida, team managers preferred to cancel the games than to allow "the nigger" on their fields. Everywhere else, Robinson was greeted with insults, hisses, and threats. Hate mail was delivered to him before the games, the pitchers aimed at his head, and once a player threw a live black cat in his face: "Hey, Jackie, here's your cousin!" Through it all, he remained silent, as he had promised.

Rickey had chosen the Royals for Robinson's debut because the team, based in Montreal, Canada, didn't often have a chance to play in the southern states that were considered the stronghold of racism. But it so happened that the Royals, champion minor league team for the National League in 1946, were opposed to the Colonels of Louisville, Kentucky, minor league champions of the American League. The first three games of the final series took place in Louisville, in such an atmosphere of rage and hate that Jackie couldn't concentrate on the game. Heartsick and close to a nervous breakdown, he did poorly, and the Royals, almost as upset, lost two of the three contests. As the two teams travelled to Montreal for the final games of the series, it seemed that the chances of winning were very slim for the Royals. But a surprise was in store for all concerned. The Canadian public, indifferent to skin color and furious at the treatment that "their" black player had received in Kentucky, proceeded to retaliate. They booed and hissed each Louisville player running to his place, and cheered enthusiastically at each Robinson hit. Grateful and happy, Jackie and the Royals regained their balance; the game changed. They won the last three games of the series with a flourish. Robinson, who had hit .400 and scored the winning run in the final game, was the hero of the hour.

A large and friendly crowd waited for him while he was changing his clothes. As soon as Jackie came out of the clubhouse, the fans engulfed him, kissing him, slapping his back, tearing at his clothes and nearly smothering him to death. "I was thrilled," wrote Robinson later, "but I was also in a hurry. I had a reservation on a plane. . . ." He was finally rescued by a Canadian motorist. Sportswriter Sam Martin, who had witnessed the scene, concluded: "It was probably the only day in history that a black man ran from a white mob [that had] love instead of lynching on its mind."

Understanding the Text

True or False? If the statement is only partly true, explain why.

1. Jackie Robinson is very special in the history of baseball because he once hit .625 in a minor league season.
2. Branch Rickey chose Robinson for his "noble experiment" because Jackie was intelligent and mild.
3. Branch's idea was to proceed in two stages: Robinson would play first in a minor league team, then he would be transferred to a major league team.
4. Even in college, Jackie Robinson was not an easy man to get along with.
5. Robinson didn't feel comfortable in his black team, the Monarchs, because he had nothing in common with his teammates besides the color of his skin.
6. In 1945 Branch Rickey announced to the press that he was trying to find a black player for the Dodgers.
7. When Robinson was with the Montreal Royals, his teammates were violently antagonistic.
8. The Canadian public did their best to support their black player.
9. When he was in college, Robinson had many illusions concerning the prospects open to a black college graduate.
10. Robinson didn't object to joining the Army in 1945.

Scanning for Details

A. *Scan the profile section you have just read, for the following details:*

1. What was the name of Robinson's sister?
2. When did Robinson and Rachel Isum get married?
3. What organization gave Robinson his first job when he left college?

4. What did Robinson say, exactly, about a man's personal dignity?
5. What football team did Robinson join in 1939?
6. Who won the broad-jumping competition at the 1936 Olympics?
7. Where exactly was the Royals' training camp?
8. When did Rickey begin to think that the time had arrived to integrate the game?

B. *Which of the adjectives on the following list could be used to describe young Jackie Robinson? After choosing the adjectives, turn to the text to find the facts supporting the choice.*

wild	easygoing	realistic
modest	self-assured	bold
appreciative	cold	lazy
bitter	shy	selfish
proper	warmhearted	basically good

The Right Order

Put the following statements in the right chronological order to make a coherent story.

__1__ In 1945 there was no black player on any major league baseball team.

_____ Finally Robinson and Rickey signed a contract.

_____ Rickey decided that Robinson had all the qualities needed for the experiment.

_____ Branch Rickey felt that the time had come to desegregate baseball.

_____ Rickey warned Robinson that he would have to face a great deal of hostility.

_____ Rickey studied the reports of his scouts, including a report on Jackie Robinson.

_____ Therefore Rickey asked Robinson to come and see him.

_____ With some reluctance, Robinson agreed to join the Royals, a white team based in Montreal.

_____ Rickey said also that, no matter what happened, Robinson would have to refrain from fighting back.

_____ Then Rickey sent scouts to observe the best players in all-black teams.

_____ To begin with, Rickey told the press that he was trying to form a black league.

_____ When they met, Rickey explained his plan to Robinson.

Vocabulary

A. *Complete each sentence with the most appropriate word from the list, which includes more words than necessary. Be sure to make all needed adjustments in articles, nouns, and verbs.*

1. A _____ is a farmer who pays a part of his crops as rent to the owner of the farm.
2. You _____ for somebody when you go to the store to buy the things that that person wants.
3. A _____ is a person sent to gather information, usually about an enemy or a competitor.
4. After the games, the athletes change their clothes in the _____.
5. Branch Rickey wanted to _____ baseball teams by mixing black and white players.
6. A _____ is the end of a bus line.
7. Quarrelsome youngsters get frequently into _____.
8. The white players on the opposite teams insulted and _____ Robinson.

retaliation	luxurious	sharecropper
scrape	breakdown	segregation
to run errands	scout	locker room
to taunt	to integrate	flourish
pitcher	terminal	to dismiss

B. *Answer the following, referring back to the profile if necessary.*

1. How does one go about giving someone the cold shoulder?
2. What happens when you have second thoughts about a project?
3. What was in store for Amelia Earhart when she left Lae in her Electra?
4. Would it be right to say that Branch Rickey was his own man? Why?
5. Jackie's offer to teach Sunday school was nothing short of heroic. Was it heroic or not?
6. Jackie was not popular on campus because of his belligerent character. From the context, would you say that belligerent is likely to mean "mild"? "Quarrelsome"? "Shy"?

The Main Idea

Check the statement that best expresses the main idea of each paragraph.

Par. 1
a) Jackie Robinson's batting average for his whole career was .342.
b) Jackie Robinson was the first Negro admitted to the Baseball Hall of Fame.
c) Jackie Robinson is famous in the United States as the first Negro to play in a major league team.

Par. 2 a) It has always been recognized that Negroes were good athletes.
b) Most white players didn't want to share rooms and showers with black players.
c) Baseball was desegregated in 1946 by the president of the Brooklyn Dodgers.

Par. 3 a) Jackie Robinson's grandfather was a slave.
b) Jackie Robinson was raised in poverty by his mother.
c) Robinson's mother worked as a domestic for several families.

Par. 4 a) Jackie Robinson was brought up in respect for religion and education.
b) The Robinson family lived in a mixed-race neighborhood.
c) Jackie's sister had to take him along when she went to school.

Par. 5 a) Jackie had a deep admiration for his mother.
b) Although he got in some mischief, Jackie grew up straight.
c) When he was in college, Jackie Robinson taught Sunday School at the neighborhood church.

Par. 6 a) In college, Robinson was a great athlete but a difficult young man.
b) In two years, Jackie Robinson won twenty-four letters.
c) Jackie Robinson was pigeon-toed.

Par. 7 a) Jackie's first job was as athletic director of a Youth Camp.
b) Robinson gave up after two years of college and went to work.
c) Robinson was drafted in 1939.

Par. 8, 9 What is the main idea of each of these paragraphs?

Topics for Discussion

1. Does it seem to you that the situation has changed since the 1940s regarding
   (a) black athletes in team sports
   (b) black people in restaurants, hotels, buses, planes, and other public places?
2. Have you noticed a general attitude about race among students?
3. Is the attitude about race different in countries that you know other than the United States?
4. Do you think that colleges and universities should offer scholarships to high school students, based only on their athletic abilities? Is it all right for college athletes to be excused from some classes in order to practice or participate in sports events? Shouldn't college athletes be held to the same scholastic standards as all other students?
5. There is presently a great interest in physical fitness: people jog, run,

swim, exercise at home or in spas, go to jazzercise classes, etc. Do you think that this is a serious change of attitude or a fad that will disappear in a short time? Do you think that the search for physical fitness involves all classes of society, all ages? What caused this interest in physical fitness? What do you do for physical exercise?

Profile
Part Two

To what kind of team did Jackie Robinson belong at the end of Part One?
Was Branch Rickey's plan working well?
What do you expect to happen now?
Skim the text to find out if Jackie Robinson remained connected with baseball until his death.

Toward the end of the next training season, in April 1947, Branch Rickey made his official announcement: Jackie Robinson had been signed to play first base for the Brooklyn Dodgers. The news that a black man had finally reached a major league team raised howls of protest all over organized baseball. Some Dodgers asked to be traded rather than play alongside Robinson; other teams threatened to strike—until Ford Frick, president of the National League and usually a mild man, let it be known that strikers would be fired. "This is the USA," stated Frick firmly, "and one citizen has as much right to play as another." The games went on as scheduled, but the mood of the players was rebellious and the crowds continued to greet Jackie's appearance with jeers and catcalls and death threats. Jackie played on, enraged but silent.

The Dodgers left him to himself; there was no friendly overture, but the players' first hostility slowly faded after the first games, as they observed Jackie's skill at the bat and his unquestionable ability to draw huge crowds of spectators to the gates. Even the most hostile baseball fan had to admit that Robinson's game, quick and dynamic, was impressive and exciting to watch. Jackie always found new ways of hitting the ball and he was a master in the art of distracting the opposing pitcher.

As the season progressed, the Dodgers also began to admire the gentlemanly silence with which their black teammate kept responding to the abuse. They were not surprised to see the pitchers aim at his head—it was an old story. But when a player from the opposite team threw his spikes in Jackie's leg, injuring him badly, the Dodgers rallied around Robinson, raising a unanimous and furious protest against the culprit. The incident, which happened toward the end of the season, in August, marked in a way the turning of the tide for the Dodgers. The "race question" simply vanished from the locker room; the players relaxed. Even Rachel suddenly found that she was welcomed without fuss among the wives for a chat before the game. Although he could feel the improvement, Jackie remained skeptical. "They did not change because they liked me any better," he said later. "They changed because I could help fill their wallets." But he was genuinely happy when, in 1948, an umpire that he had been fighting threw him out of the game as casually as though he had been an ordinary member of the team. "Jackie Is Just Another Boy Now!" proclaimed the front page of a paper the next day.

Robinson had two good years in 1948 and 1949. The Baseball Writers Association gave him its "Most Valuable Player" award for the 1949 season. *Time* magazine put him on its cover, and a national survey disclosed that Jackie was the second most admired man in the country, after singer Bing Crosby. More perhaps than the honors lavished on him, Robinson appreciated his regained freedom of expression; in the spring of 1949 Branch Rickey released him from his promise not to fight back. It would have been wise, no doubt, to remain a silent, dignified victim of racial slurs, and to continue to be admired for his fortitude by the majority of the public. But, besides the fact that he was by nature a fighter, Robinson had accumulated too much bitterness and fury during his three years of stoic silence, too much resentment from the humiliations and hardships of his travels and Rachel's loneliness among hostile white neighbors. He had paid dearly for his fame and for the success of the "noble experiment" and he was now mad at the world. His rage had the effect of making him play better, but aggressively—"like a kid with a switchblade." He was also speaking his mind, and often very loudly—contesting the manager's decisions, fighting the umpires, complaining to the press, and antagonizing sportswriters. Everyone in organized baseball and in the sports press came to agree that Robinson was a great player but a prickly, belligerent man. "The most difficult player I ever had to deal with," lamented umpire Jocko Conlan. "He wore me out!"

In 1950 Branch Rickey, Jackie's staunch ally, was replaced at the head of the Dodgers by Walter O'Malley. Robinson and O'Malley never managed to get along. Jackie found the new president "viciously antagonistic"; O'Malley referred to Jackie as "Rickey's prima donna,"[3] and never lost an opportunity to infuriate Robinson by making nasty remarks about Rickey in his presence. The bad feelings between the two men were intensified by the press which, always eager for an exciting story, reported every small incident and every uncautious remark dropped by Robinson about his new boss and about the Dodgers' management in general.

By 1954 the tension had become unbearable. All through 1954 and 1955 the Dodgers' manager kept Jackie on the bench much of the time. Robin-

---

[3] A *prima donna* is the most important woman singer in an opera. Prima donnas have the reputation of being temperamental, demanding, and capricious.

son, who had always been an active participant in all games, found his enforced inactivity hard to bear. The best solution, he finally concluded, was to quit as soon as he could secure an interesting and rewarding position in private industry. He found what he wanted in 1956, when William Black, president of a chain of restaurants named Chock Full O'Nuts, offered him the vice-presidency of the company. As Jackie was about to sign the contract with Black, the directors of the Dodgers announced that Jackie had been traded to the New York Giants for $30,000 and a pitcher. Robinson was furious: "My first impulse was to tell them that Jackie Robinson was no longer the Dodgers' property to trade!" He signed the Chock Full O'Nuts contract, refusing the Giants' offer to reconsider, and retired definitely from the game. No regrets. Wrote Robinson in his book: "The way I figured it, I was even with baseball and baseball with me. The game had done much for me, and I had done much for it."

When Robinson left the Dodgers the battle had been won; black players were being hired by major league teams without raising so much as an eyebrow. The situation had changed forever, but strangely enough, Robinson himself couldn't believe it. When it was rumored that his name was being considered for the Baseball Hall of Fame in 1962, he shook his head, declaring that he would never be selected because of his race. His name was accepted immediately, however. After the election, Jackie and Rachel were treated to a round of celebrations and testimonial dinners, complete with telegrams from the president, the vice-president, and the attorney-general. "Most fabulous of all," commented Robinson, "both my mother and Branch Rickey himself lived to see the day!"

Jackie spent seven years at Chock Full O'Nuts in pleasant association with William Black, a white man sympathetic to the Negro cause and indeed to all minority causes. Far from objecting to Robinson's involvement in outside activities, he encouraged him to do anything that he deemed important. And Jackie did enter several new fields, always leaving his mark and proving over and over again that he was very much his own man— and always a fighter.

Robinson's business undertakings included the founding of the Freedom National Bank—the first all-black bank in New York—and of Jackie Robinson Construction Corporation. The bank floundered at first, due to the dubious background of Jackie's partner and, after the departure of the man, to the inexperience of some of the top executives. The members of the board of directors, who didn't want to be drawn into unpleasant discoveries, refused to believe that anything was amiss. Robinson, however, took it upon himself to investigate the problem, determined to take unilaterally whatever action would be needed. His inquiry, which led to the forced resignation of the key administrator of the bank, saved the establishment's reputation—the only thing that really counted in Robinson's eyes.

In or out of business, his chief concern was always the dignity and welfare of his people. Even so, he tried to make clear that he was not a fanatic racist or integrationist. Mixed schools, he would explain, didn't particularly appeal to him if all-black schools could be as good as white ones; and he didn't approve of busing children far from their homes for the sole purpose of mixing races. He took pains to explain—perhaps thinking of Branch Rickey—that he had no difficulty liking and trusting white people who liked and trusted him. He disapproved, most of all, of those Negroes who turned against their country. When singer Paul Robeson defected to Russia in 1949 and proclaimed publicly that no black American would fight for America in case of war, Robinson was asked by the Un-American Activities Committee to comment on the declaration. Jackie took the opportunity to speak against discrimination, but he roundly condemned Robeson's unpatriotic position. He and other American Negroes, he concluded, had too much invested in their own country to throw it away; and in true Robinson style he added that if Negroes had to fight for civil equality they certainly didn't need the Russians' help to do so.

As a way to pursue the task that he had started on the diamond, Robinson joined the board of directors of the NAACP.[4] He had agreed to be chairman of the Freedom Fund Drive, on condition that the chairmanship would involve more than lending his famous name to the project; he wanted to participate actively in the campaign. Assisted by a young lawyer experienced in the matter of fundraising, Robinson toured the country, making speeches and raising money quite successfully. The two men even organized a $100-a-plate dinner, despite the opposition of the board, which maintained that this had never been done and surely would not work. The dinner and the campaign produced excellent results. But Robinson was becoming disenchanted by the conservative attitude of the NAACP. He felt that the "Old Guard" (as he called the top officers who had making the policies for a long time) were too timid, too cautious, and too dedicated to keeping things as they were. He complained that they were out of touch with the current problems of the Negro population, and too old to try new methods where the tried ones had failed. He thought also that the much-respected head of the NAACP, Roy Wilkins, was responsible for the lack of dynamism of the organization, and he didn't hesitate to proclaim loudly that Wilkins should pass the reins to younger and bolder hands. Having thus spoken his piece, Robinson resigned from the board of the NAACP.

By then he was embroiled in a different kind of battle—on the political front. Here again Jackie was an oddity: a Republican Negro. Since he approved of the Republicans' economic policies, he didn't think that he had any obligation to follow his fellow blacks in the ranks of the Democratic Party. Although he had occasionally supported Democratic candidates with a fine record on civil rights, the presidential campaign of 1960 found Jackie

[4] NAACP—the National Association for the Advancement of Colored People (founded in 1909).

among the supporters of Republican Richard Nixon. In the first place, Nixon's attitude on black issues had won his approval; besides, he told his disapproving friends, he wanted to remain a Republican "to keep the party from becoming exclusively white!"

His real reason may have been his admiration for the New York state governor, Nelson Rockefeller. The two men's lasting relationship had begun with a tart letter from Jackie to Rockefeller, demanding to know why there was no black man in the governor's administration—whereupon Rockefeller invited Robinson to come and see him. The meeting went well. The governor charmed Jackie, asked for ideas and recommendations, and followed them when they were given. When Rockefeller asked him to be one of the directors for his campaign for the presidency in 1963, Robinson resigned from Chock Full O'Nuts in order to work full time for his candidate. Although the campaign failed, Robinson's faith in the governor and his affection remained intact. Not only did he like Rockefeller as a person, but he considered him helpful to the black cause.

From 1966 to 1968, Robinson served as Special Assistant for Community Affairs to Rockefeller. He might have remained associated with the governor for many years if Richard Nixon, running again in 1967, had not chosen Spiro Agnew as his vice-president. Judging Agnew unacceptable, Robinson regretfully took his leave from Rockefeller, explaining that he was going to campaign now for the Democratic candidate opposing Nixon—Lyndon Johnson.

Few people would have believed that it might happen, but the years eventually mellowed Jackie Robinson. Wilfrid Sheed, who met him in the early 1970s, describes him as "gentle as a Pullman porter,[5] white-haired and prematurely old." Robinson had good reasons to look aged beyond his years—his eldest son, Jackie Jr., had just been killed in a freak accident in June 1971. Jackie Jr. had been a troubled child, then a troubled youth for many years. While his sister Sharon and brother David were growing without undue stress, Jackie Jr. had gone through many crises. He had been unhappy first to be the only black face in his Long Island school, then unhappy to be always known as "the son of Jackie Robinson"—a famous father that he was clearly not expected to emulate. A poor student, he had run away from home once in the hope of "finding himself" in California. At seventeen he enlisted in the Army, just in time to be sent to Vietnam; he came back addicted to drugs. He had just finished a successful detoxication treatment when he was killed one night on his way home, when his car ran out of control. Robinson was devastated, and never fully recovered from the shock. "You don't know what it is like," he said to a newsman, "to lose a son, find him again, and lose him again."

---

[5] The porters working on the railroads' Pullman cars (sleeping cars) were usually older Negroes with white hair and courteous manners.

In his last years of illness and grief, Robinson was warmed by the love and support of a host of admirers. The Dodgers, based in Los Angeles since 1958, held a great ceremony in 1972, in the course of which Jackie watched the "retirement" of his number, the "42" that he had worn on his uniform and that would never be worn by another player. After the Los Angeles festivities, he presided over the events of a "Jackie Robinson's Day" in Chicago. Many of his old friends and former teammates were there to fete him, as well as some of the sportswriters with whom he had fought in the old days. At the opening of the 1972 World Series, he was honored again. But this was his last celebration; ten days later he died of a heart attack brought on by diabetes. He was fifty-three.

Long before Jackie Robinson died, the integration of baseball had ceased to be a controversial topic. But because of his outspokenness and his inability to rid himself of his bitterness, Robinson himself, as a person, remained controversial much longer than the sport that he had helped to desegregate. Although he was admired and even idolized by people in all walks of life, and he enjoyed many opportunities, Robinson never forgot the price he had to pay for them. His autobiography,[6] which came out shortly before his death, closes on these words: "I have many memories. I remember standing alone at first base—the only black man in the field. I had to fight hard against loneliness, abuse, and the knowledge that any mistake I made would be magnified because I was the only black man out there. I had to fight hard just to become 'just any guy.' I had to deny my true fighting spirit so the the 'noble experiment' could succeed. When it finally did, and I could become my own man, many people resented my impatience and honesty. But I have never cared about acceptance as much as I cared about respect. . . . There is one irrefutable fact of my life which has determined much of what has happened to me: I was a black man in a white world. I never had it made."

Understanding the Text

1. Did Robinson and Rickey achieve what they had set out to do in 1946?
2. When did things go wrong for Robinson at the Dodgers?
3. Why did Robinson remain controversial and fight with so many people?
4. Was Robinson an extremist or a moderate in matters of race?
5. Why was he critical of the NAACP?
6. What was peculiar about his political position?
7. Was he involved in politics? What examples can you give?
8. What image do you have of Jackie Robinson after reading about his whole life?

---

[6]*I Never Had It Made* (New York: Putnam, 1972). The expression "I never had it made" means "I was never certain of success."

230 JACKIE ROBINSON

Scanning Exercise

Scan both parts of the profile to complete the outline of Jackie Robinson's professional life, which should include the six different fields in which he was active.

I. Education (1939)   (first field)
    Athletic director,
    Atascadero Youth Camp
    _____ (second field, or organization)
    _____ (where and in what capacity?)
    _____

III. _____ (third general field)
    A. _____
        _____ (where)
    B. _____
        1. _____
        2. _____
        3. _____
IV. _____ (field)
    A. _____
    B. _____
    C. _____
V. _____ (field)
    _____
VI. _____ (field)
    A. _____
        1. _____
        2. _____
    B. _____

Vocabulary

line 11 When he appeared on the field, Robinson was greeted with catcalls, jeers, and racial slurs.
Are any of these meant to the pleasant? What do you think cat calls sound like? In Robinson's case, what kind of racial slurs was he likely to hear?

line 25 When a player threw his spikes intentionally in Robinson's legs, the Dodgers raised a furious protest against the culprit.
Who or what is the culprit likely to be?

line 30 Although Robinson felt a change of attitude among his teammates, he remained skeptical.
Was he fully convinced or not that their feelings had changed? What in the text justifies your answer?

line 56 Robinson was regarded as a prickly, belligerent man.

	Does it seem from the context that he was considered friendly? Does <u>prickly</u> remind you of a verb that you know? What flower or plant can be described as prickly? Why was Robinson described as prickly?
line 59	Rickey had been Robinson's <u>staunch</u> ally for several years. What other adjective could be used?
lines 85–86	Nowadays nobody <u>raises an eyebrow</u> when black players are hired by major league teams. What does this seem to mean? When do people raise their eyebrows in the countries that you know?
line 104	Robinson's bank <u>floundered</u> because of the inexperience of the executives. Did it do well or not?
line 150	Robinson was <u>embroiled</u> in a different kind of battle. What other word would you use?
line 162	Robinson wrote a <u>tart</u> letter to Governor Rockefeller. Considering what he was telling the governor, was the letter nice or not very nice?

Facts, Inferences, and Opinions

The text below offers a combination of facts, inferences (from both parts of the profile) and opinions. Read it carefully in order to differentiate between them. Some statements will be debatable.

1. After signing Robinson for the Montreal Royals, Branch Rickey proceeded to complete his plan.
2. It wouldn't be possible for Robinson to share a hotel room with another Dodger.
3. Rickey, therefore, signed another black man, pitcher John Wright, to be his roommate.
4. Branch Rickey was a remarkably thoughtful man.
5. John Wright was a Southerner who had a realistic view of racism.
6. He was quiet and phlegmatic.
7. These were qualities that Robinson should have tried to emulate.
8. In 1950, Walter O'Malley replaced Branch Rickey as president of the Dodgers.
9. It was a disaster for Robinson, for Rickey had been not only a good boss, but also a supporter and a friend.
10. It seems that O'Malley disliked both Rickey and Robinson.
11. His relations with Robinson were bad from the start and became worse as time went by.
12. The tension was partly Robinson's fault.
13. He should not have criticized O'Malley in press conferences.
14. O'Malley must have told the manager to keep Robinson on the bench as much as he wanted.
15. Branch Rickey was probably retired at that time.

Topics for Discussion

1. Jackie Robinson was irritated by the attitude of Roy Campanella, a black player who joined the Dodgers a year after him. Campanella was an easygoing man who tried hard to be accepted by white people; he was quiet, always smiling, careful to show no anger and no desire to be accepted as an equal. Robinson told Campanella that he should assert himself, and fight back if he wanted to be respected.
    Which, in your opinion, is the best attitude? Would things have worked better for Jackie after his first year if he had acted like Campanella? Would he have achieved the same results for baseball, for himself? What is best for racial relations in general?
2. Robinson didn't approve of taking children far from their homes in buses in order to be sure that blacks and whites are mixed in schools. What do you think of the question? If a school is all white because of the neighborhood, should half of the students be bused to another part of town and black children brought from their own section?
3. Do you think that blacks make particularly good athletes? If so, why?

Cultural Notes for Selected Reading

The Olympic Games were originally a religious festival that took place every four years since the eighth century B.C. in the Greek city of Olympia. The festival included several athletic contests: running, wrestling, discus throwing, jumping, etc. More sports were progressively added. The games were suppressed in 394 A.D. by the Roman Emperor Theodosius I, on the grounds that they violated the spirit of Christianity.

At the end of the nineteenth century, a French sportsman and educator, Baron Pierre de Coubertin, undertook to revive the games. The first modern Olympics took place in Olympia in 1896, and were attended by athletes of several nations. The second Olympics were held in Paris in 1900; since that time many countries have hosted the Games, and the number of nations participating in the competitions has multiplied, as has the number of sports: at the Olympics of 1984 in Los Angeles, 141 nations were represented by a total of 9,000 athletes who competed in 220 sports events.

The pentathlon of ancient times was a series of five exercises (jumping, running, wrestling, throwing the discus, and hurling the spear) performed by the same contestants on the same day. The modern pentathlon comprises running, horseback riding over obstacles, swimming, pistol shooting, and fencing.

Fencing is a game of defense and attack between two contestants armed with a thin sword, or "épée." In some contests, the tip of the sword is wired to light up when it touches the body of the adversary—thus recording a "hit" without possibility of dispute.

1984: Reference is made in the text to George Orwell's famous book "*1984*" (published in 1949), which gave a somber description of life in that year in an absolutely totalitarian country.

Selected Reading

There Has Always Been Olympic Mischief
by Erich Segal

With such a title, what do you expect to find in this article?
What can you tell about the text after reading the first two paragraphs: Does the tone of the article seem to be formal, informal, negative, optimistic, serious, aggressive, respectful? What is the author setting out to do with the first words of the third paragraph? What is he going to show?

Every four years, when the Olympics roll around again, journalists seem automatically to recycle those misty-eyed notions about the "Good Old Days." They eulogize the original Greek Games as being pure and uncommercial. If we believe what we read, every ancient competitor was an amateur, and all worshipped fair play.

This is, of course, sheer nonsense. As Lord Byron quipped: "All times when old are good." In fact, the mythology of a perfect Olympics is the modern invention of snobs and self-styled purists, perpetuated by sports writers—and television commentators at a loss to fill air time.

Here is the not-so-rosy truth. From as far back as Homer's *Iliad*—which portrays games of the 12th century B.C.—Greek athletes cheated as a matter of course. Their entire ethic was based on winning—by fair means or foul. Olympic boxers hit where they weren't supposed to, and took bribes to take dives.[1] Runners jumped the gun[2] (to be precise, the Greeks used a trumpet), and they elbowed one another viciously on the curves.

The chariot racers were even more brutal, especially in the Games held under the Roman Empire. We have recorded cases of drivers *stabbing* rivals as their vehicles drove neck to neck. Perhaps most amazing of all, if it were later proved that, say, a boxer or a wrestler had dishonestly won through bribery—*he still didn't lose his title*.

Perhaps you are asking where the judges were. Oh, the Greeks had the usual referees, umpires, and so forth. But these arbiters were often susceptible to financial enticements—and treats. And even if an honest judge was stationed at the turning post that the runners had to circle, he still had

---

[1] take a dive—for a boxer, to lose a match on purpose.
[2] jump the gun—to start running before the gun signal marking the beginning of the race has been fired.

great difficulty in determining whose elbow was smashing into whose ribs, because the athletes didn't wear numbers. For that matter, they didn't wear uniforms either. Indeed, one real difference between the ancient and modern games was the fact that all the Greek athletes were obliged to compete in the nude.

You might think that this bareness would have made it impossible to commercialize the ancient Games. After all, the stars couldn't be paid to wear anybody's track shoes or sweat shirts. That much is true, but we would be naive to think that the athletes were therefore "amateurs." Then, as now, the Olympics meant big bucks (sorry, drachmas)[3] for the champions. According to a recent book by Professor David Young of the University of California at Santa Barbara, the winner of the sprint could, in fact, expect to earn the ancient equivalent of several hundred thousand dollars!

To begin with, there was the actual prize money. From at least the sixth century B.C. the Greeks openly gave cash awards for first place in the Olympics. After that there were huge fees that these newly crowned champions could demand for "personal appearances." No, I am not being anachronistic. Promoters of minor track meets—which were often held to advertise local products (!)—would fork over plenty to have the hottest runners of the day merely show up. What's more, the athletes were generally absolved by their home town from paying taxes and were given free meals for life.

Thus, even in classical times, the Olympics were a highly commercial affair. And they were also highly political. There were ferocious rivalries among the various city-states, both from the mainland and the various Greek colonies, to have one of their own win a big title.

I am not afraid to name names. The greatest sprinter in antiquity was a certain Astylos, who hailed from Crotona, a tiny Greek village in the boot of Italy. At the Games of 488 B.C. he dazzled all by winning both sprint events. Afterwards, Astylos was approached by some boys from Syracuse, then a rich and growing city in Sicily, who made him an offer he couldn't refuse. They suggested that he change citizenship so he could run for *their* city's team in the next Olympics. The price was right. And the deal paid off. In the Games of both 484 and 480, he repeated his amazing double. But he entered the record books as Astylos of *Syracuse*. Which proves that money can buy anything, including Olympic champions.

Lest I besmirch the name of a great athlete, let me hasten to say that I do not imply that Astylos really cheated. He simply accepted a lot of cash to move to a bigger base of operations. It happens all the time today with corporate executives.

---

[3] drachma—a silver coin of ancient Greece.

Let us conclude this iconoclastic survey of ancient misbehavior with two rather bizarre anecdotes. According to the authority of the great historian Plutarch, King Mithridates of Pontus (first century B.C.) poisoned the rival charioteer who dared to beat him in a race. And finally there was the multitalented emperor Nero. In A.D. 67, he had the officials hold a special Games at Olympia in his honor. He lasted about twenty yards and fell off his chariot. But he was nonetheless declared the winner. In this instance, the judges were not bribed. They were simply scared.

When the Games were revived in 1896, all the ancient shenanigans were revived with them. And as time progressed, refinements were added. It almost goes without saying that the Greeks overwhelmed their countryman Spiridon Loues, the winner of the marathon, with numerous tangible rewards. (Some accounts say female spectators threw their jewels down to him on the track.)

But let us quickly say he won fair and square. And yet when he crossed the finish line, he was a little "high" on more than joy—having fortified himself along the road with swigs of sugared wine.

By contrast, the first marathoner to reach the stadium in the St. Louis Olympics in 1904 was one Fred Lorz of the United States. Just before President Teddy Roosevelt's daughter was to give him his medal, it was discovered that Lorz had not, after all, gone the entire distance under his own steam. Having cramped up[4] at about nine miles, he accepted a ride from a passing car. But the auto also cramped up a little later, and Lorz jumped out and jogged the rest of the way to the stadium, arriving well before the other racers. This "victory" is one of the lighter moments in the history of Olympic cheating.

More ominous is the fact that distance runners very quickly began taking stimulants. Strychnine was one of the earliest drugs used for this purpose. Indeed, T.J. Hicks, the athlete who actually got the marathon gold medal after Lorz was disqualified, had sustained himself en route with large quantities of brandy and small doses of strychnine. Though his physician was not secretive about it, Hicks got to keep his medal.

Of course there were no drug tests for Olympic athletes in the early years of our century. Strychnine was again used by the runners in the 1908 London Games—during the famous marathon in which the Italian Dorando Pietri reached the stadium first and collapsed before he got to the tape. This time one of the official doctors rushed over to give him a quick injection to help him finish. But the shot nearly finished Dorando, and he had to be taken to the hospital after being disqualified for not completing the race on his own.

Since then, doctors have been hard at work trying to invent substances

---

[4]cramp—a painful muscle contraction.

that would improve performance while escaping detection. This medical research may have helped performances but it has often harmed athletes. Tragic cases like that of Knud Jensen, a Danish cyclist in the 1960 Rome Games who collapsed and died from a combination of stimulants, spurred the international Olympic Committee to initiate drug testing.

. . . In 1976, Olympic cheating entered the Electronic Age. During the fencing event of the modern pentathlon, the light on the épée of the USSR's Boris Onischenko flashed to indicate that he had scored a hit against his adversary. Unfortunately, at the time it went off, the weapon was nowhere near his opponent, Britain's Jim Fox. Upon investigation, the judges discovered that Boris had been a rather naughty boy, having rewired his sword to light at any moment *he* would deem appropriate. Boris and the entire Soviet team were immediately disqualified. The athlete himself has not been heard from since. Perhaps he has been sent to Siberia. Or to a better electronic school.

Then there is the matter of "sex cheating." This can involve women taking such large doses of male hormones to improve their performance that they lose nearly all female characteristics and should really not be allowed to use the ladies' room.(In some cases the sex of the athlete is a matter of conjecture.) There is no need to conjecture about Dora Ratjen, the German athlete who just missed a gold medal in the women's high jump in the notorious Olympics of 1936. "She" subsequently set world records in this event that remained on the books until years later, when it was discovered that "Dora" was, in fact, *Hermann* Ratjen, a mediocre male athlete, but an excellent female impersonator.

. . . As I look over what I have written, I feel that I have presented an excessively bleak picture of an inherently glorious event. Though the misbehavior described is tragic but true, I still do not share the pessimism of the writer whose most famous work has given him a near-franchise on the digits "1984." George Orwell viewed the Olympics as "bound up with hatred, jealousy, boastfulness, disregard of all rules and sadistic pleasure in witnessing violence; in other words, it is war without the shooting."

This is going much too far. The Olympics are nothing more or less than a reflection of everything that is good as well as bad in human nature. The anecdotes of ancient Greek skulduggery prove that the Games have always suffered from what we might benevolently call "human frailty."

And one might argue that our own age can actually claim a tiny bit of moral superiority over classical Greece. Very few of us, I think, would subscribe to the view of a European coach, who was recently quoted as saying: "As long as you are still alive for the victory ceremony, you should get your reward. There is no room for ethics in sports anymore."

This is cynical in the extreme. I firmly believe that the majority of spectators today watch the Olympics to see "pure" excellence. Like Mark Spitz's seven gold medals. Or the upset victory of the fresh-faced American hockey team in 1980. Or the eagerly awaited performance of Mary Decker and Carl Lewis this time.[5]

That is what the Olympics are really about.

About The Text

1. What was the author's main idea at the beginning of the article?
2. What was his general conclusion at the end of the piece?
3. Are the Olympic Games today different from the Games in Antiquity? Consider them in terms of:
   a) location
   b) participants
   c) sports
   d) professional status of the athletes
   e) morality of the athletes
   f) awards for the winners
   g) type of cheating
4. What do you think of the author's tone in the whole article? Do you feel that he is basically for or against the Olympics? Why did he write the article, in your opinion?

Vocabulary

Erich Segal has used many slang or colloquial words, easily understood from their context. What ordinary words could he have used instead of the underlined ones?

line 34 The Olympics mean big <u>bucks</u>.
line 43 The promoters of minor track meets would <u>fork over</u> plenty [of money] to have the best runners.
         What does the use of the word "fork" picture?
line 73 When the Games were revived in 1896, all the ancient <u>shenanigans</u> were revived with them.
line 140 The anecdotes of ancient Greek <u>skulduggery</u> prove that the games have always suffered from "human frailty."

Did You Guess Right?

line 8   The mythology of a perfect Olympics is the modern invention of <u>snobs</u> and self-styled <u>purists</u>. . . ."
         <u>Snobs</u> are usually people who consider themselves superior in culture, fashion and social position. What would the snobs be, here?
         The <u>purists</u> objected to the changes in the scores of famous compositions used in *Fantasia*. They would object to the improper use of words or grammatical structures. What does Segal call "purists" here, in your opinion?

---
[5] The Olympics of 1984.

line 13   Olympic boxers took <u>bribes</u> to lose.
                         What other word could you use?

line 61   Erich Segal doesn't want to <u>besmirch</u> the name of a great athlete.
                    a)   to quote
                    b)   to honor
                    c)   to dirty

line 65   "Let us conclude this <u>iconoclastic</u> survey of ancient misbehavior."
                    Has his survey been respectful or not?

line 76   The Greeks gave their countryman many <u>tangible</u> rewards (including jewelry).
                    a)   large
                    b)   small
                    c)   real

lines 85–86   Lorz didn't go the entire distance <u>under his own steam</u>.
                    What would really run on its own steam? When applied to a man, what does the metaphor mean?

Prefixes

A.   The prefix <u>eu</u> always indicates that something is good or beautiful.

     1. *Eulogizing* somebody is to say good things about the person.
     2. To be in a state of *euphoria* is to feel very good and happy.
     3. To say, "You seem to be mistaken," instead of, "You are lying," is a *euphemism*.
        How would you explain Euphemism?
     4. To kill a person who is near death and in great pain is call *euthanasia*.
     5. The right for doctors or family members to resort to euthanasia has been often debated. Why is this called *euthanasia*? (Thanatos is the Greek word for death.)

B.   <u>multi</u> (compare to *multiple, multitude*)

     1. What is a multimillionaire?
     2. What does Erich Segal indicate by saying that Nero was "*multitalented*"?
     3. What is a *multiracial* crowd?
     4. What is the difference between *unilateral* disarmament and *multilateral* disarmament?
     5. How do you understand: "The poor man had *multifarious* duties"?

C.   <u>chron</u>

     1. What do you do when you are asked to put a group of statements in *chronological* order? Obviously, *chron* or *chrono* has to do with

2. If you were asked to write the chronology of the kings of England, what would you do?
3. If you were told, "You can't trust that man; he is a *chronic* liar," what would you understand?
4. Erich Segal explained that he was not *anachronistic* in speaking of "personal appearances" of ancient athletes. But he was anachronistic when he said that ancient athletes "jumped the gun", i.e., started running before the gun signaling starting time had been fired. Why was he anachronistic then?
5. Ray Bradbury wrote *The Martian Chronicles*, a series of short stories describing several landings on Mars and other events of the colonization of the red planet. What does the name "chronicles" indicate about these stories?

Topics for Discussion

1. What do you think of George Orwell's opinion that sports are "bound with hatred, jealousy, boastfulness, disregard of rules, and sadistic pleasure in witnessing violence—in other words, war without the shooting?" Is this true of the sports in which you participate? Is it true of professional sports? Are some sports "cleaner" than others? Do you think that George Orwell is closer to the truth than Branch Rickey? Do some sports give their fans the "pleasure of witnessing violence"?
2. One of the major objectives of sporting events such as the Olympics is to encourage people to participate and to do their best. Do you think that the Olympics serve that purpose? What else do the Olympics accomplish?
3. Do you feel that people who watch sporting events on TV are stimulated to practice the sports they see?
4. Many professional athletes make a great deal of money—far more than people in most professions can hope to make. Is it right for a football player to be paid more than a surgeon, or even than the president or prime minister of a country?
5. Referees and umpires are often accused of taking bribes to make decisions favoring a certain contestant or a given team. Do you believe that the practice is really widespread?
   It was not easy to be a referee in the ancient Olympics. Is it easy to be a referee or an umpire today in a major sports competition?

Walt Disney

Introduction

Looking Ahead

- Look through the chapter.
  Are all the sections about Walt Disney?
- What does the name of Disney mean to you?
- Do you think that animated films like *Fantasia, Sleeping Beauty,* and other Walt Disney productions are still interesting today?
- What do you like or dislike about the cartoons shown on television?
- Skim the passage below: does it seem to be
  a story about animation, with anecdotes?
  a description of the process of animation?
  a history of the art of animation?
  a first piece about Walt Disney as animator?
  a comparison of animation with other arts?

Animation and the Vocabulary of Animation

Anyone who can draw can animate a scene—for example, a galloping horse. All the artist has to do is sketch on individual pieces of cardboard or paper each one of the positions taken by the body of the horse, and particularly its legs, tail, and mane, as it rushes ahead. If the draftsman stacks his drawings in the proper order and flips them like a deck of cards, the horse will seem to be galloping, or at least moving in a more or less coherent manner, depending on the skill and care of the artist. In a motion picture cartoon, each section of the film carries one of the poses taken by each of the characters involved. As the film rolls, the characters are seen to move like live actors.

It takes 10,000 to 15,000 drawings to animate a 7-minute cartoon—the length of the average *Mickey Mouse* reel. *Sleeping Beauty,* a full-length feature, required 325,000 drawings; *Bambi* had four million. One of the characters, seen on screen for one minute, needed 1,140 drawings.

The top animators of a cartoon do not waste their time and creativity on such a multiplicity of repetitious drawings. They merely trace the extremes—that is, the first and the last positions of each motion—and leave to the *"in-betweeners"* the drudgery of providing the intermediary drawings. The first drafts, made with pencil on paper, are transferred to transparent sheets, called "cels" because they were originally made of cellulose acetate. The cellulose has been replaced by more convenient material, but the name remains.

When all drawings have been transferred to cels, the inkers retrace the lines with ink and the opaquers can then paint bodies and objects with solid colors. All this work is done on glass surfaces, lighted from below and built to turn 360 degrees to allow the workers access to every part of the drawing. The cels are fragile, and attract dust so easily that the artists have to wear lint-free white gloves while working.

While the characters are thus given life, another team of artists prepares the backgrounds. The models that they make first, in oil, watercolor, or any other medium, are often works of art. Indeed, well-known painters and cartoonists have begun their careers as draftsmen and backgrounders in the Disney Studio. When the background cels are ready, each cel of the moving series is photographed in turn on top of the unchanging background.

Actually, the operations are somewhat more complicated than this sketchy description indicates. In the first place, parts of the background do not remain still—and consequently require additional cels. And the draftsmen do not trace the whole body of a moving character through all its successive positions. They draw on one cel the part of the body that is not involved in the motion; other cels carry the parts that move least and therefore go through fewer in-between positions (the arms of a walking man, for example) and other cels carry the parts that move most—the legs. The various cels are then piled up with great precision on top of the background—body first, then one position of the arms, then the corresponding position of the legs. The whole affair, which constitutes a frame, is then photographed by the cameramen. There will be a frame for each in-between position of the legs, the cels carrying the arms being replaced less frequently. Everything is done by hand, with great care. Needless to say, the process is time-consuming, which explains why an animated feature is more expensive to make than a live-action film of the same length. And let's not forget that we have not struggled with synchronization, which is an art in itself.

We shall see in Walt Disney's profile that the creator of Mickey and Donald Duck eventually had to give up making cartoons and turn to another kind of fantasy world.

Summing Up

Suppose this class wants to make a cartoon.

a) What different kinds of artists will be needed? What will each group do?
b) What equipment will be needed? How is it used?
c) What is needed besides artists and material for the drawings?
d) How will the cartoon be put together?

Logical Reasoning—Connectors

Some of the groups of two sentences below express a cause and its effect, to be indicated by because. *The other groups present a restriction, to be expressed by* although *or* unless.

Combine the two sentences of each group, using the connector that indicates their relationship. The connector will have to be used either in the first or in the second sentence.

Examples: A. The transparent sheets used by the animators are called cels.
They are not made of cellulose acetate any more.

could become:

The transparent sheets used by the animators are called cels *although* they are not made of cellulose acetate any more.*

B. He is a very good draftsman.
He is not creative enough to be a top animator.

would become:

Although he is a very good draftsman, he is not creative enough to be a top animator.

1. The author says that anyone can animate a scene.
   It is not really easy to do.
2. It is not easy to animate a scene.
   You can draw pretty well.
3. Many young artists went to work as cartoon animators.
   The pay was rather poor.
4. They were eager to become animators or even in-betweeners.
   The work gave them plenty of practice.
5. Young Gus Arriola became animator in the cartoon department of the MGM** Studios.
   He had no previous experience in that line of work.
6. He was eager to be hired.
   He was very interested in animation, and he needed the salary.
7. Arriola left that job after a year and a half.
   He didn't like to work under pressure, as animators do.
8. Arriola never worked at his best.
   He had time, peace and quiet.
9. Arriola quit his first job at MGM.
   He remained with the studio, in a different department.
10. MGM was not often so accommodating.
    The bosses recognized talent in their dissatisfied employe.

---

*In this particular case, it would be just as good, from the point of view of logics, to say: "*Although* the transparent sheets used by the animators are called cels, they are not made of cellulose acetate any more.

**Metro-Goldwyn-Mayer—one of the major studios in Hollywood.

Profile
Part One

Born December 5, 1901
Died December 15, 1966

What kind of man, in your opinion, could have created the Disney cartoons and films and Disneyland?

Skim the text to find out the answers to the following questions:
- Did Walt Disney draw the characters of his cartoons himself?
- Was Mickey Mouse his first cartoon?
- Did Walt Disney come from a family of artists?

Walter Elias Disney was born in Chicago. The location was rather a matter of chance, for the boy's father, Elias, was the kind of man who never meets with success for long and who keeps moving from place to place, always convinced that the grass will be greener in some other part of the country.[1] Elias had a sour disposition and a remarkably slow sense of humor. He listened, poker-faced, to the jokes that young Walter always tried on him; he would turn away without a word, then came back to his son several days later, saying: "You know, I have been thinking about the joke that you told me, Walter. It's funny, very funny!"

Elias tried his hand successively as a farmer, a businessman, an orange grower, a carpenter, a mechanic, a hotel owner, and a house builder. He could also, when times were hard, make a living of sorts[2] by playing the fiddle[3] at the door of a local saloon; he remained outside, however, for, as a religious man, he didn't care to set foot in such a sinful place. Whatever he did, Elias expected all members of his family, no matter how young, to spend most of their waking hours working for him without any compensation. Moreover, he didn't believe in letting them spend whatever little money they managed to earn on the side. His two eldest boys, Herb and Ray, deserted the household as soon as they could, leaving behind the two younger brothers, Roy and Walter, and baby Ruth. Roy, who was eight and a half years older than Walter, played an important part in his brother's life, first as companion and protector, then as advisor, supporter, money supplier in difficult times, and eventually as business manager and president of the Walt Disney Corporation.

During Walter's childhood and adolescence, Elias operated first a farm

---
[1] an allusion to the proverb, "The grass always looks greener on the other side of the fence."
[2] a living of sorts—some kind of living (connotation: not very good).
[3] fiddle—a violin, but the term has a derogatory meaning. It might be used to refer to a bad instrument, or, often, to a violin used to play folk music, as opposed to classical.

in Marceline, Missouri, then a newspaper-delivery business in Kansas City, and finally a jelly factory in Chicago. In all three enterprises, Walter and Roy found themselves toiling endlessly before and after school. In Kansas City they had to get up at 3:30 A.M. to receive the newspapers from the truck and deliver them from door to door. The boys tried to do some business of their own by buying an extra stack of papers to sell in town. Elias had no objection to their enterprise, but he demanded their profits "for safekeeping," and the boys never saw their money again. Walter then found a job sweeping a candy store during his lunch hour, but having learned his lesson, he carefully refrained from declaring his new revenue to his father.

Disney was never heard in later years to complain about his hardworking youth, but he seems to have been marked by his childhood. He never learned to play or to relax; he never lost the habit of working at least fourteen hours a day. Nor did he seem able to form friendships outside of his family circle, having never had the time or the opportunity to do so in his youth. He either inherited or learned from his father the art of making people work for the smallest salary he could talk them into accepting. One of Disney's best animators, who had worked for him in the thirties, was to describe him without rancor as "a good and pleasant taskmaster and a terrible paymaster."

Walter was not a very good student—his mind wandered off too easily. But he loved to read, and he particularly enjoyed the works of the great storytellers: Charles Dickens, Robert Louis Stevenson, Mark Twain, and Sir Walter Scott. And he discovered early—almost by accident—another source of pleasure. In an ill-advised fit of youthful spirits, Walter had once painted some forms with black tar on the white wall of his father's farm. The unamused Elias made him sorry for this outburst of creativity; but the incident inspired one of Walter's aunts to present the boy with crayons and drawing pads. Walter played with these and became so interested that he asked one of the teachers at school for instruction. He became pretty good— one of his sitters paid him 25 cents for his portrait and a drawing of his horse, and the local barber thought enough of young Walter's production to give him free haircuts in exchange for a drawing a week—which the barber put in his window. At fourteen, Walter received permission from his father to attend Saturday morning classes at the Kansas City Art Institute, on the ground that it was "educational."

Although he shared some of his father's values as an upright worker and a conservative citizen, Walter was vastly different from Elias in his appreciation of the lighter sides of life—a blessing that he must have owed to his mother, a hardworking woman with a sense of humor. Walter loved jokes and gags,[4] which he collected and filed for further use. He enjoyed

---

[4] gags—jokes, or amusing tricks or situations.

circus parades so much that he organized some with the participation of his schoolmates and neighbors. He learned to do magic tricks. As a teenager he discovered vaudeville[5] and motion pictures, and earned some money doing imitations of Charlie Chaplin. None of these activities, surely, met with Elias' approval.

In the spring of 1917 Walter graduated from McKinley High School in Chicago. All of his brothers, including Roy, were already in the Army or the Navy. Either because he was feeling left out or because he didn't care to remain alone at home, Walter did exactly what Ray Kroc was about to do: he lied about his age to join the Ambulance Corps. Curiously enough, Kroc and Disney both ended up in the same ambulance company in France, but they didn't get to know each other. By the time Walter was shipped to France, the war was over. Once overseas, however, he had to wait until the spring of 1919 to be brought back home. When he finally reappeared in Chicago, Walter announced, to Elias' acute displeasure, that he had definitely made plans about his future: he was going to be an artist.

Walter returned alone to Kansas City, full of ideas and impatient to start a career, preferably as political cartoonist for the *Kansas City Star*. Since the *Star* was pleased with the cartoonist that it already had, young Disney had to resign himself to a less glamorous job as a plain draftsman, first with the Kansas City Advertising Studio and afterwards with the Kansas City Slide Company—a firm that made animated "commercials" for the local cinemas. Although he didn't remain long with either outfit, Walter gained much through his apprenticeship. At the studio he made friends with a talented draftsman named Ub Iwerks, with whom he remained associated, on and off, through a good part of his career. At the Slide Company, Walter learned the elements of animation and began to make some short reels of his own with a camera borrowed from his employer. These shorts, which he called "Laugh-o-grams," made fun, in cartoon form, of local problems and scandals. They sold well enough to give Walter and Iwerks the courage to go into business for themselves.

But the Laugh-o-grams didn't hold Walter's interest very long. He had a new idea to try—a series of cartoons illustrating updated fairy tales. The cartoons that he and Iwerks produced were not bad by the standards of the day, but Disney never got paid for his films. He then embarked on a fresh project, a series of funny shorts featuring a child actress and animated characters. He called it *Alice's Wonderland*. Money was so scarce at that point that Walter was living in his studio and eating on credit. He did earn $500 by making a film on dental hygiene for a dentist—to which he was able to add the small sums that Roy occasionally managed to send him.

All he could produce with such meager funds was a pilot film for the *Alice* series. Then, completely broke, he had to reconsider his position.

---

[5]vaudeville—humorous variety show.

Kansas City, he reasoned, was not the most favorable place for the kind of future to which he was aspiring. California was the place to go. For one thing, it was the most likely place to "break into movies" as he wanted to do. Besides, his uncle Robert, established in Los Angeles, might be moved to lend some assistance; and better still, Roy was there, recovering from a bout with tuberculosis. Having sold all his worldly possessions, Walter bought a one-way ticket (in first class!) to Los Angeles. With one small suitcase and $40 to his name, he presented himself to Uncle Robert, who agreed without excessive enthusiasm to provide room and board for $5 a week, and to let his nephew use the garage as a studio. Walter rented a camera and set to work on the *Alices*.

Even by the standards of 1923 the first six *Alices* were not very good, and only the novelty of the technique (mixing cartoons and live characters) helped them sell at all. A realist under his dreams, Walter was well aware that he was not a good enough draftsman to make them better. He had a wealth of ideas, he could invent gags and adventures, but he needed a first-class animator to give shape to his characters. With some difficulty, he persuaded Iwerks to give up his steady job in Kansas City to join him in his uncertain venture. With Iwerks at the drafting board, the quality of the *Alices* improved enough to make them easily marketable.

Through these ups and downs, both Walter and Roy got married—Roy to his Kansas City sweetheart Edna, and Walter to Edna's maid-of-honor Lillian, who was working as an inker at the Disney Studio. But since there was no time (or money) for honeymoons, work went on pretty much as usual at the studio. Walter was too engrossed in his ideas to think of taking time off anyway. With sixty *Alices* completed he felt that the line was exhausted, and with Iwerks' help, he began a new all-cartoons series, featuring a new hero, *Oswald the Lucky Rabbit*. *Oswald* caught on immediately. Its main character was more appealing than Alice, the story line was stronger, the situations funnier, the characters better drawn. *Oswald* sold so well that, in the glow of the resulting prosperity, the Disney brothers built their first houses—an unusual step for the brothers, who so far had lived most frugally, plowing most of their profits back into the production of their lucky rabbit.

As it turned out, they were soon to need their savings. In 1926, Disney went to New York to renew his contract with *Oswald*'s distributor Charles Mintz, and to ask for a raise in his percentage. But Mintz announced coldly that there would be a cutback in the studio's share of the profits. He added that if Disney refused to sign, he would have to do without four of his best animators, who had been hired by Mintz at higher salaries; he would also lose the right to produce *Oswald,* since the name of the cartoon, according to custom, was the distributor's property. Disney refused to sign. The Mintz episode surely did not diminish his innate distrust of business people, and it had much to do with his determination from then on to keep personal control of all the rights attached to his cartoons—control that Walt Disney Productions has kept to this day.

Disney was deflated at first, but not for long. In the train that was taking him and Lilly back to Los Angeles, he came up with a character and the first scenario for a new series. The hero would be a mouse looking very much like Oswald without the ears, and named Mortimer. Lilly vetoed Mortimer as too formal; "Mickey" would sound much better, she said; and Mickey it was. Walter, Iwerks, and the few loyal draftsmen left in the studio went to work on the mouse at once, and the soon-to-be-famous Mickey Mouse took shape under the pencil of Ub Iwerks.

Three reels were already completed when the first sound movie, *The Jazz Singer*, was presented in Hollywood, shaking the motion picture industry profoundly. Disney understood immediately that the era of silent pictures was over, and that Mickey had to be a talking mouse if he were to place himself ahead of the competition. He rushed with his reels to Kansas City to get a background score from a musician friend (whom he hired on the spot for the Studio); then to New York to synchronize cartoon, score, and Mickey's voice—which was Disney's own and remained his to the end. He concluded what looked like a good deal with Pat Powers, the owner of the Cinephone [Sound] System, who agreed to provide Disney's studio with the necessary equipment and to distribute the future cartoons.

It turned out that Powers had plans of his own. Although he did distribute the *Mickeys,* which were instantly successful, he never sent Disney his full share of the profits. When Walter demanded them, he was faced with the same kind of blackmail that Mintz had tried with *Oswald:* Disney was to stop producing his cartoons independently and to start working for Powers at a fixed salary—if he refused he would be ruined because Iwerks, the indispensable Iwerks, father of Mickey, had agreed to leave Disney's Studio to launch a series of his own, financed by Powers.

Even if Disney had been by nature inclined to yield to blackmail, Powers' attempts to take over the production of Mickey would have convinced him of the great value of his series and given him a good reason to hold firm—as he did. Back at the studio, he pushed the production of the shorts, to which he added a new series, entitled *Silly Symphonies*. Iwerks, he found out, was not indispensable after all. Good craftsmen were now working at the studio, more were eager to join. The work went apace. By 1930 the Disney cartoons, and particularly Mickey, had become immensely popular. Always cheerful, always on the brink of disaster, and always bouncing back with new calamitous schemes, the Mouse with the squeaky voice had caught the public's fancy. Movie houses had to include a new cartoon in every program. Mickey Mouse Clubs were opening everywhere, newspapers were devoting columns to the beloved character, and even *Time* magazine honored the Mouse with a feature article in 1931. Mickey, by then, was an international celebrity.

Understanding the Text

1. Are there points of resemblance between Walt Disney and Ray Kroc? Between Walt Disney and Walter Cronkite? Walt Disney and Ray Bradbury?
2. Is it difficult to understand why Walt Disney was an obsessive worker all his life, and a hard taskmaster?
3. Why is Roy Disney important in the story of his brother?
4. How did Walt Disney learn to be a tough businessman?
5. Why is *The Jazz Singer* so important in the history of motion pictures?
6. What was Walt Disney's part in the creation of *Mickey*?
7. Why was Disney more indispensable than Iwerks at the Studio?
8. What did the Disney Studio produce in the early 1930s?

Scanning for Details

1. Did Disney break with Charles Mintz in 1924 or 1925?
2. What positive qualities can you find in Elias Disney, either expressed or implied in the text?
3. What was the name of the sound system used by Disney in the first *Mickeys*?
4. What did Disney's animator say, exactly, about his former boss?
5. In what company did Disney work first when he came back to Kansas City after the war?
6. Why was *Oswald the Lucky Rabbit* more appealing than *Alice*?
7. What was the total amount of art training that young Disney received?
8. When were the first *Alices* produced?

Facts, Inferences, and Opinions

The following statements express either facts, inferences or opinions. Read them carefully to differentiate. As usual, some statements will be debatable.

1. Walt Disney listened to Lilly's advice.
2. She was right to suggest "Mickey" instead of "Mortimer."
3. Disney must have felt that he was not getting enough from the profits of the *Mickey* cartoons.
4. *Mickey* had been doing very well.
5. Since Powers had been slow in sending the money he owed, Disney should have guessed that something was wrong.
6. When Disney met with Powers, he was planning to ask for a larger share of the returns.
7. Powers announced that he would not pay unless Disney agreed to work for him as an employee.

PROFILE 251

8. If Disney refused, said Powers, he wouldn't be able to produce *Mickey* because Iwerks was leaving the Studio.
9. It must have been a painful shock for Disney to learn of Iwerks' betrayal.
10. Iwerks was not a reliable friend.
11. Before Powers, Mintz had tried to blackmail Disney.
12. Disney was not lucky in his choice of distributors.
13. And distributors do not seem to be a very honest breed.
14. Iwerks was a fool to leave the Disney Studio.
15. After a year of trying to launch his own series of cartoons he had to give up.
16. He must not have found very good positions afterwards.
17. A common friend eventually talked Disney into taking Iwerks back on his team.
18. No doubt it was humiliating for Iwerks to go back to work for his former friend.
19. Disney had agreed to hire Iwerks, but he never spoke to him again.
20. He should have forgiven him.

Which of the statements above are clearly opinions? Facts? Inferences? Which statements do you find debatable?

Vocabulary

A. 1. Scientific books have to be updated frequently. How do you update them? What expressions does "updated" remind you of that could be used in the sentence: *The textbooks had to be replaced because they were* _____.
   2. What is remarkable in the face of a poker player (or a player in any other serious game) that led to the expression "poker-faced"?
   3. From Mintz' and Powers' attempts to blackmail Disney, what explanation can you give of the word *blackmail;* how and why do you blackmail a person?
   4. From the context, what is a hard taskmaster?

B. *The following statements include, in a different context, words that were encountered in the text. Give your own synonym for the word if you can, or choose the word of identical meaning in the list.*

   1. Once, when the Studio was in serious financial difficulty Disney announced that everybody would have to take a 34 percent cutback in salary.
   2. Since most of the workers knew that the problem was real, they accepted the cutback without rancor.
   3. Being aware of the novelty of their production, they realized that it would take time to be successful.

252　WALT DISNEY

   4. They continued to work <u>apace</u>.
      One of the animators, however, got mad and expressed his displeasure to his boss in very strong terms. Disney forgave him this <u>outburst</u> of bad temper.
      Iwerks, a splendid draftsman, didn't have any of Disney's <u>innate</u> flair and sense of timing.
      Neither did he possess that business sense that is <u>indispensable</u> to marketing a new product.
      But he couldn't help feeling an <u>acute</u> desire to start a cartoon series of his own.
      His attempt to do so proved <u>calamitous</u>.

show	reduction	excellent
explosion	in another place	remorse
disastrous	quickly	discussion
bitterness	newness	useless
from birth	sharp, strong	expense
absolutely essential		

Prefixes

<u>Syn</u> and <u>sym</u> mean "with" and by extension, "like" and "together." *Sympathy,* for example, is the ability to feel "with" another person, to share the person's feelings.

   1. What did the technicians do when they *syn-chron-ized* drawings, voice and music for a Mickey cartoon? What does *chron* indicate here?
   2. If somebody says: "Let's *synchronize* our watches," what will we have to do?
   3. Some plants live in *sym-bio-sis*. This is the case for mistletoe and the oak, for example. What does "bio" indicate, and what does "symbiosis" refer to?
   4. If you *analyze* water, you will find hydrogen and oxygen. How do you *synthesize* water?
   5. What is the difference between ordinary rubber and *synthetic* rubber?
   6. Some scientists and industrialists are meeting for a *symposium* on waste disposal. What is symposium more likely to mean:
      a) condemnation
      b) general study
      c) promotion?

The Right Order

Put the following sentences in the right chronological order to make a coherent story.

   __1__ Elias Disney bought forty-five acres of land that he hoped to turn into a prosperous farm.

_____ Finally the overworked Elias fell ill and had to keep to his bed.

_____ At first he refused to use fertilizers because he believed that they were not good for the plants.

_____ As a final blow, a severe drought destroyed his crops.

_____ The young men resented their father's demands and his lack of generosity.

_____ From then on Elias used fertilizers, with good results.

_____ Roy, who was only sixteen, couldn't keep the farm going all by himself.

_____ He made his elder sons work hard and refused to let them have money of their own.

_____ Roy and Walter cried when they saw their favorite animals auctioned off.

_____ But his neighbor showed him the difference that fertilizers could make on a patch of corn.

_____ Elias had to resign himself to selling the farm and its equipment.

_____ One night they slipped out of the house and caught the train to Chicago.

_____ Without his two grown sons Elias found it difficult to work his forty-five acres.

Topics for Discussion

1. The author spent a great deal of time on Walt Disney's father and the circumstances that surrounded Walt Disney's early life. The same was done about Imogen Cunningham, Katharine Graham and others.
Do you think that too much importance is given to such factors—family and background?
Do you know people who are very different from what one might have expected from their family and childhood?
2. Should a father pay for the fulltime work that his sons and daughters do for him? Should the father take the money earned by the children on the side? Should he get that money for safekeeping to prevent the young people from using it on what he'd consider "unwise" purchases?
3. Do you know a proverb similar to the American saying: "The grass always looks greener on the other side of the fence."?
What non-American proverbs do you know?

Profile
Part Two

Skim the text to find the answer to the following questions:
- Does this part of the profile provide much information about Disney's family life?
- Does it provide information about some of his cartoons and films?
- Does it describe the development of Disneyland?

Walt Disney never drew a character after 1926. He knew that the outstanding draftsmen now working for him could design and animate the cartoons much better than he ever had, and it made more sense for him to concentrate on what he alone could contribute. Disney's strength was his imagination, his ability to come up with original ideas, to create amusing characters, to expand the gags for maximum length and effect, and to carry the project through. A first-class editor, he had a talent for rejecting needless details from a cartoon, keeping just enough to make it rich and entertaining but not so much as to interfere with the comic line. Ub Iwerks, for all his skill, had failed miserably when he was on his own, because he lacked Disney's editing flair and genius for organization.

Another side of Disney's character explains both his spectacular triumphs and his numerous brushes with disaster: he was never satisfied with repeating a successful formula—new techniques, new dreams beckoned him, and neither the lack of precedent nor the shortness of money would give him pause when he felt like experimenting with something new. He went cheerfully ahead on the wings of his new idea, undaunted by Roy's or Lilly's stern lectures. And so he experimented with sound, then color, bold new projects—and eventually with amusement parks and cities of the future.

The results were not always financially rewarding—far from it. In fact, the Disney Studio was chronically short of cash or in debt for most of its existence; new projects always started on enthusiasm and borrowed money. In 1945, Roy announced glumly to his brother that his latest venture had put the company $4.5 million in debt. Walter burst out laughing. As Roy watched, petrified with surprise and no doubt wondering about his brother's sanity, Walter managed to explain: "Do you remember when we couldn't borrow a thousand dollars? And now we owe four and a half million dollars! I think it's pretty good!" Roy couldn't help laughing too. But even with a sense of humor, the situation at the Studio was often unpleasantly precarious. One of the reasons was Disney's insistence on perfection and constant improvements. He never allowed shoddy work or shortcuts that would cut down the cost but weaken the quality of the animation. The research work was extensive and costly. And he refused to have anything but the best of everything—artists, equipment, surroundings for "his people." To train the apprentices and help the draftsmen, in 1934 he installed in the Studio an Art School, which merged in 1962 with the Los Angeles Conservatory of Music to form the California Institute of the Arts.

Pleased as he was with the overwhelming popularity of his Mouse, Disney began to worry in the early thirties about being trapped in the *Mickey* series. Not only did the public clamor for more *Mickeys*, but it was impossible to make the slightest modification in Mickey's appearance or character without being deluged with angry letters from the fans. To bring some variety in the cartoons, Disney introduced new characters: Pluto the Dog, then the two great winners, Goofy and Donald Duck. The bad-tempered Donald, who quacked in fury through an endless series of frustrations and misadventures, eventually replaced Mickey in the heart of the public.

Without slowing the production of the Mickey shorts, Disney began in 1932 to use color in the *Silly Symphonies*. The first color cartoon, *Flowers and Trees*, created a sensation and brought Disney the first of his twenty-one Academy Awards (the record number of awards received by one person in Hollywood). From then on the whole production was made in costly Technicolor, with the exception of Mickey, who remained black and white until 1935. This extravagance paid off when the *Three Little Pigs* came out in 1932. It was the Studio's biggest success up to that time. Movie theaters kept the cartoon on for weeks, and its theme song, "Who's Afraid of the Big Bad Wolf?," was sung, hummed, whistled, and played throughout the world. The *Pigs* was followed by a succession of splendid shorts, most of which are now considered classics. They include the black and white *Band Concert*, in which band leader Mickey and his musicians try to give their rendition of the *William Tell Overture* in the midst of a tornado. The *Concert* was a favorite of Toscanini,[1] who saw it six times and wrote Disney about it.

Walt Disney was now as much a celebrity as Mickey, Donald, and Goofy, but he was not comfortable with his exalted status. Apart from his compulsive dedication to his work, Disney's interests centered around his family—his parents, Roy and Edna, and above all Lilly and their daughters Diane and Sharon. He had no taste for socializing, although he did enjoy attending the Academy Awards ceremonies to collect more Oscars. Even Walter's favorite sport, polo, and his attempts to play golf, were not conducive to social contact, since he only practiced in the early hours of the morning or in the evening—usually with some members of his staff who shared his tastes.

While the team was rolling out one fine cartoon after another like a well-oiled machine, Disney was quietly pondering an idea that had been in his

---

[1] Arturo Toscanini—famous Italian conductor who died in 1957.

mind since 1934: the making of a full-length animated movie. He had the subject—it would be a fairy tale in full color about Snow White and the Seven Dwarfs. When he gathered his artists, as he always did to introduce a new project, acting out the whole story for them and explaining its length and composition, the animators were appalled. The technical problems involved seemed insurmountable. No attempt had ever been made to give a three-dimensional quality to large backgrounds, or to draw human characters that would not be caricatures. To Roy the idea seemed ruinous. And no one but Disney believed that a cartoon, however good, could sustain the public's interest for an hour and a half. It had never been done! In the industry the new project was soon known as "Disney's Folly." Neither Roy's remonstrations nor the unhappy questions of his draftsmen discouraged Walter. Since Roy was so reluctant to go ahead, he took upon himself the burden of securing the necessary loan from the Studio's usual, but worried, lender—Bank of America—and a team was put on the project forthwith.

Snow White and the Seven Dwarfs premiered on December 21, 1937, in time to be seen by the large holiday audiences. The film was cheered and applauded by the same crowd of stars and movie producers that usually greeted new movies. From there it went on to an international career that grossed $8 million on its first run. The film received a special award—a large Oscar surrounded by seven small ones. Roy would have enjoyed *Snow White*'s triumph much more if his brother had not disclosed to him his plans for the future. Walter had concluded that if one long film was a good thing, three of them could only be better; the thing to do, therefore, was to start three long features that would be completed more or less simultaneously. Over Roy's distraught protests, three teams were put to work on *Pinocchio, Bambi,* and *Fantasia*. And since the old studio, overcrowded by its enlarged staff and the multiplication of offices, was bulging at the seams, Disney ordered a larger, more convenient building to be erected in Burbank.

While the new studio was going up under Walter's watchful eye, *Pinocchio* and *Fantasia* were completed in February and November 1940 respectively. Neither one turned out to be a moneymaker. *Bambi,* in which great pains had been taken to draw the animals as realistically as possible, did better financially and the next film, the low-budget *Dumbo,* was even more satisfactory. But the good returns from *Snow White* were not sufficient to offset the cost of the new building and of the unsuccessful cartoons. When the Disneys found themselves facing that $4.5 million debt that made Walter laugh, they had no choice but to sell some of the stock to the public. In April 1940, the Disney Studio became Disney Productions, Inc.

Pinocchio is generally considered to be Disney's masterpiece. But *Fantasia,* with its mixture of animated stories and classical music, was the most original and ambitious project of that period. Originally, Disney had only planned to make a short cartoon to bring Mickey back into the favor of the public. The story he had chosen presented Mickey as an apprentice magician who starts a trick that he cannot control. Paul Dukas' *Sorcerer's Apprentice* would serve as background music. Leopold Stokowski, then conductor of the Philadelphia Orchestra, offered to conduct the piece. His enthusiasm and Disney's fired-up imagination progressively expanded the short cartoon into a full-length feature that included music by Bach, Beethoven, Tchaikowsky, Mussorgski, and others—all of them being illustrated by a variety of cartoons, ranging from abstract lines for Bach's Toccata and Fugue in D Minor, to a hilarious ballet of tiptoeing crocodiles, elephants, ostriches, and hippos in tutus[2] and satin slippers for Ponchielli's *Dance of the Hours*. *Fantasia* confused the public and drew scornful judgments from the highbrows,[3] who objected to the modifications made in the scores to fit the action. The film remained in the background for years, an interesting if unsuccessful experiment. But it proved durable—it is now enjoying a good second career.

The creation of the Disney Productions Corporation relieved the company's financial woes, but the relief was short-lived. It was impossible to compensate for the loss of the foreign market (45 percent of the total revenue) due to the beginning of the war in Europe. The situation was further complicated in 1941, when the United States entered the conflict and the Army requisitioned part of Disney's new building, including the sound stage, to lodge an anti-aircraft unit. The Corporation survived by producing short training films for the Army and the Navy, documentaries for the Department of Agriculture, propaganda cartoons, and even a film for the Treasury Department exhorting all good citizens to pay their taxes promptly. In 1941, Walter agreed to accompany Nelson Rockefeller on a goodwill tour to Mexico and South America, a trip that gave him the inspiration for two features illustrating the adventures of Donald with his pals Panchito, the Mexican Rooster, and Jose Carioca, and Brazilian Parrot. *Saludos Amigos* and *The Three Caballeros* were well received at home and south of the border. But the war years were lean years nonetheless for the Disney Productions.

Not only were they lean, but they were painful in other ways. In the old days the work had been done by a small team of draftsmen in a happy, informal atmosphere—even when the studio was cramped and Disney too demanding and tightfisted. But the staff had grown considerably since those early days. A large number of new employees had joined the old-timers in the spacious Burbank establishment. They were too numerous now to be known individually by Disney and he himself had changed a great deal since he had become "Walt Disney." He was not one of the boys anymore. A

[2]tutus—the very short white skirts worn by classical ballet dancers.
[3]highbrow—a person with tastes and interests considered to be superior.

strike of his unionized employees demanding higher salaries showed him, in 1941, that he had indeed lost his former happy relationship with his people. The strikers won. And both their victory and the fact that they had struck against him left a bitter taste in Disney's mouth. He never forgot that in the course of the conflict he had been accused of "capitalistic greed" and "workers' exploitation," and he never felt the same about his staff afterwards.

Disney had always had a fine appreciation of the public's changing tastes, as well as a keen business sense. After the war, he began to feel that fairy tales and funny cartoons were losing their appeal to the audience. Moreover, animated features were getting so expensive to produce that the shorts couldn't break even any more, and the long films didn't net enough. The short cartoons were discontinued in 1956. Of the long features produced in the early fifties, only *Cinderella* brought large profits. *Lady and the Tramp* and *Sleeping Beauty* did moderately well; *Peter Pan* and *Alice in Wonderland* were disasters. By that time, Disney had turned to other sources of wealth and success: adventure films, including *Treasure Island* and *Robin Hood* (made cheaply in England with the funds frozen in that country) and *20,000 Leagues Under the Sea*, documentaries such as *Seal Island* and *The Living Desert*, and other live-action films.

Even without that string of films, Disney Productions would have remained in the public consciousness through the Disney television programs and the flood of books, comics, hats, toys, spoons and bric-a-brac bearing Mickey's or Donald's portrait or name—all of which constituted a considerable source of revenue for the corporation. Disney had ventured cautiously into television with two Christmas shows. Those were so well received that a regular Disney program was promptly devised. It was aired every weekday, first in black and white by ABC, then in color by NBC. The shows attracted two-thirds of the total television audience from 1954 to 1963—and unequalled advertisement for Disney's new films and new ventures. Meanwhile, the Mickey Mouse Club was keeping young fans glued to the screen and singing the Mickey Mouse song.

No extra publicity was needed, however, for the smash hit of 1963, *Mary Poppins*, which happily combined live action (with stars Julie Andrews and Dick Van Dyke) and cartoon characters. To date the film is reported to have grossed about $120 million. It was Walt Disney's last great triumph, although he did release several good films after *Mary*. *The Jungle Book* was in production when Disney died on December 16, 1966, of circulatory problems after an operation for lung cancer.

Disney's death was felt keenly by his millions of fans, and warm tributes came pouring in from all over the world. For over thirty years he had enchanted old and young with his whimsical fantasies, his magical world where flowers sang and ducks got entangled in tires while repairing automobiles, where baby elephants learned to fly and where everything—anything—was possible. Without being a great artist, he had created, in the words of the *London Times*, "works of incomparable artistry and of touching beauty." He was a man of inexhaustible imagination, a creator, and undoubtedly one of the great entertainers of all times. While the short cartoons are now rarely available to the public, and the major features released mostly in video cassettes or every few years in movie theaters, Disney's two greatest creations are enjoyed year round by millions of visitors. They are of course, Disneyland in Anaheim, California, and Walt Disney World near Orlando, Florida.

210

Understanding the Text

1. What was Disney's contribution to the making of a cartoon or film?
2. Why was Disney Productions so often short of cash?
3. What was special about *Fantasia*?
4. Why was the war such a disaster for Disney Productions?
5. How did the Company survive the war?
6. What different reasons did Disney have to stop making cartoons and animated films?
7. Why were Disney's animators so worried when he announced the production of *Snow White*?
8. What image of Walt Disney emerges from his profile?

Scanning for Details

A. *Scan the profile section you have just read, for the following details.*

1. Who composed *The Sorcerer's Apprentice*?
2. How and when was the California Institute of the Arts formed?
3. What film brought Walt Disney his first Academy award?
4. Which of Johann Sebastian Bach's works was used in *Fantasia*?
5. When did *The Three Little Pigs* come out?
6. What is the name of the parrot in *The Three Caballeros*?
7. What exactly did the *London Times* say about Walt Disney?

B. *Fill in the information in the categories below. This exercise requires scanning of both parts of the profile.*

Walt Disney

Full name _____
Date of birth _____
Place of birth _____
Names of brothers and sisters _____
_____

Marriage(s) _____
Children _____

Jobs _____

Types of Production _____

Cause of death _____
Date of death _____

Vocabulary

Complete each sentence with the most appropriate word from the list, which includes more words than necessary. Be sure to make all needed adjustments in articles, nouns, and verbs.

1. The new buildings in Burbank were well planned and spacious. Disney's artists, who had been complaining about their _____ working areas in the old studio, were delighted to have all the space they needed.
2. Roy objected that it would be difficult to find a loan for such an expensive project. But Disney assured him that the difficulty was not _____ . And he began _____ (at once) to look for a sympathetic banker.
3. Disney wanted perfection. He didn't keep draftsmen who seemed to be satisfied with _____ work.
4. Disney's cartoons had many fans among intellectuals, who would not have disliked the idea of using classical music as a background for an animated feature. But these _____ were displeased by the changes that had been made in the scores to fit the stories of *Fantasia*.
5. When *Fantasia* _____ on November 13, 1940, the movie critics praised it, but the music critics looked down their noses at the strange production.
6. *Fantasia* didn't make much money at first; in fact it seemed for years that it wouldn't even _____ .
7. After the tornado, Mickey's musicians of the *Concert Band* were scattered all over the park; some were dangling from trees, others were _____ in tubas and drums and other large instruments.
8. Disney was never stopped by financial problems. But the high cost of animated films after the war _____ (made him hesitate). After much reflection, he decided to try live-action movies.
9. After *Snow White*, the Disney Studio entered a period of relative prosperity and security. Until then the financial situation of the Studio had always been _____ .

discontinued	to endure	precarious
highbrow	insurmountable	to break even
shoddy	to boost	cramped

PROFILE 261

    forthwith   to tiptoe   to give pause
    entangled   to premiere   capitalistic
    to premier

The Main Idea

Check the statement in each group that best expresses the essential idea of the paragraph.

Par. 1 Walt Disney stopped drawing cartoons in 1926.
        Disney's great gift was the ability to invent and develop good stories.
        Although he was a talented artist, Iwerks didn't succeed on his own.

Par. 2 Disney was always trying new ideas.
        Both Roy and Lillian objected to Disney's new ventures.
        Disney was often close to disaster.

Par.3 Disney was very amused when he found out that he owed $4.5 million to his banker.
        Disney always insisted on using the best of everything.
        The Studio's financial problems were due to Disney's vision and perfectionism.

Par. 4 Disney soon introduced new characters to avoid boring his public.
        Donald Duck is a bad-tempered but likable character.
        Disney could not change anything about Mickey without irritating his public.

Par. 5 Disney received his first Academy Award for *Flowers and Trees*.
        The Studio produced very good cartoons in the early thirties.
        The *Three Little Pigs* and their theme song were a big success.

Par. 6 In spite of his fame, Disney always remained a private man.
        Disney tried to play polo and golf before or after work.
        Walter and Lilly had two daughters named Diane and Sharon.

Generalizations

Which of the following statements express a generalization rather than a particular fact (supporting statement or example)?

1. In animated films, human characters are never drawn as well as animals and imaginary characters.
2. The rabbits, the squirrels, and the dwarfs of *Snow White* are far more appealing than Snow White herself.
3. The Prince is particularly flat and blank.
4. Disney stopped producing cartoons when they became too costly.
5. The problem with animated features is that al the work is done by hand.
6. Anything done by hand is expensive to produce.

7. *Snow White* cost $1.5 million.
8. *Davy Crockett,* the story of a hero of the American West, was planned as a series of three TV shows.
9. The first show, and particularly its theme song, the *Ballad of Davy Crockett,* were tremendous successes.
10. Every little boy wanted to wear a coonskin cap like Davy.
11. Disney Productions manufactured and sold over ten million of those hats.
12. Disney had strict rules for the products sold under his name.
12. They were all of good quality and authentic to the period.
13. He vetoed the sale of "Davy Crockett Colt .45" because, he said, "They didn't have Colt pistols in Davy Crockett's time!"
14. Frontiersmen like Davy Crockett wore leather coats with long fringe.

Taking Notes for a Summary

Skim though the two parts of Walt Disney's profile, and note down all the facts that you can find or infer about Roy Disney.

Write a brief summary, without details, but including all the essential facts.

Topics for Discussion

1. Whether you have seen *Fantasia* or not, do you think that critics are justified in condemning the film because the famous scores have been altered?
2. Can you contrast the tastes of highbrows and lowbrows in books, music, amusement, food, drinks, clothes, manners, etc.? Do their tastes ever coincide? Are there comparable differences in countries other than the United States than you may know? Give examples. How do you explain the word *highbrow*?
3. Was Disney unreasonable to resent the strike of his workers? Should the employees have simply approached him for a raise rather than join a union?
4. What Disney films have you seen and what do you think of them? Are full-length animated films interesting?
5. Was Walt Disney an artist?

Reading
Disney's Worlds

What is this section about?
Is it a history of the development of Disney's Worlds, or a description?
Which paragraph mentions the main criticisms against Walt Disney and his productions?

Being a dutiful father, Walt Disney used to take his small daughters to amusement parks, where he would wait patiently while they enjoyed the rides. As far as he was concerned, there was not much that was truly enjoyable about such places; the grounds were dirty, the material shabby, the parents bored. And so it is that, around 1934 or '35, the idea began to form in his mind that perhaps something could be done to bring more pleasure to children and adults alike. It was a modest idea at first. When Disney brought it out in the open in 1948, he was merely proposing a small amusement area in a corner of the Burbank lot—eleven acres all told. Even so, the plan was not modest enough for Roy, who vetoed it instantly, lecturing at length about loans, debts, and extravagant dreams.

Walter kept dreaming, nonetheless, and adding to his first concept. There should be more than rides and merry-go-rounds, he thought; it would be nice to have shops for the parents, soda fountains and theaters for all, a horse-drawn street car, plenty of things to do and see. Wherever he went, either in the United States or abroad, he visited parks, county fairs, circuses, carnivals, open air attractions of all kinds—and above all, zoos. Eventually, Lilly announced that she would not travel with him any more if it was to visit another zoo. Most of the places that he saw looked dirty and sad to Disney. The only amusement park that met his approval was Copenhagen's Tivoli Gardens, because they were clean and cheerful, with friendly attendants and brightly painted attractions.

The more he thought about his project, the more enthusiastic Disney felt about it. Although he was not blind to the business side of such a venture, the park represented more than a moneymaking device for him. He was envisioning it as "a place for people to find happiness and knowledge . . . a place for parents and children to share pleasant times in one another's company; a place for teachers and pupils to discover greater ways of understanding and education." There, he thought, the older generation would recapture the nostalgia of days gone by, and the younger generation would "savor the challenge of the future." All would be able to see and understand the wonders of nature and human ingenuity.

Since Roy couldn't be persuaded to cooperate, Disney borrowed $100,000 on his insurance policy. Then he gathered a number of his most imaginative designers and assigned them to the planning of his park. The group was called WED (for Walter Elias Disney); the park already had a name in Walter's mind: it would be Disneyland.

In the hands of the inspired team, the plans took shape swiftly, and even Roy began to be caught up in the general feeling of optimism that prevailed in the studio. When Disney hit upon the idea of raising money for Disneyland by selling a television program to one of the networks, Roy capitulated and flew to New York to find a buyer, which turned out to be ABC. In return for a series of shows and a 35 percent ownership of the future Disneyland, the network agreed to guarantee a loan of up to $4.5

million. Neither ABC nor Disney himself suspected at the time that the project would end up costing over $11 million.

With the funding assured, Disney proceeded to search for a location. After a painstaking study of the flow of population and the existing access routes, the choice fell to 160 acres of orange groves in Anaheim. WED announced bravely that Disneyland would open there in the summer of 1955—and the construction began. Disneyland did open on a blistering day in July 1955. It was a total disaster, referred to at WED as "Black Sunday." People had come in unexpected numbers, the roads were hopelessly clogged with traffic, rides collapsed under the excessive weight, restaurants and stands ran out of food, and a gas leak forced the personnel to close a whole section of the grounds. After repairs and improvements, Disneyland re-opened for good in October, to become America's top vacationland—the year-round wonderland that Disney had wanted. It still draws about 5 million visitors per year, most of them from California.

Disneyland fulfilled all the promises made in the WED's publicity folders. The "Good Old Days" are recaptured in a reproduction of a quarter of New Orleans; in a Frontierland illustrated by Western streets, pack mules, and log cabins; and most of all in an idealized version of Main Street, U.S.A., complete with ice-cream parlors, curio shops, a horse-drawn trolley, and antique cars. Adventureland offers a safari on an African river infested with programmed hippos and crocodiles; Fantasyland has its Sleeping Beauty Castle and Tomorrowland its rockets to Mars and other wonders. Visitors ride the vintage train, bobsled down the Matterhorn, dive in submarines to meet mermaids and electric eels, or visit the world of atoms and molecules.

Visitors are usually impressed by the near-fanatical neatness of the place, as well they should be. Disney had firmly established the rules from the beginning: the attendants had to be handsome, healthy, and impeccably friendly, forever smiling and helpful. A brigade of "sanitation attendants" wander around picking up litter the moment it touches the ground; streets and buildings are scrubbed every night, the targets in the shooting galleries repainted, the plants constantly replaced to look fresh at all times. Whatever the marvels of Disneyland, the most extraordinary facts about it are unfortunately beyond the visitor's knowledge. The problems that had to be overcome during construction; the ingenuity of the planners, engineers, architects, and decorators spurred by Disney's vision and his insistence that "of course there is a way to do it!"; visual tricks that go unnoticed, but, for example, make the 77-foot castle look imposing; and the avant-garde technology that keeps the machine purring smoothly; are all, in a way, much more fascinating than the park itself.

But the engineering miracles of Disneyland pale when compared with those of Walt Disney World in Florida. Although he had talked since 1954 of opening a second Disneyland "somewhere in the East," Disney had a larger concept in the back of his mind—a vision of urban planning that would combine modern living and entertainment. It may have been vague at first, but circumstances encouraged Disney to give it flesh. In the first place his WED team—the men he called his "imagineers"—told him that it was practically impossible to improve on the California Disneyland; except for a few details that might be perfected, they had already achieved the ultimate in the realm of pleasure grounds. Although their opinion was gratifying, it took all the fun out of building Disneyland II. Then the search for an ideal location for year-round entertainment revealed that Florida's weather was making it the top spot. Since the whole population of the state is about 6.5 million, the new park would have to draw its attendance from the rest of the country. It would therefore have to offer more than Anaheim did. Disney already knew what attraction he would provide: a whole new world, a City of the Future "where people could live like human beings" and send their children to model schools. He wanted to keep enough space open around his pleasure grounds for Americans to build their homes there and enjoy the most advanced conveniences that science and technology had to offer. And he would show them what those advances were.

Secretly, so as not to upset the price of land in the Florida swamps, Disney visited Florida and bought, in November 1965, twenty-seven thousand acres of ground near Orlando. In the one year that he had to live, Disney did all the planning for his new Park and its Experimental Prototype Community of Tomorrow (EPCOT), for which Ray Bradbury was hired as a consultant. The "fun area" consists of a World Showcase—a re-creation of foreign cities (from Mexico to China), spread like a fan around the central lagoon. On the other side of the water, the World of the Future is dominated by a 180-foot geodesic sphere—Spaceship Earth. The sphere is surrounded by a number of pavilions housing entertaining displays of future possibilities in the fields of energy, transportation, agriculture, mariculture (sea exploitation) and technology. Spaceship Earth is devoted to information and communications from dinosaur time to the 21st century.

EPCOT, built by imaginative technicians, made use of the latest technical and scientific advances, and provided some of its own. It is impossible to depict briefly the daring and inventiveness of the experts who were involved in its completion. But Peter Blake, an architect who is editor of *Architectural Forum,* wrote after his tour of the grounds: "In a great many respects, the most interesting New Town in the United States is Walt Disney World. It is interesting not only because it is huge—27,000 acres, or twice the size of Manhattan . . . or because it is so well financed ($400 million invested to date), or because it is so unabashedly corny[1] (i.e., such enormous fun). It is interesting also, or even primarily, for what it can teach every architect, planner and urban designer about any number of things that may have escaped his or her attention in the past. . . . Walt Disney

---

[1] corny—commonplace, silly, and overly sentimental.

didn't know that such things as vast urban infrastructures, multi-level mass-transit systems, People Movers, nonpolluting vehicles, pedestrian malls and so forth, were unattainable, and so he just went ahead and built them. In doing it he drew on all kinds of resources that no other city planner had ever before considered seriously, if at all. . . . It seems unlikely that any American school of architecture will ever again graduate a student without first requiring him or her to take a field trip to Orlando."

Peter Blake is not the only person who has used the word "corny" to describe Disney's productions. Even though the early Mickey cartoons are considered classics and revered by highbrows and lowbrows alike, the films and the amusement parks have often been objects of ridicule, and their creator derided as a farm boy of dubious taste and no appreciation of the fine arts. His animals, say the critics, are "cute,"[2] the human characters "phony"; *Snow White* has been described as "animated vanilla custard," and art critic John Canaday, although an admirer of the early cartoons, has charged Disney with "reducing our best fairy tales to the ultimate banality." As for the two Disney Worlds, they are usually dismissed as "plastic" worlds of make-believe for the unsophisticated masses. None of this seems to dim the enjoyment of the millions of people who go to see the periodically-released Disney films and who flock to Anaheim and Orlando. Even the blase critics have to admit that "Disney's America is the only one we seem to want to escape to, these days" and that although aware of "the plastic, cutesy, make-believe phoniness, you ask yourself why you enjoy Disney's [imitation] world." Disney knew what was said and written about his achievements; it didn't worry him much. "Maybe it's corny," he said to one of his daughters who had applied the word to a new cartoon, "but millions of people eat corn. There must be a reason why they like it so much." And to a group of French cartoonists, he gave his own advice:" Don't go for the avant-garde stuff. Be commercial. What is art, anyway? It's what people like. So give them what they like. There's nothing wrong with being commercial." He had never claimed that he wanted to create art for the connoisseurs,[3] or elevate people's minds. He wanted to give them good clean fun and to introduce them to the wonders of human discoveries that fascinated him. Mostly, he wanted to give happiness to all. Who can maintain that he didn't succeed?

Understanding the Text

1. In what ways did Disney want his amusement park to be different from the places he had seen?
2. Was he planning to amuse children?

---

[2] cute—sometimes derogatory, meaning "too pretty" and rather silly.
[3] connoisseurs—knowledgeable people.

3. What is the difference between Disneyland and the Walt Disney World in Florida?
4. Why did he choose Florida?
5. Why did the Florida project need stronger attractions than Disneyland?
6. Why should a student of architecture or city planning visit EPCOT?
7. What is there to see in Walt Disney World?
8. Why could it be said that the best of Disneyland is not seen?

Scanning for Details

1. What kind of sphere is Spaceship Earth?
2. What is the name of the art critic who condemned Disney's treatment of fairy tales?
3. When did Disney unveil his first plans for Disneyland?
4. What did Disney say exactly about Disneyland: "a place for people _____ in one another's company."
5. How high is Sleeping Beauty's Castle?
6. When did Disneyland open for the first time?
7. What does EPCOT mean?
8. What is the word that means "sea exploitation" or "sea farming"?

Appraising the Text

1. Have you found words or expressions in the text that should not be taken literally?
2. In your opinion, why did the author choose to devote so much space to this one aspect of Walt Disney's production? Do you think that the amusement parks deserve that much attention?
3. Do you feel that the author is biased for or against Disney, or neutral?
4. Do you agree that Disney's films are "corny"?
5. What do you think of Disneyland if you have been there?
6. Do you agree with Disney that:
   a) Art is what people like
   b) There is nothing wrong with being commercial?
7. In your opinion, was Disney unsophisticated?
8. What, do you think, is a "People Mover"?

What Is Important?

Check the six statements, among the fifteen listed below, that express the most important facts to remember about Walt Disney.

1. Walt Disney's father moved his family several times during Walter's childhood and adolescence.
2. Walt Disney had three brothers, all older than himself, and one sister.
3. By heredity and by training, Walt Disney was a conservative, hard-working man with middle-class values.

4. Walt Disney had a good sense of humor and a talent for using it well.
5. When he was still a child, Walter's aunt gave him some crayons and drawing paper.
6. Disney had a certain gift for drawing but no outstanding artistic talent.
7. Throughout Walter's life, he had the support and help of a good businessman, his brother Roy.
8. Disney was above all a man of great imagination and vision.
9. Although he was nice enough to work for, he was not very generous with his employees.
10. Disney's films and amusement parks have been widely criticized as corny and artificial.
11. Eventually Disney's visions went far beyond entertainment, toward city planning and the improvement of life through the bold use of technology.
12. Disney chose Orlando, in spite of its drawbacks, because the Florida weather allowed year-round entertainment.
13. Through his enthusiasm and his energy, Disney accomplished more than a better artist might have.
14. It is not Disney, but Ub Iwerks, who drew Mickey Mouse as we know him.
15. Disney was in debt throughout most of his career.

John Mauchly

Introduction

The Vocabulary of Invention

The curious youngster, the <u>crack</u> student who gets nothing but A's in math and sciences, the bright and inventive <u>whiz kid</u> who frightens his or her schoolmates, sometimes becomes an <u>inventor</u> that the world will honor forever for devising an important machine, improving an old process, or making a major <u>breakthrough</u> in the search for the cure for some disease.

It is rare nowadays to see one person alone invent something entirely new and startling. More often, a number of researchers are working on a problem that has been studied by others for some time; a pioneer has laid the <u>groundwork</u>, probably, and his or her successors are building on it, step by step.

Scientists, engineers, and technicians are a competitive lot; they often have a clear idea of what is afoot in each other's laboratories, and they do their best to beat their rivals to the final glorious discovery.

Some inventors are neither scientists not trained technicians; they are merely <u>tinkerers</u> who play with an idea, working in a amateurish way but with great imagination and skill. While they <u>tinker</u>, they might stumble, entirely by chance, upon some major fact that they had not at all expected. The faculty of making such lucky but unplanned discoveries is called <u>serendipity</u>. Neither the word "serendipity" nor the occurrence that is expressed are very common. Usually discoveries are the fruit of hard work and obstinate, <u>dogged</u> perseverance. Thomas Edison, who invented the electric light bulb and the phonograph (among other things) said that genius, which brings discoveries, is 10 percent inspiration and 90 percent perspiration.

It is not enough to announce one's invention to the world, as we have seen in the case of young Imogen Cunningham. The inventor should protect his or her <u>brainchild</u> against <u>pirates</u> who may steal the idea and make practical use of it. To establish ownership and rights, the wise inventor applies to the Patent Office for a <u>patent of invention</u>. If someone <u>infringes</u> on the patent, by copying part or all of a method, for example, the patented inventor can appeal to the courts. The <u>litigation</u> may be slow, but it is usually thorough.

Miracles, Menaces—The 21st Century As Futurists See It
U.S. News & World Report, July 16, 1984

With such a title, what could this chapter be about?
Skim the article: What will be bringing "miracles and menaces"?
What kind of people are quoted in the article?
What two types of machines are considered in the article?

Why is this article interesting to students and working people?

Peering into the 21st century, authorities on the future see extraordinary changes that will make today's world seem as outdated as the era of the Model T.[1]

Experts attending a recent World Future Society Convention in Washington, D.C., and other futurists interviewed by *U.S. News & World Report* paint this picture of life ahead as the new century approaches:

TECHNOLOGY: IS IT MACHINE OR HUMAN?

New scientific breakthroughs will allow machines to take on more tasks that the human brain has traditionally done.

Computers, which once only remembered data, will make more decisions. Machines that tell doctors today what symptoms their patients have may soon be recommending surgery. Others will design new buildings after questioning buyers about their preferences. Increasingly, human thought processes and even values are being programmed into computers, according to Earl Joseph, president of Anticipatory Sciences, a Minneapolis consulting firm. "Imagine machines which are smarter and more intelligent than humans and, with their embedded initiative, can't wait to tell you about it," he says.

In everyday life, the future will mean talking directly to computers without pushing buttons. Just tell a toaster, stove or other kitchen device what to do, and it will hear the message. The oven may even decide itself how long to cook the roast. Tell the television: "I want to watch Channel 12 at 8 P.M., but store the show for next week," and the job will be done.

The computer will talk back too. Already some soft-drink machines complain loudly if you don't deposit enough cash. At home, a bedside machine may someday tell you: "You forgot to turn off the basement light."

Computers are already embedded in such household devices as television sets, telephones, stereos, and thermostats. Some of them provide home message delivery and banking information.

Consumer psychologist Robert Lee envisions audio-visual encyclopedias that combine text, pictures, and sound. For example, call up Beethoven on the computer screen and the student reads texts, watches a short film, and hears the symphonies themselves.

Increasingly there's talk of viewer participation in television. Two-way TV programs will make it possible to take part in a soap opera or football game as if the viewer were there. The spectator will be given choices to make, and once a football play or an alternative plot is selected the story will resume. . . . Bridge and other card games, social events and business

---

[1]The Model T was the first mass-produced automobile, manufactured by Henry Ford from 1908 to 1927, at which date it was replaced by a more advanced model.

conducted long distance by computer will change the way people make friends. . . .

Away from home, the automobile of the future will think for itself. Ove Sviden, an automotive consultant, predicts that drivers will feed destinations into a computer that would then explain what route to take and even tell where parking spaces are available. A city's traffic control system might instruct the car computer how fast to go in heavy traffic and whether to change lanes. "The cars would be like electronically coupled trains," he explains.

WORKPLACE: ROBOTS TAKE DANGEROUS JOBS

Machines and foreign competition will replace millions of American jobs. But work will be plentiful for people trained in the occupations of the future. The Labor Department predicts a net increase of 25 million new jobs in the United States in 1995, with service-industry jobs growing three times as rapidly as factory jobs. "Work will shift its emphasis from the fatigue and monotony of the production line and the typing pool to the more interesting challenge of the electronic service center, the design studio, the research laboratory, the education institute, and the training school," predicts Canadian economist Calvert.

Jobs in high-tech fields will multiply fastest, but from a low base. In terms of actual numbers, more mundane occupations will experience the biggest surge: custodians, cashiers, secretaries, waiters and clerks. Yet much of the drudge work will be taken on by robots.

The number of robots performing blue-collar tasks will increase from 3,000 in 1981 to 40,000 in 1990, says John E. Taylor of the Human Resources Research Organization in Alexandria, Va. Robots might also be found on war zones, in space—even in the office, perhaps making coffee, opening mail and delivering messages.

One unsolved problem: what to do with workers displaced by high technology and foreign competition. Around the world "the likelihood of growing permanent unemployment is becoming more accepted as a reality among social planners," notes David Macarov, associate professor of the Hebrew University in Jerusalem. Meantime, the percentage of time people spend on the job is likely to continue to fall. Robert Theobald, author of *Avoiding 1984*, fears that joblessness will lead to increasing depression, bitterness, and unrest. "The dramatic consequences of such a shift on the Western psyche,[2] which has made the job the way we value human beings, are almost incalculable," he comments.

Because of the constantly changing demand for job skills, Ron Kutschner, Associate Commissioner of the Bureau of Labor Statistics, offers this advice for today's high school students: "Be prepared with a broad ed-

---

[2]psyche—the Greek word for *mind* or *soul*.

ucation, like the kind pre-college students get—basic math, science, and English. Prepare yourself to handle each new technology as it comes down the road. Then get technology training for your first job. That is the best stepping stone to the second and third jobs."

85

Understanding the Text

1. Basically, what is the main point of the article?
2. What will be new in the role of computers in the future?
3. In what fields does the article announce great advances?
4. What kinds of computers are expected to assist in offices and factories?
5. What will be the consequences for human workers?
6. What is the article's final advice to high school students?

Commenting on the Text

1. What is your reaction to the article; does it make you feel uncomfortable, hopeful, happy, enthusiastic, sad? Why?
2. What do you think of the people quoted—are they in a position to know what is going to happen and what the effect on people will be?
3. Turn back to the text to make a list of the kind of activities in which computers and robots are expected to help or replace humans. In which field(s) will the machines be most welcomed?

Scanning for Details and Examples

1. The article predicts that there will be a great increase in mundane jobs. What jobs are mentioned?
2. What is the source of this article?
3. Who wrote *Avoiding 1984*?
4. Computers will make decisions, says the article. What examples are given?
5. Who is Earl Joseph?
6. How many robots are expected to be in service in 1990?
7. What could robots do in an office?
8. Why would permanent unemployment be hard on Westerners, according to Robert Theobald?

Vocabulary

Complete each of the following definitions, either from memory or after consulting the list below.

1. A _____ is a device that regulates the temperature in a house.
2. A _____ is a major advance in technology.

3. _____ work is an unpleasant and boring task.
4. A _____ occupation is a very ordinary occupation.
5. _____ jobs include repair work, maintenance, cleaning and other similar tasks.

> embedded   mundane   emphasis
> symptom   consulting   thermostat
> anticipatory breakthrough service
> drudge

Prefix

psych (psyche)

1. What is the name of the science that studies the mind and its processes?
2. A number of diseases end with the letters *is*, among them *arthritis, tuberculosis, colitis, hepatitis*. If you see an article concerning certain types of *psychosis*, what can you assume about the subject of this article?
3. What kind of hospital is a *psychiatric* hospital?
4. Drugs like LSD and mescaline are called *psychedelic* drugs. Why?

Logical Reasoning—Connectors

Some of the groups of two sentences below express a cause and its effect, in which case the two statements should be linked by since *or* because. *In the other groups, the statements could be linked either by* and *or by* but *depending on their meaning.*

Combine the sentences in each group, using the appropriate connector, and making the necessary adjustments.

Examples: A. Until now, computers have performed all kinds of tasks.
The computers have performed those tasks much faster than a man could.

could become:

Until now, computers have performed all kinds of tasks *and* have performed *them* much faster than a man could.

B. The computers have filed and remembered data and obeyed the instructions given to them.
The computers have not been capable of making decisions.

could become:

The computers have filed and remembered data and obeyed the instructions given to them *but they* have not been capable of making decisions.

C. It is getting increasingly expensive to recover oil. Homes and workplaces of the future will be designed to capture the heat of the sun or to draw power from nuclear plants.

could become:

Since it is getting increasingly expensive to recover oil, the homes and working places of the future will be designed to capture the heat of the sun or draw power from nuclear plants.

or:

The homes and working places of the future will be designed to capture the heat of the sun or to draw power from nuclear plants, *because* it is getting increasingly expensive to recover oil.

1. The name Singer has been synonymous with sewing since 1851.
   The Singer Company has little to do with sewing these days.
2. The Singer Company has turned to aerospace and high-tech business.
   Modern women do not sew as much as their grandmothers did.
3. Today, sewing machines represent only 24 percent of the company's sales.
   Sewing machines bring the company none of its profits.
4. The computers of the future might be more intelligent than men.
   The computers of the future will certainly be much faster and more reliable.
5. The American automobile and textile industries have to make full use of computers and robots.
   If they don't, they'll be unable to compete with foreign countries.
6. The automobile industry was slow in understanding that it had to use automation.
   The industry is now automating in a big way with computers, robots, and laser technology.
7. The industry will still need a large number of workers.
   The workers must have technological skills.
8. Many factory workers who lost their jobs during the recession are not trying to learn new skills.
   They don't understand that there is no hope of going back to their old jobs.
9. The experts expect the world population to swell from 4.6 billion to 10 billion by year 2100.
   It will be necessary to farm the sea and to find new forms of food.

Topics for Discussion

1. Will it be good or bad if computers and robots ever reduce man's labor to such an extent that people work only a few hours a week, or not at all? What would happen? Would you look forward to permanent (paid) unemployment?
2. Will machines ever be more intelligent than man?
3. Will it be good to have computers diagnose diseases and recommend therapy? Do you like the idea? Why would anyone want to study medicine?
4. Do you like the idea of playing cards, chess, or other games with a computer?
5. In the near future, the article predicts a net increase of 25 million new jobs in the United States in 1995, with a shift from monotonous jobs to creative ones. Is this entirely satisfactory? What will be the problem and what solutions can you see for it?

Cultural Notes for Selected Reading

April Fools' Day is the first day of April. In many Western countries it is customary to play tricks on people that day—perhaps pinning something on their back or giving them false news.

Phi Beta Kappa, founded in 1776, is the oldest Greek Letter honor society in the United States, and a very prestigious one. Membership is based on high scholastic standing. Sigma Chi, also mentioned in the profile, is a purely social organization.

Selected Reading

He Changed The World *(Part One)*
by John Costello (*The Washingtonian,* December 1983)

Considering what you have read so far in this chapter, what kind of man do you expect to find portrayed in this profile?
Skim the text:
- Who changed the world, and how did he do it?
- Is this text very technical? Is it written formally or informally?
- What was the profession of the man portrayed in the text?
- As you read the text, check in the margin the passages or sentences that you consider irrelevant to the main line of the story.

When he died, *Time* magazine gave him a mere twenty lines of obituary. Yet, the electronic device that transmitted that very story might not have existed without him. Indeed, the multibillion-dollar computer industry now touching the lives of most of us owes much of its origin to him, to John W. Mauchly, earnest son of a physicist father from Chevy Chase.

Nobody paid much attention when on February 16, 1946, the U.S. Army announced that a couple of scientists from the University of Pennsylvania School of Electrical Engineering had concocted[1] this "automatic computing machine of unprecedented speed and capabilities," which they called ENIAC. John Mauchly and his co-inventor, J. Presper Eckert, displayed a roomful of electronic equipment that could condense into days what a Ph.D. could not do in a lifetime. The Army had wanted a device to solve complex ballistic problems. It got that, and the world got a revolution.

Revolution or not, reporters who showed up on that Saturday thirty-seven years ago were not much impressed. They found a cumbersome giant of forty separate panels, weighing thirty tons, occupying more than 15,000 feet of floor space. Some papers didn't even run the story; others cut it to a brief. The *New York Times* was one of the few that acknowledged the invention's potential.

The inventors were as lusterless as the machine. A photo of Mauchly from that period depicts him as a pleasant-faced, slender man with oversize ears, and warm, deep eyes (he was nearsighted). Mauchly was very much the product of his background and times: an electronic tinkerer blessed with the American virtues of curiosity, dogged perseverance and unquenchable optimism. Even after he had laid the groundwork for a new era, after he and his co-inventor had sold their patent to Remington Rand for a song, after a judge ruled that he had borrowed his computer idea from another scientist—even then he was not bitter.

"Bill" Mauchly, as his family called him, grew up in small town America—in Chevy Chase, back in the days when it literally was a cow town, although not your average cow town. Mauchly's father was a physicist with the Department of Terrestrial Magnetism at the Carnegie Institution. Mauchly was born August 30, 1907, in Cincinnati. He was nine when his family moved to Chevy Chase, near Washington. It was all country then, great fields of corn, pumpkins, kitchen gardens. The Mauchlys raised chickens, fifty of them. "My father believed in living off the land," says Betsy Westphalen, John Mauchly's sister. "It was my brother's duty to clean the chicken coop every Saturday morning. He hated it."

Mauchly preferred to tinker. "On April Fool's Day," his sister Betsy recalls, "he wired the front door bell so that when you rang it, you got a little shock." He also rigged a remote alarm from the staircase to his room to

---

[1] concocted—means "put together." It is an informal word, and implies a lot of work, and perhaps a lot of ingredients when one is *concocting* a dish, for instance.

alert him if an adult was heading upstairs, giving him time to quash his post-curfew reading light. And on the Fourth of July, Mauchly recalled, "I'd fix up some electrical contraptions so that when I pressed a button the fireworks would go off fifty feet away."

By age thirteen or fourteen, John was earning summer money by wiring neighbors' homes, caddying at nearby Columbia Country Club, or picking up tips for watching members' Buicks, Stanley Steamers and Packards in the club parking lot.

Most of the social life for Mauchly and school chums like Gus Winnemore and Win Stone centered on Chevy Chase Presbyterian Church. Gus grew up to become a teacher in the District high schools. Win, later Dr. George Winfield Stone, is a well-known theater historian recently retired as dean of libraries for New York University.

During the school year, John and Gus would board the trolley at the Chevy Chase Country Club. It clanged its way down Connecticut Avenue to Rhode Island Avenue where McKinley Vocational High School stood. McKinley in those days was, among other things, a prep[2] school for engineers, and that's where Mauchly figured he was headed.

He was a crack student, a whiz at math and physics. Gus Winnemore remembers physics teacher John Adams telling Mauchly: "John, you made 100 on your homework and assignments, 100 on all your tests, and 100 in your class recitations. But nobody is perfect, so I'm giving you a grade of 99 for the year."

In the fall of 1925, John entered Johns Hopkins on a state scholarship to study engineering. But after a couple of years, he knew that it was not for him. "The problem was that my friends and my father's friends were not just garden-variety[3] engineers; they were scientists. They were over at Johns Hopkins taking Ph.D. courses. Even in the mid-twenties, Hopkins was a center of scientific learning of international repute. Washington in those days had no institution to rival it."

Engineering looked to Mauchly like "cookbook stuff." He was out to do big things and the biggest thing he ever saw an engineer do was "design a girder by looking it up in a handbook published by U.S. Steel." He switched his major to physics, and by 1932, at age 24, had acquired a Ph.D. as well as membership in Phi Beta Kappa and Sigma Chi, the science honor fraternity.

Mauchly's specialty was molecular spectroscopy, not a big seller in the midst of the Depression. Also he was newly married, to Mary Walzl, whom he had met while at Hopkins. He got lucky, landing a job at his alma mater[4] photographing and measuring the spectra of molecules. The job had elements he would later use in devising the computer. "The first thing you

---
[2]prep—preparatory.
[3]"garden variety" engineers—ordinary engineers.
[4]his alma mater—the college that he attended.

have to do is go down to the laboratory and get a photograph of the spectrum. Then you go into a dark room and optically measure the lines on those plates." A single molecule, for example, might have 20,000 spectral lines.

Mauchly learned how to work vacuum equipment and make high-voltage sparks. To measure, he had to do sophisticated computations. He remembered: "Not on the electronic computers you know today. I used a little mechanical computer, a desk machine which Merchand manufactured. It could multiply if you pushed the right buttons and pulled a little handle that looked like a lima bean. I spent hours on that lima-bean computer. I sort of got fed up[5] but I did learn how to guess the mathematics, the cleverer way of getting the computation done faster."

The search for a cleverer way to compute gradually moved to center stage, obscuring and finally overtaking Mauchly's interest in molecules and atoms. In 1933, he took a $2,400-a-year job teaching physics at Ursinus College, a friendly little co-ed college in Collegeville, Pennsylvania, population 878, outside Philadelphia. It had a handsome 140-acre, tree-shaded campus, about 500 students, and good academic standards. There he attracted a cluster of enthusiastic students who were drawn to his intellect and restless scientific curiosity.

One of Mauchly's interests was statistics and their application to solar-system research and weather phenomena. Whatever direction he pursued, it somehow came back to measurements—in this case, how to absorb mountains of meteorological data. He had put together his own mechanical analogue computer for problems such as computing the effects—if any—that the planets have on sunspots and that sunspots have on Earth's weather. After dark, when the day's work was done at Ursinus, the lights were often on in his downstairs lab at Pfahler Hall.

John Chapline, a Mauchly disciple, remembers: "I was one of the young pests who hung around there. Mauchly built several gadgets of note with cheap neon blubs. They had interesting ignition and extinguishing characteristics. Bring the bulb up to a certain voltage, say 72 volts, and the thing fires. It glows and ionizes. Then lower the voltage to, say, 51 volts, and it goes out, it de-ionizes. So John's mind went to work, and he concocted a coding machine. He put it together with these neon bulbs and some flat cardboard boxes that held cod-liver-oil capsules you gave children. Each capsule came in a little round hole stamped out of the cardboard frame. John used the frame to mount his neon bulbs, each one representing a letter of the alphabet. His machine had three sets of complete alphabets plus one null, each arranged in three rows of nine. He could encode messages by changing the setting of eight switches on the machine to change circuits. It was a most ingenious machine. I think that John built it as a

---

[5]to be fed up (slang)—to be tired of.

kind of intellectual exercise. What he did was see the logic of the circuits and the special electrical properties of these neon bulbs. Some of the ideas he used to design that gadget could be related ultimately to computer circuitry.

"He also took two of these bulbs and made what he called his railroad-crossing signal. He took a simple DC battery out of a flashlight and hooked it up to two NE-2 neon bulbs mounted on two pieces of cardboard fastened to a quarter-inch dowel. The dowel was stuck into something like the cardboard top you find on a round container of Chinese food. Somehow he had the bulbs go *plink, plunk,* lighting back and forth like a railroad crossing signal. He had made an oscillator out of a DC battery. But what he really did was make a diode flip-flop. That was a binary device that leads right into the computer.

"Another device he made when I was there was a ring-counter. He took a little piece of masonite, mounted four tube sockets in it, interwired them, and got an oscillator that made the tubes count. The oscillator was set at 1,000 pulses a second. The tubes, AO-4G vacuum tubes, were arranged in a square. As each pulse came in, it turned on one tube and turned off the tube behind it that had been lit. So we had a four-stage ring-counter. Later, in ENIAC, they had ten-stage ring-counters. Twenty-four ten-stage counters in fact. This is the equipment that makes that lab deserve a plaque.[6] Because that's where our electronic computer began."

Mauchly the scientist was on to something: neon bulbs that retained charges long enough so you could make them count numbers. He was getting a glimmer of how to solve problems electronically. But there was still another step.

"What I was wishing for," Mauchly remembered, "was a machine that would *store* the numbers you stuck into it. Then, once it got the stuff, it ought to be able to do anything you wanted with it. And it should know a set of directions that tell it what to do."

But with a $600 annual equipment budget, Ursinus was not the place for major breakthroughs. In 1941, Mauchly took a job as an instructor at the Moore School of Electrical Engineering, a division of the University of Pennsylvania. A few months before joining the faculty, he took a side trip that was later to have fateful consequences. At an earlier meeting of the Association for the Advancement of Sciences in Philadelphia, Mauchly had met John Atanasoff, an Iowa State College professor, who said he had a device he hoped would be able to compute electronically. In May 1941, Mauchly drove out to Iowa to see it.

Mauchly remembered that, in the three days that he spent there, Atan-

---

[6]a plaque indicating that someone important has lived there or that something important has happened.

asoff could not get the device to work. He remembered it as a "gizmo[7] that looked like a bread box."

The move to Moore coincided with the start of World War II, a confluence of events that would prove serendipitous. Moore College, in association with Aberdeen, Md., Proving Gounds,[8] was a principal center for compiling artillery firing tables crucial to the war effort. The technique was ponderous and often inaccurate. It involved the use of a mammoth mechanical computer—10 feet by 35 feet—designed by the scientist Vannevar Bush, which was little more than a mechanical engineer's slide rule. It was called, appropriately, the Bush Differential Analyzer. Each new gun design involved plotting thousands of correct trajectories to compensate for such variables as wind, temperature, and distance. Each calculation took several hours.

Before long, the backlog on the Bush Analyzer—called "Annie" at Moore— was so great that the Moore School had to hire hundreds of women, working with hand calculators, to try to keep abreast of the critically needed calculations.

Mauchly, convinced that the whole operation could be geometrically accelerated, proposed that Moore develop an electronic computer using high-speed vacuum tube devices. Such an instrument, he said, could move numbers from one column to another by moving electrical pulses through wire circuits. Such circuits, he rhapsodized,[9] "are capable of counting electric pulses at rates in excess of 100,000 per second." In that split second, poor Annie couldn't blink, let alone count.

The idea was not an instant hit with Moore's conservative faculty. But J. Presper Eckert, Jr., liked it. Eckert was a brilliant electrical engineer, twelve years younger than Mauchly's thirty-four, but stamped from the same can-do mold. Eckert was a graduate student in electrical engineering at Moore, and he and Mauchly had often discussed the possibility of an electronic computer. Mauchly's proposal to the Moore School faculty owed a lot to Eckert.

"Those conversations," Mauchly said, "gave me confidence that I wasn't on a wild goose chase.[10] Eckert convinced me that the models and other things I had been making with neon tubes weren't too practical. They were too slow. "If you want to do this thing right," Eckert said, "Let's do it with vacuum tubes. They respond a thousand times faster." He had a point of view which, I think, was rare in those days of electronics. His idea was that, if you designed your circuit right, you could more or less avoid the

---

[7]gizmo (slang)—a thing, a device (rather derogatory).
[8]Aberdeen Proving Grounds is a large military reservation.
[9]rhapsodized—said with great enthusiasm and at length.
[10]a wild goose chase—a foolishly useless undertaking.

problem of reliability. So it didn't scare him to think about something that might have a couple of thousand tubes in it, whereas most people were scared of it." 205

Understanding the Text

1. What kind of information does this part of the profile offer about John Mauchly?
2. Were Mauchly's parents and early friends likely to be surprised when he turned out to make a major invention?
3. What was Mauchly's profession?
4. Why didn't he become an engineer?
5. Why did he go to Iowa?
6. Why did the author introduce J. Presper Eckert?
7. What circumstance was to bring Mauchly in touch with the Army when he was teaching at Moore School?
8. What was the problem and how was Mauchly proposing to solve it?

Appraising and Commenting

1. Did you find passages or statements that seemed irrelevant to the main line of the story? Consider each "irrelevancy" mentioned by students and try to imagine why the author included it in the text—is it really irrelevant? Does it serve a purpose—such as giving warmth or humor to the narration, suggesting another side of Mauchly's character, or adding to the story in any way?
2. What is the author's attitude toward Mauchly? Why do you think he undertook to write this "article," which is really a condensation of an intended book?
3. Does anything in the text suggest that Mauchly may have been intellectually arrogant, or at least that he felt intellectually superior?
4. The author describes Mauchly and Eckert as "lusterless" in 1946. Does the text show that Mauchly was neither attractive nor interesting in his early career?
5. What is the tone of the story: formal, informal, serious, ironic?
6. Did you understand the technical passages:
   a) about Mauchly's work in molecular spectroscopy?
   b) about his research about the solar system?
   c) about his early devices with neon tubes?

   Is understanding those technical passages essential for understanding Mauchly's career and abilities? What was the purpose of showing Mauchly working on spectral lines and meteorological data in his first jobs? Why show him building a coding machine with neon tubes and the cardboard boxes that held cod-liver-oil capsules? Do those cardboard boxes suggest something?

Vocabulary

A. Paraphrasing: *How would you express, in your own words:*

1. Chevy Chase was just a cow town.
2. The question of finding a job moved to center stage for young Mauchly.
3. He quashed his light when he heard his parents coming.
4. John would have liked to spend half the night reading; but his father told him that curfew time would be 10 P.M.
5. Mauchly said that engineering was cookbook stuff.
6. Like Eckert, Mauchly had a can-do attitude.
7. One wonders why Mauchly finally sold his idea for a song.

B. Did You Guess Right?

line 25   Mauchly was blessed with unquenchable optimism
Does it seem that his optimism could be crushed or not?
How would you understand: "I had to drink three glasses of water to quench my thirst"?

line 24   He worked with dogged perseverance. Is this likely to mean:
  a) short-lived perseverance
  b) steadfast perseverance
  c) no perseverance at all

line 41   Young Mauchly rigged all sorts of devices that his mother didn't appreciate.
  a) he built them
  b) he bought them
  c) he described them

line 147   Mauchly was on to something (after experimenting with neon bulbs). From the context, this is likely to mean:
  a) he was sitting or standing on something
  b) he had discovered something
  c) he was holding something in his hands

line 168   Mauchly moved to Moore school and World War II started; the combination of events was to prove serendipitous.
  a) it proved disastrous
  b) it became a source of success for Mauchly
  c) it led to unexpected and fortunate discoveries

line 170   They were trying to compile firing tables
  a) to collect
  b) to compare
  c) to invent

line 178   The backlog of work was so great that the school had to hire hundreds of workers.
  a) the work done
  b) the work left to be done
  c) the work that was expected to come

What Is Important?

Check the six statements, among the fifteen listed below, that express the most important facts to be remembered from the text. [Instructor's Note: If the students do not all agree on the statements chosen, they can discuss them one by one and establish a final list.]

_____ Mauchly was born in Cincinnati and grew up in Chevy Chase, near Washington.

_____ Eckert was seventeen years younger than Mauchly.

_____ John Mauchly has not been given enough credit in the development of computers.

_____ ENIAC had 24 ten-stage ring-counters.

_____ Mauchly was not interested in engineering because it was not challenging enough.

_____ Mauchly had been brought up among intellectually stimulating people.

_____ John Mauchly went to work at Moore school in 1941.

_____ He managed to concoct a crude coding machine with neon tubes and cardboard boxes.

_____ When he was young, Mauchly earned money by wiring neighbors' homes or caddying at a country club.

_____ Mauchly was a curious, inventive, and persevering man who loved to tinker and experiment.

_____ Before 1946, people had to use mechanical computers that were large, slow, and not very accurate.

_____ Mauchly was led to dream up a fast, accurate computer through his own need and the need of the school where he was teaching.

_____ Some molecules have 20,000 spectral lines.

_____ John Mauchly had a brilliant mind that attracted other gifted people.

_____ Mauchly was a Ph.D. and a married man at 24.

Taking Notes for a Summary or an Outline

Go over the text carefully and note down the main facts of Mauchly's professional life after he received his PhD: where he worked, what job he had there, and (without details) the other important activities he engaged in in each place. The object of this summing up is to get a clear picture of what intellectual work Mauchly had done up to the time when he worked on the ENIAC.

Present the facts either in a brief summary or in an outline.

Topics for Discussion

1. Do you know of any custom marking either April 1st, or the beginning of spring or another traditional date in the first months of the year? Do you know any occasion in countries other than the United States, on which people play light tricks on each other?
2. What do you think of video games such as Pac-Man:
   Are they interesting?
   Do you think that they can develop the intelligence or other skills of the young people who play them?
   What bad effects do the games and video game galleries have—if any?
   Are video games losing their appeal?
3. Are you opposed to the idea of colleges doing research for the Defense Department? Is it good for the college? For the researchers? For science? For the general public?

Selected Reading

He Changed the World *(Part Two)*

> *Note:* This part of Mauchly's profile contains a number of words that are slang words, or that at least belong only in informal speech. Try, as usual, to understand the general meaning of the text without stopping to check these words, marked with the sign °, to which we shall return after reading the text.
>
> What was Mauchly doing at the end of the first part of the profile?
> Can you guess what is going to happen now to his idea?
> Skim the text to find out if you have guessed right.
> Was the ENIAC ready in time to help the artillery in wartime?
> Did Mauchly ever make another kind of computer?
> Where does the text explain why Mauchly's trip to Iowa turned out to be disastrous for him?

Despite the fortuitous teaming of Mauchly and Eckert, it took a deus ex machina[1] to rescue the computer project from oblivion. It seemed that neither Annie nor her back-up squad of women cranking their hand calculators could quench Aberdeen's appetite for firing tables. Thus, in September

---

[1]deus ex machina—the "god" who descended from the "sky" on a machine at the end of Greek and Roman plays to bring a happy ending to a hopeless situation.

1942, Aberdeen sent Lieutenant Herman Goldstine to see if he could speed up the work. Goldstine groused° about Annie's shortcomings and was informed that a couple of academics° had another idea. Goldstine, who had been a math professor before the war, was impressed. "Why can't we spend a million on this?" he said. "If it doesn't work, we'll scrap° it. If it does, we're in°!" He didn't get a million, but Aberdeen came through with° $150,000 (later upped to $400,000) to bankroll° a shot° at the world's first electronic digital computer. And in June 1943 the Moore School got the green light. Eckert and Mauchly went to work on their brainchild. They dubbed the infant ENIAC, short for Electronic Numerical Integrator and Computer.

Mauchly and Eckert put together a team of engineers, housewives on the production line, and moonlighting² telephone wiremen. "They gave us very good wiring," recalls Eckert. "They were fairly slow but very neat and accurate. And accuracy was what we needed." As with so many part-time workers and moonlighters, people came in when they could. "It was a free-for-all³ sort of thing," one worker recalls. "They might show up at 11 A.M. then work until midnight. In fact the work went on almost 24 hours a day." Eckert, the chief engineer, worked at it full-time, putting in long hours. Mauchly carried a full teaching schedule as well. Fortunately both of them were night owls. After classes, Mauchly would go to the Lido restaurant, just two blocks from the Moore School, eat dinner, then come back and work on the ENIAC until one or two in the morning.

Over a thirty-month period they tackled° one tough problem after another. As word got around about the progress of the new wonder toy, the scientific world perked up its ears. Enrico Fermi, the brilliant physicist and Nobel prize winner, was working frantically to beat Germany to the A-bomb and, like any other scientist, was painfully aware of the need for a high-speed calculator. Fermi was especially curious about this electronic computer under construction. How many tubes will it have? he wanted to know. "About 18,000," he was told. "In our scaling circuits," Dr. Fermi said, "we have about 100 tubes. And the circuits fail X number of times a day! Multiply that failure rate, per tube, by 18,000. I doubt if it will go long before it breaks down." Eckert would say: "I think we can design so you don't have to worry about tube failures. We can run the tubes a little under the graded voltage and make them last longer. We can get heftier° resistors that won't heat up too much and go bad. If you design properly, you can get reliability."

By July 1944, a year after it started, the team had completed two working devices that foreshadowed the success of the ENIAC. Called electronic accumulators, they could add and subtract numbers up to ten digits long

²moonlighting—working at night on a second job.
³a free-for-all is usually a fight in which anyone can join.

and store the results in their vacuum tubes. When finished, ENIAC would have twenty of these.

Only a year and a half later, ENIAC was complete—too late for World War II but in time for the new age. It had forty panels, each two feet wide and eight and a half feet tall, half of them accumulators. The other twenty panels included master programmers, a divider and a square-rooter, high-speed multipliers, function tables, and panels hooked up to a punch-card reader and printer.

The Army and Moore School unveiled ENIAC at a press conference to a lukewarm reception. But the *New York Times* bubbled[4] that ENIAC was "one of the war's top secrets, an amazing machine. . . . Leaders who saw the device in action heralded it as a tool with which to rebuild scientific affairs on new foundations." Eckert and Mauchly, looking slightly uncomfortable, posed for the pictures.

Few people recognized ENIAC's potential. In the late '40s, electronic computation was still an exotic notion, not yet reclaimed from the realm of science fiction—much like television when it was first introduced before World War II. Indeed, it would take another thirty years for the full promise of the computer to seep down to the popular culture.

Inside the profession, there was a more sophisticated realization that something was afoot—so much so that Mauchly and Eckert found themselves in battle with the Moore School over patent rights. They won the right to apply for patents in their names, and they did so in July 1946. But the struggle left a bad taste,° and the two scientists left Moore to establish their own computer manufacturing company. It was a sad period for Mauchly. Mary, his wife of sixteen years, drowned in a swimming accident in September 1946. Two years later, Mauchly married Kathleen McNulty, a mathematician who had worked on ENIAC.

ENIAC continued to work for the Army, first at Moore and later at Aberdeen, churning up° thousands of firing tables until its plug was pulled° in 1955. It could solve the complex ballistic problems of a shell flight in less time than it took the actual shell to hurtle from gun to target. It could do other tasks as well. Soon after the war, scientists from Los Alamos, looking for some fast early calculations on the H-bomb project, turned to ENIAC with great success. The lumbering giant performed calculations that would have taken a single mathematician 100 years to solve.

Mauchly and Eckert set up shop in an office over a clothing store on Philadelphia's Walnut Street, hoping to perfect and market a commercial version of their computer. First they called themselves Electronic Control Company, then the less modest Eckert-Mauchly Computer Corporation. They managed to win a government contract to create a computer for the

---

[4]bubbled—the word connotes enthusiasm.

Bureau of the Census, but they were too thinly capitalized to get very far.

This time, a friendly angel came to the rescue: Henry L. Strauss, chief stockholder of the American Totalisator Company, which manufactured tote-boards[5] for racetracks. Mauchly met Strauss in the summer of 1948—two men in the business of totaling things. Strauss, an electrical engineer who understood technology, was impressed enough to kick in° $400,000 from his company's funds for a large chunk of Eckert-Mauchly stock. That, with a commitment of $270,000 from the government, enabled the two scientists to begin work on what was to become UNIVAC I, the world's first commercial computer.

But several more plot twists lay ahead. In October 1949, Henry Strauss died when his company's Beechcraft crashed near Fort Deposit, Maryland, in a violent storm. The surviving stockholders of American Totalisator, always skeptical of old man Strauss's computer adventure, quickly sold their Eckert-Mauchly stock to Remington-Rand for $375,000.

A few months later, the dispirited scientists sold their interest, along with the patent rights, to Remington. "Each of us wound up with $200,000 or $250,000 out of that deal," Mauchly said later. He and Eckert joined Remington to continue perfecting UNIVAC, which came off the line in 1951 for delivery to the Census Bureau.

UNIVAC carried the ENIAC concept to new heights of sophistication. It was faster and more powerful, able to add 237,000 five-digit numbers in one minute, check for errors in its own problems, and handle information other than numbers. But its most important attribute was the stored-program concept which, simply put, provided for side-by-side storage of both data and instructions about what to do with data. The concept laid the foundation for the programming function of future computers.

And it became the source of bitter controversy, one of the disputed discoveries of scientific history. Working with Mauchly and Eckert on the stored-program concept was the great mathematician John von Neumann, who later received credit for its creation. Mauchly and Eckert claimed that the stored-program idea was already in place when von Neumann came on the scene. They never forgave von Neumann, who died in the fifties, for failing to acknowledge their central role.

The Bureau ordered two more UNIVACs from Remington. But even then, the company didn't realize what it had gotten hold of. Mauchly related that he sometimes felt Remington thought it had acquired a lemon.[6] the early days, the company thought there might be a market for about a dozen computers throughout the country—the government, universities, a few giant corporations.

But Thomas Watson, Jr., newly installed president of IBM, read the fu-

---

[5]tote-boards (totalisator boards) register the bets on horses at race tracks.
[6]a lemon—something worthless.

ture correctly. When the Census Bureau ordered its third UNIVAC, Watson once said, "We went into an absolute panic. Here was our traditional competitor, whom we had always been able to handle quite well, and now, before we knew it, they had five of these beasts installed, and we had none."

Watson corrected that disparity. IBM made the commitment to computers, and the rest is history. Remington never maintained its initial lead in the field. Mauchly stayed on as director of UNIVAC applications research before forming his own consulting business.

But the final indignity was yet to come. In 1967 Remington, now known as Sperry Rand, sued Honeywell, Inc., for infringing the ENIAC patent. In the course of a five-year litigation, U.S. District Court Judge Earl R. Larson ruled the original patent invalid on a technicality, stating that ENIAC had been used by Los Alamos for H-bomb calculations more than one year *before* the patent was applied for. Patents are invalid when the invention has been in public use more than one year before the application is filed.

Then, the judge unloaded the bombshell: Mauchly and Eckert, said Judge Larson, had not invented ENIAC in the first place! Mauchly, he said "had derived" his idea from Atanasoff, the Iowa State College professor he had visited briefly in the spring of 1941.

Mauchly defenders protested that Atanasoff's electronic computer device had never been functional, that its original purpose had been merely to solve linear equations. Dr. Nancy Stern, a computer historian, pointed out that Atanasoff "was never able to get [his device] to work," that it could not even do arithmetic. Stern, assistant editor of the *Annals of the History of Computing,* concluded: "Despite the Court's decision, Mauchly and Eckert are clearly entitled to be considered the inventors of the first fully operational electronic digital computer."

The judge's ambiguous ruling had acknowledged Mauchly and Eckert as the inventors of the first working computer, but awarded the concept to Atanasoff. The ruling ignored all the computation Mauchly had been doing before he met Atanasoff, notably the work at Ursinus (Sperry Rand was not interested in pressing that at the trial). Mauchly, who already felt robbed of the credit for the stored-program concept, now felt robbed of credit for the entire computer concept as well. It was a smashing blow.

Mauchly tried to sound philosophical about the whole thing. "Lawyers," he said, "are not out after the truth; they are after winning the case for their clients. I didn't have any great reason to think that life would be otherwise."

Stripped of all legal claims to his achievement, Mauchly retired in 1974, a year after the judge's decision, emerging only occasionally from his Ambler, Pennsylvania, home to do some consulting work for Sperry Rand.

But to the end, Mauchly retained a lively interest in computer development. He used a pair of personal home computers to pursue his lifelong interest in weather predictions. And he spent considerable time writing and publishing articles to clarify his role in computer history. He tried, in vain, to buy back the ENIAC patent. He continued to be recognized in the profession, but his reputation clearly had been tarnished by the spate of books and articles inspired by the controversy.

Mauchly believed that his biggest deficiency was that he was a poor self-promoter. He remained convinced that history would ultimately assign him and Eckert their rightful place.

In January 1980 he died in surgery, of a failed heart. He was 72. At his funeral, his partner, Eckert, then vice-president and technical advisor at Sperry-Univac, gave the eulogy: "John saw things for what they were, and not what people told him they were. And there is a big difference between those two things when you come to try to invent something. . . ." Said his wife, Kay, who continues to write and to campaign to assert her husband's legacy: "He did influence many, many people. He was an inspiration. I just want to see his place in history restored. I feel justice has not been done."

Understanding the Text

1. Would it be right to say that Mauchly's life was extremely successful and happy?
2. Are ENIAC and UNIVAC interesting only from a historical point of view, or were they good computers? What proofs can you offer?
3. Why did Mauchly and Eckert leave Moore College?
4. How did they manage to finance the research and development of UNIVAC?
5. Why did the two inventors have to join Remington-Rand?
6. Why were Mauchly and Eckert mad at mathematician John von Neumann?
7. What did Judge Larson conclude at the end of the litigation over the ENIAC patent?
8. What happened to Mauchly after the judge's decision?
9. What happened to (Remington) Sperry Rand, as a computer company?

Your Opinion

Does it seem absolutely certain that Mauchly and Eckert were indeed the inventors of the first electronic computer? [Instructor's Note: The class can be divided in two groups—the supporters of Mauchly and those who have doubts about his role. Each group will skim the two parts of the profile to list the facts that can be used to support its position. Then they will debate the question with the help of these notes and of any ideas that might come to the members of the group.]

SELECTED READING 291

Vocabulary

A. *How would you express in a less informal way, either with a synonym or an entirely different sentence, the following:*

line 6 Lt. Goldstine groused about Annie's shortcomings and about the backlog.
line 7 He heard that a couple of academics had a better idea.
line 9 "If it doesn't work, we'll scrap the project."
line 10 "If it works, we're in."
line 10 Aberdeen came through with $140,000.
line 11 Aberdeen came through with $140,000 to bankroll a shot at making the first electronic computer.
[Mauchly said: "I am not sure that it'll work, but let's have a shot at it."]
line 28 Over a thirty-month period Mauchly and Eckert tackled all sorts of tough problems.
line 75 ENIAC was churning up thousands of firing tables.
[The normal meaning of "to churn" is "to stir over and over"—for example: to stir cream to produce butter. What does churning suggest in this case? What is the connotation?]
line 92 Henry Strauss kicked in $400,000 from his company's fund to help Mauchly start his UNIVAC.

B. *For each of the following, find the meaning of the underlined words.*

line 1 The meeting of Mauchly and Eckert at Moore College had been fortuitous. The fact that Mauchly happened to be teaching at Moore when Moore embarked on a project that would need a computer was fortuitous also. Is fortuitous more likely to mean:
a) hoped for
b) happening by chance
c) unlucky

line 1 The deus ex machina rescued the computer project from oblivion. It can be said also that John Costello's article was written to rescue John Mauchly from oblivion. From oblivion must mean:
a) from its problems
b) from being remembered
c) from being forgotten

line 3 The back-up (supporting) squad of women working with hand calculators must be:
a) a group
b) a room
c) a table

line 6   Goldstine complained about Annie's <u>shortcomings</u>.
           a)   qualities
           b)   faults
           c)   small size

line 40   To avoid tube failures, Eckert said that they could use <u>heftier</u> resistors that would stand the voltage better. *Heftier* is likely to mean:
           a)   stronger
           b)   lighter
           c)   smaller

line 64   It took thirty years for the meaning of the computer to <u>seep through</u> to the nonprofessional people.
           a)   to strike
           b)   to rush
           c)   to go down slowly

line 102   After Strauss's death and the loss of their stock to Remington-Rand, Mauchly and Eckert felt <u>dispirited</u>. Were they likely to be in good or bad spirits? Does the prefix <u>dis</u> seem to indicated a good or a bad thing? Can you think of other words starting with <u>dis</u>?

line 132   Since Remington had five computers and IBM had none, IBM's president was eager to correct that <u>disparity</u>. How do you compare <u>dis-par-ity</u> to <u>on a par</u> ("the accomplishments of Ray Kroc were on a par with the accomplishments of Andrew Carnegie")?

C. *Paraphrase or explain the meaning of the following statements:*

ENIAC was Mauchly's and Eckert's <u>brainchild</u>.
Both Mauchly and Eckert were <u>night owls</u>.
As word went around about the progress of the new computer, the scientific world <u>perked up its ears</u>. [Is this literal?]
The scientists and engineers knew that something <u>was afoot</u> at Moore College.
Mauchly and Eckert happily completed their work on UNIVAC. But several more <u>plot twists</u> lay ahead—the death of Strauss, the sale of the stocks, the dispute with von Neumann, the litigation between Sperry-Rand and Honeywell, etc.

Facts, Inferences, and Opinions

Read the following passage carefully, differentiating between facts, inferences, and opinions. Some statements will be debatable.

     Mauchly and Eckert employed a large number of people to work on the ENIAC. Some were qualified technicians, some were not qualified at all. The moonlighting telephone wiremen were slow—which is not surprising from people who have been working all day at their regular job. It is remarkable that they could work as well as they did, as a matter of fact. Eckert, apparently, was not a student anymore; as for Mauchly, the college had not relieved him from his teaching duties. Mrs. Mauchly must not have seen much of her husband.

The news that research was going on steadily spread rapidly among scientists. Apparently the rumor reached the physicists working on the A-bomb in an isolated corner of New Mexico, near Los Alamos. One of them, Dr. Fermi, made inquiries about the computer. Such a device would have been a great help to the Los Alamos team, which had been working under pressure since 1942 on very complicated problems. It is rather surprising that the team had not tried to put together a computer of its own. They certainly had enough brains to do it. But they had to build the A-bomb without benefit of computers, for ENIAC was not unveiled until seven months after the explosion of the first bomb. Late or not, the first electronic computer was a tremendous achievement.

What opinions did you find in the text?
Which statements express an inference? What justifications do you find in the text text for those inferences?
Did you find ambiguous statements that could be classified in two categories?

Prefixes

fore

The good performance of the first accumulators *foreshadowed* the future success of the ENIAC, and those who saw the accumulators' performance could *foretell* how good the ENIAC would be. What does this mean? What is fore likely to indicate?

1. Do you know where the *foreword* of a book is likely to be found?
2. The *forefathers* of von Neumann came from Germany. Where did your forefathers live?
3. Is it good or bad to have the gift of *foresight*?
4. In a picture, what is the difference between the *background* and the *foreground*?
5. Do you think that Mauchly would have gone to Iowa to see Atanasoff if he had had *foreknowledge* of the consequences of that trip?
6. Why do they say that swallows are the *forerunners* of spring?
7. Elvis Presley was the *foremost* pop singer in the 1950s. Who is the foremost pop artist these days?

hind is the opposite of fore

1. What is the difference between the *forelegs* and the *hindlegs* of a horse?
2. When the judge ruled that Mauchly had taken his ideas from Atana-

soff's computer, Mauchly could have said: "I see now, with hindsight, that visiting Atanasoff was a bad idea." Why do people say, "Hindsight always has 20/20 vision"?

Topics for Discussion

1. "Lawyers are not after the truth; they are after winning the case for their clients," said Mauchly.
   Do you agree with him?
   Should the lawyer of an accused man be concerned with anything but his client's interests? If not, what should he consider?
2. Sometimes a lawyer who knows that his client is guilty (of murder, for instance) loses the case after doing his best, and the client is convicted. Should the lawyer, who knows that justice is truly being done, give up the case at this point? Or should he or she try to use any possible technicality to demand a second trial or get the conviction rejected by a court of appeal? What reasons do the lawyers have to keep trying?

Reading
In-Between

Skim the text:
- What is the meaning of the title?
- What kind of fresh information does it provide about computers?
- Does the text mention any particular brand of computers?

Mauchly's ENIAC, conceived for one sole purpose, performed its task well and kept performing it to everyone's satisfaction until 1955. But it was a pioneer, a first-try prototype, a one-function system without memory and without the capacity of being programmed. It was also a monstrous piece of equipment (30 tons, 100 feet long and 10 feet high) requiring 15,000 square feet of space to house its 40 units. It used 18,000 tubes, 7,000 resistors, 6,000 switches, and generated enough heat when in use to bring the room temperature to 120 degrees. The much simpler UNIVAC, with 5,000 tubes, marked a definite progress. It was more sophisticated and more versatile. It could store about 1,000 twelve digit figures or words, compared with the 12 ten-digit figures stored by ENIAC. UNIVAC was just as durable as its older brother; the Census Bureau's UNIVACs worked around the clock for twelve years without flinching—and without making a mistake.

Although Tom Watson pushed IBM very hard into the production of smaller and better computers, the results were disappointing for several years; only in the early fifties did IBM put on the market its Model 705, a multipurpose computer that could perform all the tasks desirable in business management—writing, calculating, filing and retrieving data, etc. The 705 was still a hefty machine, however, the kind of towering contraption that cartoonists love to draw, with revolving reels of tape, rows and rows of buttons, keys, switches, and blinking lights. There was no way at the time to design anything smaller.

But as the computer fever spread among engineers, physicists, and technicians, research began to move forward at an accelerated pace. It was done mainly in the small California area known as the Santa Clara Valley. The valley, which stretches for about 15 miles south of San Francisco, from the Stanford University campus to San Jose, was a pleasant, prosperous agricultural region, covered with apricot, plum, almond, and pear orchards. A few small engineering concerns, attracted by the research facilities of the university, settled in the vicinity of the campus in the 1950s. Larger research centers for IBM, General Electric, Xerox, and Burroughs were also establishing themselves among the fruit trees. And here and there a handful of tinkerers or Ph.D.s were pursuing their own research in shacks and garages. One such group manufactured the first transistor, under the direction of the man who had invented its principle and received a Nobel Prize for his achievement. The transistor was long-lasting, generated little heat and, although fifty times smaller than a vacuum tube, one transistor alone could replace all the tubes of an old-fashioned computer. It was now possible to build smaller systems; a new era was opening.

But the transistor itself was soon superseded. In another dilapidated building of the valley, a few dissidents from the "transistor group" had achieved another miracle by developing the silicon chip. In 1959 the first chip—the size of a fingernail—could carry an entire electrical circuit; by 1964 it was carrying ten circuits, and 1,000 circuits ten years later. By then, small computers were popping up everywhere, the Santa Clara Valley had become known as "Silicon Valley" and its orchards were gone, replaced by a sea of ultra-modern factories, plants, and buildings of all types, with banks to finance the explosion, restaurants to feed the workers, real estate agents to shelter them, and hot-tub salesmen to see to their relaxation. The age of the small computer was on.

Computers today come in a wide range of sizes, shapes, capacity, sophistication—and price. Enormous "mainframe" computers (including the new UNIVAC) are still the mainstay of large organizations such as the Internal Revenue Service, the Social Security Administration, the Department of Defense, and the large banks and insurance companies—not to mention NASA,[1] whose rows of computers guide astronauts and unmanned spaceships. Besides these intimidating systems, the field has been

---

[1]NASA—National Aeronautics and Space Administration.

taken over by the ubiquitous "personal" computer, small, affordable, and easy to handle. The versatile personal computer does payrolls and inventories, predicts production and profits, draws charts, teaches math, calculates taxes and occasionally plays games with the family. The heaviest models sit on their own supports, the lightest of them all, the twelve-pound "portable," travels in a soft case like a common typewriter. Needless to say, the competition is fierce among manufacturers, notably between the giant IBM (which makes about 38% of the sales) and the maverick Apple Computers Corporation.

The story of Apple Computers has caught the imagination of the public, partly because of its unlikely start in business, partly because of the excellence of its first product. Furthermore, the company's founder and president, Steve Paul Jobs, has been extremely skillful at keeping fresh in the mind of the public the humble and endearing beginnings of the corporation in a corner of his mother's garage.

Jobs was a resident of Silicon Valley when it was still Santa Clara. The adopted son of a middle-class couple, he went through a normal, happy childhood. But in the sixties he was attracted by the counterculture,[2] experimented with drugs, and dropped out of school. He worked for a time as a video-game designer for Atari. As none of these activities seemed to satisfy him, Jobs one day shaved his head and headed for India to seek higher truth on the banks of the Ganges.

After a year of meditation and sightseeing, Jobs came back home in 1975 and soon got in touch with an old friend, Stephen Wozniak, a 26-year-old tinkerer working for Hewlett-Packard. Wozniak was a technical genius who had built his own computer at the age of thirteen. The two friends, both dark, heavily bearded, and casually attired (to say the least) looked more like a pair of hippies than like proper high-tech experts. They knew very well what they were after, however; they wanted to build a small, simple, easy-to-use computer. It took them about forty weeks to design it and only six hours to actually build the first model in Mrs. Jobs's garage, using secondhand and discarded pieces that they managed to find in the area. Their computer finished, they left it for display in a store specializing in electronic equipment.

The first week brought fifty orders. Since there was no capital to start manufacturing, Steve sold his car and Stephen sacrificed his Hewlett-Packard calculator; with the $1,354 thus collected, the two friends went back to the garage to start production. They called their model the Apple—reportedly because Jobs, a natural food devotee, was on a fruit diet at the time. The first year's sales came to a mere $100,000, with a 20 percent

---

[2]counterculture—the culture of hippies and other persons antagonistic to authorities, beliefs, social conventions and the like. "Counter" means "anti," "against."

profit. The second year produced $6 million and 30 percent profit. From there the sales climbed to $18 million in 1978 and $983 million in 1983. Since 1980, Apple, Inc. has been a corporation, with plants in several states and several countries overseas, notably in Taiwan.

But for Apple Computers, as for all other computer manufacturers, the period of expansion seems to have come to a close. One of the reasons may be that the extent of the market was overestimated and that most of the people interested in personal computers have acquired one in the first flush of enthusiasm. Another factor in the slowdown is the large number of computer manufacturing companies, which, having happily multiplied in the boom years, are now competing for a shrinking market. At any event, the manufacturers have suddenly found themselves with a large stock of unsold computers on hand as sales have dwindled and prices plummeted. Even the mighty IBM has felt the effect of the business slump.

At Apple Computers, Inc., the year 1985 was, despite a large volume of sales around Christmas, particularly painful. The members of the board of directors had become acutely aware that a large corporation doesn't run efficiently on the kind of informal, relaxed, decentralized, and capricious arrangement that had been so successful when Jobs and his handful of geniuses were putting together the first Apples. When the board, led by its president and chief executive John Sculley, insisted on a drastic reorganization, chairman Jobs resigned. He is now reported to be forming a new, smaller company to manfacture basic computers for businessmen and scientists. Meanwhile, the surviving computer manufacturers are cautiously limiting their production, discontinuing their less successful models, and concentrating research on software.[3]

But the scientists now have further goals. One of their present dreams is to create a base for the electronic circuitry that would be much smaller than the microchip that is the building block of small computers. The building block of the future, the experts predict, will be a molecule, bred to perform some electronic functions. A billion three-dimensional molecules would take no more space than one silicon chip, and the molecular computer would work a million times faster than existing computers. Those molecular systems, explains ABC journalist Gordon Williams, would not be wasted on mundane chores; they could be implanted in our bodies to monitor our health and improve our intelligence. Others would guide the spaceships of the future to distant stars. Although developing such microscopic objects wouldn't be easy, the scientists are confident that it can be done with the help of increasingly refined computers. Molecular computers are indeed feasible, they say, and the model already exists; it's the human brain.

[3]software—the various programs of instructions that direct the operation of computers.

Understanding the Text

1. The subject of the first paragraph was : ENIAC and UNIVAC. As briefly as possible, what was the subject matter of each of the other paragraphs in the essay?
2. What are the two great differences between the early computers (ENIAC, UNIVAC, IBM 705) and today's personal computers?
3. What two great inventions allowed the manufacture of small computers?
4. What small computers can you name, based on the text and on your own knowledge?
5. What do the experts hope to achieve in the future?
6. How could it be done?
7. Why does the author call Apple Computers Corporation a "maverick" corporation and then proceed to describe its history?
8. What is Silicon Valley and how did it get that name?
9. What brought the first researchers to Silicon Valley?

Vocabulary

line 3   ENIAC was a prototype; so was UNIVAC, and so was the first Apple built by Jobs and Wozniak. A prototype is most likely to be:
  a) a lemon
  b) an electronic device
  c) the first model

line 13   UNIVAC worked round the clock for twelve years without flinching.
  a) without weakening
  b) without producing anything
  c) without repairs

line 19   Computers can file and retrieve data.
  a) move
  b) produce
  c) find again

line 54   The mainframe computers are the mainstay of large organizations. The mainstay must be:
  a) exclusivity
  b) pride
  c) chief support

line 59   Nowadays the personal computer is ubiquitous. A journalist was saying that Cronkite's ubiquity on television explains his popularity. Ubiquitous must be the quality of:
  a) being good looking
  b) being seen everywhere
  c) being interesting

line 111   The price of personal computers has plummeted.

a) increased
b) fallen
c) remained stable

Sequencing

Put the following statements in the right order to make a coherent summary of the history of computers.

__1__ Until the mid-forties, the only computing devices known were mechanical machines, which were slow and of limited use.

_____ Presently, IBM dominates the market for personal computers, with 38 percent of sales.

_____ Two great discoveries then transformed the computer industry.

_____ Five years later the two men completed the more versatile UNIVAC for Remington-Rand.

_____ The giant corporation's main competitor in the field is Apple Computers, makers of Apple II and McIntosh.

_____ The first operative electronic computer was completed in 1946 by Mauchly and Eckert.

_____ The importance of computers was understood at that time not by Remington, but by the new president of IBM, Tom Watson.

_____ The second was the invention of the silicon chip, as small as a fingernail.

_____ Under Watson's direction, IBM produced a good "business" computer, Model 705, which could perform more tasks than Mauchly's second computer.

_____ It seems, however, that Apple, Inc.'s fantastic growth has slowed down and that the company is experiencing some difficulties.

_____ The first one was the invention of the transistor, which made it possible to build smaller and more versatile computers.

_____ The microchip led to the manufacturing of small "personal" computers, cheap enough to be accessible to small businesses and individuals.

Topics for Discussion

1. Many educators are concerned by the frequency with which students use pocket calculators instead of solving problems on their own. They think that new generations are going into the world without having

acquired arithmetic skills. Do you agree that calculators should be totally forbidden at school? Do you think that they should be authorized at a certain level of education, and at what level?
2. What do you think of the computer age? Do you find computers exciting, or do you think that they are taking too much place in our lives? Some people see computers as a threat to privacy because the information about individuals stored in the machines of organizations such as the Social Security Agency, the Internal Revenue Service, the police, etc., is available to anyone who has access to a computer. Are you concerned about this?
3. Many people are already doing at home on computers the work that they would have done in an office ten years ago. They receive their work, do it, and transmit it by computer without seeing either their boss or their fellow employees. What are the good points of such a job? Is there a bad side to the arrangement?
4. Ray Kroc, Walter Cronkite, Walt Disney, Steve Jobs, and Stephen Wozniak were school dropouts. Does this prove that it is not important to finish school?

J. Presper Eckert, standing by ENIAC.

Word List

The following list includes the words that were introduced in the preliminary vocabulary of each chapter (V), explained in footnotes (F), or studied in the exercises (E). For words in the last category, the page on which the word first appeared is also indicated.

about
   what she is about, 204F
abreast, 44, 48E
abuse, 218, 298E
abyss, 43, 47E
"academics," 286, 291E
acrobatics, 95, 99E
acute, 247, 252E
adamantly, 130, 133E
addicted, 62, 66E
ad lib, 154V
admonition, 94, 99E
advertiser, 154V
aesthetics, 68V
affiliate, 154V
affluence, 126, 132
afoot, 270V
afresh, 168, 174E
airfield, 88V
alienation, 73, 77E
alma mater, 278
alone
   let alone, 7, 10E
altimeter, 103, 110E
anachronism, 238E
anachronistic, 234
anchorman, 154V
animate, 242V
animation, 242V
animator, 242V
announcer, 154V
apace, 249, 252E
apprised, 104, 109E
approach
   direct approach, 16, 19E
arduous, 167, 174E
arrangement, 198F
arthritis, 4, 10E
askance, 112F
askew, 158, 164E
assorted, 60, 65E
auto-, 39E
   autobiography

autogiro
autograph
automatic
autonomy
avant garde, 196F
avuncular, 155, 164E

backbone, 158, 164E
backlog, 281, 283E
ban, 30V
bankroll, 286, 291E
base, 210V
bat, 210V
batter, 210V
batting average, 210V
be
   to be on to, 280, 283E
belligerent, 216, 222E
benign, 73, 77E
bent, 197, 201E
besmirch, 234, 238E
bio-, 39E
   biocide
   biodegradable
   biography
   biological
   biology
blackmail, 249, 251E
blase, 97F
blow
   to blow one's top, 249, 251E
blue
   out of the blue, 96F
blue collar, 111F
bonus, 15, 19E
boom, 2V
boy
   to be one of the boys, 113F
brainchild, 270V
break even, 258, 260E
breakthrough, 270V

bribe, 233, 238E
brink
   on the brink, 155F
bubble, 287F
buck, 234, 237E
budding, 189, 193E
bulletin, 154V
bully, 61, 66E

calamitous, 249, 252E
called upon, 138, 142E
camera, 182V
cameraman, 243V
carnival, 58V
cartoon, 242V
cartoonist, 242V
catcall, 224, 230E
cel, 242V
chain, 2V
chaperone, 49F
"character," 188F
chase
   wild goose chase, 281F
chemical, 30V
chron-, 238E
   chronic, 239
   chronically, 254
   chronicles, 239
   chronological, 239
   chronology, 239
   chronometer, 239
churn, 287, 291E
-cide, 48E
   biocide
   fratricide
   genocide
   herbicide
   homicide
   insecticide, 30V
   pesticide, 30V
   suicide
circulation, 122V
"class," 137V

cockpit, 88V
cold shoulder, 219, 222E
columnist, 122V
commanding, 161, 165E
commentator, 158, 164E
compile, 281, 283E
compulsive, 35, 38E
concocted, 277F
conform, 61, 66E
congenial, 35, 38E
connoisseur, 266F
consecutive, 44, 47E
contraption, 94F
contrite, 191, 194E
contrive, 95F
counterculture, 296F
convey, 36, 38E
corny, 265F
cosmic, 155F
crabby, 196F
crack, 200F
crack student, 270V
cramp, 235F
cramped, 257, 260E
crisscross, 15, 19E
crummy, 198, 202E
crusade, 130, 133E
culprit, 224, 230E
cumbersome, 162, 164E
cure, 13, 18E
curfew, 278, 283E
cutback, 248, 251E
"cute," 266F

daily, 122V
dark room, 184V
deficient, 160, 164E
definitive, 205F
depth
    out of one's depth, 42V
deus ex machina, 285F
develop (photo), 183V
diabetes, 4, 10E
diaphragm, 182V
diligently, 128, 133E
discomfiture, 168, 174E
dismantle, 94, 99E
disoriented, 136, 142E
disparaging, 5, 10E
disparity, 289, 292E
dispirited, 288, 292E

dispossess, 137, 142E
dive
    to take a dive, 233F
dogged, 270V
dowdy, 126, 133E
draft, 242V
draftsman, 242V
drawback, 159, 164E
drive, 13, 18E
drive in, 2V
drive up, 2V
drudge, 272, 274E
drudgery, 242V

earthling, 69, 76E
ecological, 30V
ecology, 30V
editor, 122V
editorial, 122V
effacement, 15, 19E
embroil, 227, 231E
endorse, 100E
endorsement, 97
engrossed, 34, 38E
engrossing, 42, 47E
enjoin, 138, 142E
enlarge, 184V
entangle, 258, 260E
entice, 73, 77E
environment, 30V
epigraphy, 39E
escapism, 58V
esprit de corps, 15F
ethics, 68V
eu-, 238E
    eulogize, 233
    euphemism
    euphoria
    euthanasia
evocative, 36, 38E
exemplary, 158, 164E
exposure, 183V
exterminate, 30V
extinction, 30V
eyebrow
    to raise an eyebrow, 226, 231E

fanatic, 6
fanatically, 10E

fancy
    to take a fancy to, 188, 194E
fauna, 43, 47E
feature, 242V
fed up, 279F
felony, 19E
fey, 58E
fiddle, 245F
film, 182V
flair, 158, 164E
flinch, 294, 298E
flippant, 58E
flounder, 226, 231E
flunk, 159F
focus, 182V
fore-, 293E
    forefather
    forefront
    foreknowledge
    foremost
    forerunner
    foreshadow
    foresight
    foretell
    foreword
fork over, 234, 237E
formidable, 127, 133E
forthright, -ly, 102, 109E
forthwith, 256, 260E
fortuitous, 285, 291E
frame, 243V
franchise, 2V
fraternities, 31
fratricide, 48E
freak, 58V
frivolous, 104, 109E
front page, 122V

gag, 246F
gall bladder, 4, 10E
"garden variety," 278F
gaudy, 24, 27E
genocide, 48E
geology, 39E
get somebody wrong, 14, 19E
giddy, 139, 142E
go for broke, 74F
goggles, 88V
going over, 96F

WORD LIST   303

...aphy, 39E
...epigraphy
...stenography
...avity, 68V
...egarious, 196, 202E
...oss (revenue), 2V
...oundwork, 270V
...ouse, 286, 291
...n
   jump the gun, 233F
...ts, 218F
...y, 5F

...abitat, 30V
...alf-hearted, 5, 10E
...ang around, 7F, 10E
...angar, 88V
...atch, 30V
...ave a shot at, 286, 291E
...ave it made, 222F
...eadline, 122
...eadstrong, 93, 99E
...elm, 133, 142E
...erbicide, 48E
...igh brow, 257F
...ind-, 293E
   hind legs
   hindsight
...o hum, 200F
...oldings, 14, 19E
...omicide, 48E

...iconoclastic, 235, 238E
immaculate, 23, 27E
immunity, 30V
impart, 33, 38E
impetus, 162, 165E
implication, 8E
imply, 8E
impromptu, 104, 109E
inarticulate, 127, 133E
in-betweener, 242V
incompatibility, 196, 202E
indiscriminate, -ly, 30V
indispensable, 249, 252E
infer, 8E
inference, 8E
infringe, 270V
injunction, 138F
inker, 242V
innate, 248, 252E

installment, 138, 142E
instrumental, 168, 174E
insurmountable, 256, 260E
integrate, 215, 222E
invention, 270V
inventor, 270V
I.Q., 61F
irrefutable, 5, 10E
irrelevant, 37E
irrepressible, 199, 201E

jeer, 224, 230E
jukebox, 2V

kick in, 288, 291E
kid, 158F

landmark, 206F
laurels
   to rest on one's laurels, 199F
lavish, 43, 47E
layout, 122V
league, 210V
"lemon," 288F
lens, 182V
let alone, 7, 10E
limelight, 102, 109E
lineman, 60, 65E
litigation, 270V
locker room, 214, 222E
logic, 68V
long-hand, 43, 48E
lousy, 16, 19E

made
   to have it made, 229V
mainstay, 295, 298E
mal-, 19E
   malnutrition
   malpractice
mark
   to make one's mark, 129, 133E
marketing, 2V
masse
   en masse, 114F
maverick, 71, 76E
media, 154V
medium, 243V
merge, 122V

merry-go-round, 58V
metaphor, 9E
-meter, 120E
   altimeter
   barometer
   chronometer
   dynamometer
   speedometer
meticulous, -ly, 13, 19E
mettle, 6, 10E
mind
   to speak one's mind, 137, 142E
mis-, 19E
   miscalculation
   misdemeanor
   misinformed
   misspell
   mispronounce
   mistreat
momentous, 169, 174E
monitor TV, 200, 201E
monster, 58V
monstrous, 58V
moonlight, 286F
morbid, 75F
moronic, 46, 50E
"mug," 155F
multi-, 238E
   multifarious
   multilateral
   multiracial
   multitalented
mundane, 272, 274E
mystic, 188, 193E

negative, 183V
net, 2V
network, 154V
newscast, 154V
no
   take no for an answer, 7, 10E
nostalgia, 70, 77E
nothing
   make nothing of, 64, 66E
novelty, 248, 251E
nudge, 200, 202E
nuts
   to go nuts, 200F

oblivion, 285, 291E
odd (forty-odd), 63F
odds and ends, 94F
offbeat, 205F
offset, 14, 18E
omen, 45, 47E
omni-, 11E
   omnipotent
   omnipresent
   omniscient
   omnivorous
opaquer, 242V
orient, 142E
orientation, 142E
ostentation, 93, 99E
ostentatious, 98E
out-, 143E
   outdated
   outdo
   outflow
   outlive
   outlook
   outnumber
   outweigh
   outwit
out of one's depth, 42V
out of the blue, 96F
outburst, 246, 252E
outlandish, 188, 194E
outlet, 2V
outskirts, 24, 27E
over-, 143E
   overcrowded
   overextended
   overnight
   overrate
   override
   overripe
   overseas
   overweight

par
   on a par with, 4, 10E
parody, 68V
parsimony, 160, 164E
partisan, 130, 133E
pass out, 112F
patent of invention, 270V
patronizing, 126, 132E
pause
   to give pause, 254, 260E
pedantry, 36, 38E

per se, 108F
pest, 30V
pesticide, 30V
phrenologist, 8, 39E
phrenology, 39E
pigeon-toed, 216F
pirate, 270V
pitcher, 210V
plate, 182V
plot, 288, 292E
"plum," 161, 165E
plummet, 297, 298E
point, 42F
   to make one's point
pollute, 30V
portfolio, 189, 194E
pose, 184V
pre-, 77E
   precedent
   prefix
   prehistory
   preliminary
   premature
   premeditated
   preshrunk
   preventive
   previous
precarious, 254, 260E
premiere, 256, 260E
premonition, 70, 77E
preposterous, 71, 76E
press, 122V
pressman, 122V
prickly, 225, 230E
prima donna, 225F
print, 183V
profit, 2V
prolific, 206F
prosaic, 190, 193E
prototype, 294, 298E
proximity, 44, 47E
psych-, 272, 274E
   psychedelic
   psychiatric
   psychosis
purist, 233, 237E

quash, 278, 283E
quench, 283E, 285
quota, 60, 65E

racket, 104F
rancor, 246, 251E

ratings, 154V
real estate, 2V
red
   to be in the red, 130F
regalia, 88V
re-instated, 168, 174E
relentless, 5, 10E
relinquish, 14, 19E
reluctance, 6, 10E
repercussion, 138, 142E
reporter, 122, 164E
retouch, 184V
revenue, 2V
reversal, 169, 174E
rhapsodize, 281F
robot, 272, 273E
rodent, 30V
roller coaster, 58V
royalty, -ies, 34, 39E
run
   to run errands, 215, 222E

sanctuary, 30V
scoop, 154, 173E
scrap, 286, 291E
scrape, 216, 222E
sea
   to be at sea, 42V
second thoughts, 218, 222E
self-, 134E
   self-aggrandizement
   self-centered
   self-conscious
   self-effacement
   self-made
   self-styled
serendipitous, 274E
serendipity, 270V
shenanigans, 235, 237E
shoddy, 254, 260E
short
   nothing short of, 216, 222E
shorthand, 58E
shot
   to have a shot at, 286, 291E
shutter, 183V
sitter, 183V
skulduggery, 236, 237E

sloppy, 206F
slur, 218, 230E
small talk, 35, 38E
snob, 233, 237E
socialite, 96, 99E
soda fountain, 2V
software, 297F
solo, 88V
sort of, 79V
sorts
   of sorts, 245F
speleology, 39E
speak
   to speak one's mind, 137, 142V
spic and span, 6F
sponsor, 154V
spur on, 183V
squad, 285, 291E
stall, 88V, 99E
steam
   under one's own steam, 235, 238E
stenography, 39E
stipulate, 13, 18E
store
   to be in store, 218, 222E
stunt, 88V
subsidiary, 154V
suicide, 48E
summa cum laude, 34F

tackle, 286, 291E
tangible, 235, 238E
tart, 228, 231E

taskmaster, 169, 174E
taunt, 218, 222E
tele-, 77E
   telegraphy
   telepathy
   telephone
   telephotography
   telescope
   television
terminal, 217, 222E
thermostat, 271, 273E
thick
   in the thick of things, 130, 133E
thyroid, 4, 10E
ticker tape parade, 88V
tide pool, 35, 39E
tight-fisted, 196F, 202E
tinker, 270, 277E
tinkerer, 270V
tomboy, 93, 99E
tongue in cheek, 9E
top
   to blow one's top, 169, 174E
top notch, 168, 174E
totalitarian, 61, 66E
trick, 58V
trivial, 170, 174E
tutu, 257F
twist, 288, 292E
tycoon, 127, 133E

ubiquity, 155F
umpire, 210V

uni-, 110E
   unicell
   unicorn
   unilateral
   unisex
   unison
un-materialistic, 197, 202E
unquenchable, 277, 288E
up
   to be up to, 127F
update, 247, 251E
uproot, 94, 99E
upshot, 160, 164E
ups and downs, 5, 10E

vegetarianism, 188, 193E
visionary, 5, 10E
volition, 102, 109E

waves
   to make waves, 170, 174E
weird, 58V
whiz kid, 270V
wild goose chase, 281F
wily, 13, 18E
wobbly, 136, 141E
wont, 168, 174E
wrong
   don't get me wrong, 14, 19E

zest, 96, 99E

Continued from copyright page.

JAMES H. ROSENFIELD   For excerpts from his speech delivered at the annual convention of the Maine Association of Broadcasters, September 23, 1983. Reprinted by permission.

SIMON & SCHUSTER, INC.   For an excerpt form *The American Diamond* by Branch Rickey and Robert Riger. Copyright © 1965 by Branch Rickey and Robert Riger. Reprinted by permission of Simon & Schuster, Inc.

TRIANGLE PUBLICATIONS and ERICH SEGAL   For "There Has Always Been Olympic Mischief" by Erich Segal from *TV Guide*® Magazine (July 28, 1984). Copyright © 1984 by Triangle Publications, Inc., Radnor, Pennsylvania. Reprinted by permission of Triangle Publications and Erich Segal.

TRIANGLE PUBLICATIONS and ISAAC ASIMOV   For an excerpt from "Ray Bradbury" by Isaac Asimov from *TV Guide* Magazine (January 12, 1980). Copyright © 1980 by Triangle Publications, Inc., Radnor, Pennsylvania. Reprinted by permission of Triangle Publications and Isaac Asimov.

U.S. NEWS & WORLD REPORT   For excerpts from "Miracles, Menaces—The 21st Century as Futurists See It" from *U.S. News & World Report* (July 16, 1984). Copyright © 1984 by U.S. News & World Report, Inc. Reprinted by permission.

ILLUSTRATION CREDITS

p. 1   Courtesy McDonald's Corp.; 29   HBJ Picture Library; 31   © 1984 United Features Syndicate, Inc.; 57   Wide World Photos; 87   HBJ Picture Library; 121   UPI/Bettmann Newsphotos; 153   Courtesy CBS News; 181, 205, 207   © The Imogen Cunningham Trust; 209   Culver Pictures; 241   Courtesy Walt Disney Productions; 269   UPI/Bettmann Newsphotos; 300   Courtesy IBM.